To Zelda
and
To Phyllis Bennett, Dudley Dudley, and Nancy Sandberg

SMALL TOWN, BIG OIL

The Untold Story of the Women Who Took on the Richest Man in the World—And Won

DAVID W. MOORE

DIVERSIONBOOKS

Diversion Books
A Division of Diversion Publishing Corp.
443 Park Avenue South, Suite 1008
New York, New York 10016
www.DiversionBooks.com

For more information, email info@diversionbooks.com

First Diversion Books edition March 2018.
Paperback ISBN: 978-1-63576-188-7
eBook ISBN: 978-1-63576-187-0

LSIDB/1801

CONTENTS

Acknowledgements vii

Prologue xi

1. The Stranger 1
2. Early Alert 10
3. Devising a Strategy 18
4. SOS Emerges 27
5. Abandoning the Dream 36
6. The Man Behind the Throne 44
7. The Man on the Throne 55
8. Meeting Olympic 62
9. Touring Durham Point 75
10. Town Meeting 84
11. Pursuing the Dream 90
12. Petitions and the Governor 96
13. The Oil Refinery—Nineteen Articles and Reports 100
14. Campaigning for Oil 107
15. The Richest Man in the World 112
16. The Oil Man Cometh 122
17. New Year, New Woes 135
18. More on the Petitions 144
19. The Economic Bonanza Myth 148
20. Rye Surprise 152
21. Saving the Dream 158
22. The Other Greek 166
23. SOS Panic Time 172

24. As Rich as Croesus   180
25. Final Preparations   186
26. Dudley's Hearing   196
27. Olympic Refineries Presentation   205
28. The Town Speaks   217
29. Concord Speaks   226
30. Immediate Aftermath   234
    Epilogue   239
    Photo Credits   245
    Notes   247
    Index   257

ACKNOWLEDGEMENTS

While much information about the Onassis Oil Refinery contro-versy was provided in *Publick Occurrences* and other newspapers, this account would not have been possible without the personal interviews I conducted with Phyllis Bennett, Dudley Dudley, and Nancy Sandberg. Other people who also provided helpful infor-mation and encouragement include Sharon Meeker, Ray Belles, David Meeker, Bob Nilson, Clif Horrigan, Art Mathieson, Dale Valena, Patrick Bennett, and Meredith Bennett. I am greatly indebted to them and grateful for their support.

I am also grateful to my agent, Rita Rosenkranz, for her wise counsel and diligent efforts on my behalf.

Special thanks to my writing group—Noreen Kilbride, Shannon Huffman, and Brad Bolton—for their constructive cri-tiques and unfailing encouragement.

Thanks also to the many people who allowed their photos to be included in this book (please see "Photo Credits" for a complete list).

Much appreciation to Lia Ottaviano of Diversion Books for her insightful edits and suggestions and her enthusiastic support.

As always, my greatest debt is to Zelda…

New Hampshire is rich in natural beauty. Its eighteen miles of beaches and rugged coastline are fed by a web of rivers and estuaries that fuel the economy for many New Hampshire communities.

This is a story about legacy and how the actions of ordinary people can impact the lives of many for generations to come.

It is also a story about recognition—of the often underappreciated leadership role that women play in society.

And it is a story about today—balancing the reality of our energy needs and understanding our responsibility to our community and to our descendants.

But to understand this responsibility, we must first take a step back into the past.

Jim Horrigan,
University of New Hampshire Professor of Economics[1]

PROLOGUE

In the spring and summer of 1973, the United States and the rest of the world were in the midst of the worst economic crisis since the Great Depression. Economic growth was sluggish at the same time that prices were increasing, giving rise to stagflation—stagnation of growth, accompanied by significant inflation. Increases in food and energy prices were particularly acute, compounded by shortages in various kinds of foods and in heating oil for homes. In a radio address to the country the previous February,[2] President Nixon pointed especially to the energy problems faced by the country: "The energy crisis was dramatized by fuel shortages this winter. We must face up to a stark fact. We are now consuming more energy than we produce in this country."

Bad times for some people are good times for others. For Aristotle Onassis,[3] owner of the world's largest private shipping fleet and reputedly the richest man in the world,[4] the spring and summer of 1973 represented an "exhilarating" time. His fleet of more than one hundred ships was producing close to $50 million a month in profits (in today's currency). With world oil consumption increasing by about eight percent a year, he saw a great opportunity to expand his fleet, ordering four more Very Large Crude Carriers (VLCC) from Japan and two more Ultra Large Crude Carriers (ULCC) from France.[5]

Onassis also continued his search for a location to construct an oil refinery, an objective he had pursued for years. In 1968, during the period in which he was honeymooning with his new wife,

Jacqueline Kennedy Onassis, he had signed an agreement called the Omega Project, which included construction of an oil refinery, with the Greek government. For various reasons, the deal finally collapsed in 1971, leaving the shipping magnate disappointed but not defeated.[6] One of the men who had worked with him on the Omega Project was Robert Greene of Purvin and Gertz, an independent energy consultancy in Houston founded in 1947. Constantine Gratsos, Onassis's trusted friend and confidant, had sent Greene to Nova Scotia in the quest for a suitable refinery site. Then, from out of the blue, Gratsos was contacted by a longtime friend, Peter Booras, who suggested that New Hampshire would be a good location for a refinery. Booras, a Republican who ran unsuccessfully for the US Senate in 1972 and was a close colleague of New Hampshire Governor Meldrim Thomson, reported that Thomson was eager to locate a refinery in the state. Booras himself had no experience in the oil business. He owned a small printing and greeting card shop in Keene, and was busy trying to sell his invention of the Booras Endless Bread System—essentially, a crustless bread. His interest in the refinery, he said, lay solely in trying to bring together two parties who shared a common interest.[7]

Gratsos was excited by the information and, along with Booras, met with Thomson to discuss the idea. The governor was equally excited about the project, reassuring Gratsos of his strong support, as well as the support of William Loeb, publisher of the only daily statewide newspaper, the *Manchester Union Leader*. Gratsos in turn called Onassis and told him the good news. He had found what seemed to be the perfect location. Plus, he had the enthusiastic backing of the governor, which meant there probably would be "no problems, no red tape." Onassis gave the go-ahead.[8]

Gratsos now ordered Greene to go immediately to New Hampshire. The "briefing" Greene received was "unusually succinct," he later recalled. Essentially: *Onassis wants a refinery in New Hampshire. Find a site.* "Obviously Onassis had the ships, and if he could find somewhere to move the oil to, he could tie them up okay," Greene said. "But the way Gratsos put it, it was just like ordering a Cadillac."[9]

With no background about the geography of the land, Greene met up with Booras and flew all over the state in a helicopter looking for a suitable site. New Hampshire has only an eighteen-mile-long seacoast, so locating a possible port hardly demanded a lot of thought. The supertankers required a draft of at least ninety feet, so the Isles of Shoals, nine miles off the coast, seemed to be an ideal docking location. The closest land point was Rye. An underwater pipeline would take the oil from the docking station to Rye, and from there an overland pipeline would carry the crude oil to be processed. Ideally, the refinery would be located in an area of about three thousand relatively underdeveloped acres, and as close to Rye as possible. The helicopter flights suggested that Durham Point was the area that best met those criteria.[10]

In the late summer, Gratsos and Booras sent out a team of brokers, mostly Greek-Americans, to buy up options of land in the areas where the refinery and the pipeline were to be located. They were to purchase the options without revealing the true purpose of the transactions. They were told, "the fewer people who knew what the land was wanted for, the cheaper it would come."[11]

• • •

The assumption that because the governor and the newspaper publisher supported the project, there would be "no problems, no red tape," was, to put it mildly, not well-founded. Not only ignorant of the geography, but also of the history and culture of the state, Gratsos and Greene believed that whatever problems they faced could be solved with money. They took into account neither the state's form of government nor the will of the people.

Perhaps their most egregious oversight was New Hampshire's three-hundred-year-old history of feisty voters demanding citizen participation in policy decisions. The first Assembly in the state was established in 1680, and right from the start, its members refused to kowtow to the demands of the governor, even denying him a salary until he stopped trying to impose unwanted taxes.[12] The first constitutional convention in the world was held in New Hampshire, where elected representatives formulated rules allowing the citizens to govern themselves.[13] And the constitution that was finally accepted by the voters ensured that the chief executive would have limited power, with most power located in the legislature. New Hampshire adopted the first free constitution in American history in January 1776, six months before the Declaration of Independence was signed. So intent were the framers on keeping the citizens involved in the affairs of government that the first House included one elected representative for every one hundred families. As the population increased, so did the number of House members, reaching a high of 443. In 1942, the limit was set at four hundred, which has continued to this day.[14] The Senate consists of twenty-four members. The New Hampshire legislature is thus the largest legislative body in the country apart from the US Congress.

It is not, however, what political scientists would call a "professional" law-making body. The salary for legislators for a two-year term is a meager $200. Clearly, they do not seek office because of the money. One might think that such representatives would be more susceptible to being bought off by lobbying groups, given their almost nonexistent salaries. But in practice, that has not been the case. In 1934, Walter Davenport wrote an article titled "You Can't Fool New Hampshire" for *Collier's Weekly* about the size of the legislature, voicing comments that are still applicable today:

> Just try to put something over on the Legislature of New Hampshire. You can't do it. For one thing, it's too big— nobody could afford to bribe the boys even if they could all be seen. Besides, politics is a pastime, not a business, in New Hampshire.
>
> In session it is healthily suggestive of the old-fashioned town meeting, a form of government still to be found without much seeking in New England. As numerically it has the

unwieldiness of the true Republican form, in action it comes as close to the old Jeffersonian idea as any legislative body you'll find anywhere.

Apart from the legislature, many citizens in 1973 lived in towns that still held annual town meetings, and all significant town business was voted on by the citizens. Such business would include not only town spending and tax revenues, but other items such as town zoning—and whether an oil refinery could be located within the town limits. Whatever the governor, or even the legislature, might want, ultimately the town of Durham itself would have a crucial say.

• • •

What most Americans who paid attention to the news probably knew about Onassis was that he was old and rich, and that he had married President Kennedy's young widow, Jackie Kennedy, much to the derision and shock of most of the world.[15] What only the really attentive observers might have also known was that he was, as one of the women who knew him best recalled, ruthless, manipulative, irascible, and vengeful—a monstrous figure.[16] As his men fanned out across the seacoast area to persuade people to sell their land by deceiving them about the true purpose of the sale, Onassis clearly expected the state legislature and Durham residents to fall in line with whatever their governor decreed and the state-wide newspaper supported.

He was in for a big surprise.

1

THE STRANGER

Nancy Sandberg was startled when a large dark sedan crept its way up her driveway past the oak trees. She wasn't anticipating company, her friends would have called before coming over, and she wasn't wild about talking with any strangers. She had seen the car earlier, as it wound down the road toward her neighbors, and had expected it would simply pass by on its return. That it was now coming directly toward her made her mildly anxious. She was working in her garden and looked a mess, her dark hair curling all over the place, her old shorts spattered with paint. It was a hot and humid August day, typical for that time of year in Durham, New Hampshire, and she was perspiring, hardly a condition for socializing with anyone, much less someone she didn't know.

A tall man wearing a dark suit and sunglasses, but no hat, emerged from the car. *A city slicker*, she thought as he approached her, maybe lost and needing directions. He was dark complexioned, looking like maybe he was from some place in the Mediterranean. He greeted her in a friendly tone, asking if she was Mrs. Sandberg. Knowing her name, he was clearly not lost. He was interested in buying some property, he told her. He didn't need a lot of acreage, just a little for a house for himself and his family. He seemed so out of place, she couldn't imagine him actually building a house and living there, the bucolic life at complete odds with his whole persona.

She told him she couldn't sell the land. The land and the farm still belonged to her grandmother, who had suffered a stroke and was in a nursing home. Nancy and her husband were living there just to take care of the property, she told him. She *didn't* tell him that they expected to live there permanently, that eventually she expected her grandmother to give the land to her father, who would give it to her. That was none of his business.

Yes, he said, he knew about the actual ownership of the land, but certainly the occupants must have some control or influence on any decision to sell some acres. Nancy was startled by the level of his knowledge about her property, realizing that he must have been to the Town Hall to look at the tax map. This was no casual encounter. He said he realized there were forty acres around the farmhouse, but farther away was a woodlot of thirty acres. Couldn't he buy a few acres of that? Again, she said no, and again he claimed he needed only a small area for a home. Surely, she could afford to give up some part of the land for a reasonable price. Several times he reiterated his requirements in different ways, not so much asking, it seemed, as insisting, as though he had some right to acquire what was not his.

She thought maybe she wasn't being direct enough for him to get it through his head that there was no way she was going to sell any part of her grandmother's farmland. When her intentions finally became clear, he asked if he could talk with her husband. When would he be available? She was relieved at the request, because she knew Mal would back her up completely. Maybe he could be more forceful. Some men only listen to men, thinking women don't have the judgment necessary to make sound decisions about their own lives. The fact was, of course, that Mal had no legal or moral right to make any independent decision about the disposition of the land. He wasn't the one who had come here every Christmas as a child, as she had since the age of five, taking the fourteen-hour-long car trip from New Jersey with her parents and younger sister, loving to be with her grandmother and in her grandmother's house, her own room situated at the top of the stairs overlooking the grandfather clock, which was so tall it extended into the stairwell above the second floor. During the holidays, she and her sister, her parents and grandparents, all played in the snow, sledding and making snowmen and snow angels, and afterward coming into the kitchen for warm apple cider. They would all open their presents on Christmas morning. She remembered that one year, she and her sister had gotten up before dawn and were chomping at the bit to open their presents when their grandmother came down, happy as always, sharing their eagerness, and let them open some of their presents right then. Her parents were annoyed when they later came down to find they had missed some of the excitement. But her grandmother just waved off their objections with a laugh.

The original farmhouse was built by Jacob Mathes in 1861, on the site of an Army garrison established two centuries earlier, with some of the wood in the new house actually taken from that fort. Her grandparents had bought it from the Mathes family in 1916, and her dad had been raised there with his siblings. Not one of the kids in his generation had any interest in returning there when their mother had the stroke. Her dad was pleased when Nancy and Malcolm, who had just finished getting his degree at Boston University, volunteered to live at the farm and take care of it. Mal sought teaching jobs all over southern New Hampshire and eventually found a position at Exeter High School, about a half hour away. Nancy stayed home to take care of the house and the land, to help make the farm pay for itself with produce, and to raise their daughter, Betsy, who was now four years old. Nancy had a large garden of vegetables, and was taking care of an apple orchard that she and Mal had begun planting when they first arrived, two hundred new apple trees every spring, so that now they had eight hundred. It was hard work, but she couldn't imagine not living there. She was *rooted* there, as surely as the oak trees in the front yard, and she could never part with any portion of the land.

She agreed to meet with the man again, *Peter Booras*, he said, his Greek name confirming her instinct about his origins. The visit bothered her. His desire for a small piece of land didn't ring true. If that's all he wanted, there were lots of homes for sale in Durham. So why did he insist on having part of her farmland? Later, she picked up Betsy from nursery school and came home to fix the dinner. When Mal arrived, he told her about his day at school, preparing for the beginning of the new academic year. She told him all about the visit from Peter Booras. Who was he? She didn't know. He never said what he did or why he wanted the land, other than for his family. Mal agreed there was something fishy about Booras's request to buy some part of their land, and suggested that when the man came the next time, they should ask him some pointed questions and tape record what he told them. They considered whether it would be practical or wise to record him without his knowledge, but decided that if he was in their house, anything he said was a matter of record.

They bought a small recorder and set it up in their kitchen area. The meeting took place the next week, in the evening after dinner, Booras wearing a suit, but no tie, his white shirt open at the neck. He was tall and smooth and said he could stay for only a short time. They all sat on the chairs around the kitchen table as he reiterated his desire for some small piece of land, not much, just for a house for him and his family. Mal was firm in saying they would not, in fact could not, did not have the authority, to sell any of the land, and wouldn't do so even if they could. But when Mal began grilling Booras about why he was so intent on obtaining some part of their property, Booras gave vague answers about how beautiful their location overlooking the Oyster River was, and that other places didn't suit his needs. When he left, they realized they had nothing of use on the recorder. But the meeting reaffirmed their suspicions that Booras was not telling the whole truth. There was some secret agenda that he refused to reveal.

• • •

Over the next couple of weeks, Nancy talked with her neighbors and found that many of them had also been approached about selling their land. But it wasn't always the same man. Another man with a Greek name, George Pappademus, also claimed he was seeking property and had approached several households. The coincidence of the Greek names and vague reasons for wanting property on Durham Point Road led Nancy to believe that something else was going on. She contacted Francis Robinson, a fellow resident on Durham Point and a former, longtime Town Moderator to see if he would preside over a neighborhood meeting to exchange stories. As it turned out, Pappademus had also tried to buy some of Robinson's property, so Francis was quite willing to grant Nancy's request.

One couple that had not been approached was Sharon and Dave Meeker, who had moved into a small, seven-acre ranch just down the road from the Sandbergs. Dave started teaching math at the university a couple of years earlier, and for two years the Meekers had lived in Dover, a small city less than ten miles away. But as their children were getting close to school age, they decided to move into the Oyster River School District, which included Durham and two other adjacent towns. The first person to visit and welcome them was Nancy, and they had been friends with both Sandbergs since. At their new ranch on Durham Point, Sharon and Dave had a couple of horses for them and their kids to ride. "We are both from out west," Dave later recalled. "We both rode horses and we wanted our children to have the same opportunity."

Before moving to New Hampshire, the Meekers lived in a community housing complex in New Jersey overseen by a federal agency, Housing and Urban Development (HUD). A major conflict arose between the tenants and the supervisors of the complex over the quality of the services that were supposed to be provided to all the residents. Sharon was heavily involved in the conflict, working on behalf of the tenants, keeping them informed of negotiations with HUD officials and providing the press with the latest updates. When Nancy informed her about the strange series of visits by Booras and Pappademus and suggested the neighborhood meeting, Sharon's political antennae told her something important was probably happening. She was eager to attend the meeting, to lend her skills and whatever knowledge she had gained from her experience in New Jersey. She and Dave assumed they had not been approached to sell their land because it was so small compared with the other properties being sought. "But I sensed right away there was something big going on," Sharon would say later. "Another case where the powers that be try to screw the common folk."

• • •

At the evening meeting in the UNH library, the neighbors shared stories of their encounters with the men who wanted to buy their land. To Sherwood "Woody" Rollins, whom Nancy had known for a long time, Pappademus said he wanted the land for "a game preserve"; to Connie Kitfield, a math teacher at Oyster River High School, Pappademus claimed he was "not in the real estate business—he just wanted a nice farm"; to Sam Smith on Durham Point Road, the man said he was just interested "in an older house"; and to the Langleys, Nancy's next door neighbors, he said there "absolutely would be no development." But Evelyn Browne's story was perhaps the most troublesome.[17]

Ev, as Nancy called her, was also promised by the men who approached her that there would be no development.[18] She was a professor of physical education at the University of New Hampshire, and lived on "Salty," a 170-acre estate that bordered Little Bay—an extension of Great Bay, a tidal body of water several miles inland from the Portsmouth coastline. Ev had been living on Salty with her partner, Marion Beckwith, also a UNH physical education professor, since 1948. The main house on Salty was originally built almost two centuries earlier, but it was virtually rebuilt by the two women after they bought it from the Rollins family. The property initially consisted of just eighteen acres, but over the years the two women had gradually added to it, buying up available parcels when they could afford to do so. Now, a decade and a half later, they had no intention of selling it.

Ev and Marion were first approached by two men on either Thursday or Friday, September 20 or 21—Ev couldn't remember which. The men identified themselves as Chris Booras (who, they later discovered, was the brother of Peter Booras) and a Mr. Belhumer, who owned the Hampton Motel in Hampton, New Hampshire. Ev recounted that the men "said they were looking for property for a friend who was looking for 'isolation.'" Ev told the men that Salty was not for sale. When they asked her if she had any other property for sale, Ev said she did—Ambler Acres, consisting of thirty-five acres and a two-apartment house, which she had listed for sale several years earlier. "However," she told the group, "I have resisted selling to real estate developers, as I did not want a Wedgewood [a new housing development in Durham at the time] down here." The men said they would report back. They never mentioned their client's name.

On Friday evening—either the same day or the day after the first encounter with the two men—Ev received a phone call from a man who identified himself as Mr. George Pappademus of Hampton, New Hampshire, the client who wanted to buy Salty and Ambler Acres. "I would like to see you tomorrow morning," he said. "My wife and I have been down there and you were not at home, and we walked around and peeked into your windows and we just love your big, wide boards."

The notion that these people were poking around her house and property while she was gone did not sit well. "I already told those two men, Salty is not for sale," Ev told him. "If you want to discuss Amblers, I will meet with you. But I won't sell Salty."

Pappademus replied, "Little lady, I'll bet that we will buy your wide boards right out from under you."

• • •

Clearly, the arrogance and persistence of these men portended something of great consequence. For the next couple of hours, the neighbors engaged in animated conversation in the UNH library as they tried to figure out what might be happening in their neighborhood. Most certainly, there was some plan underfoot that threatened to change the character of Durham Point. Most probably, they thought, it would be a major housing development, because the scenic views of Little Bay and the Oyster River were certainly to die for. That the men were being so secretive about their intentions, and the fact that they were seeking so much property, suggested this was no small undertaking, but something major. Still, they didn't really know what they were fighting against.

"We need to have a name for our group," someone said. And that started an extended conversation about what the name could be. Someone suggested "Save Our Shores," which had the nice acronym of SOS—Help!—but others thought it was premature and perhaps not even relevant. Was it really their "shores" that needed saving, or was it more extensive, the whole area of Durham Point? Sharon Meeker liked the name, loved the acronym, and argued strongly for such a name that, from a public relations perspective, immediately conveyed the problem the neighbors faced. But wasn't that just the problem, someone argued, that SOS was really limited to only their neighborhood, and so could be seen as just another case of the NIMBY phenomenon—where people liked the advantages of economic development, as long as it's not in my back yard?

It was getting late and they had argued long enough. "We need something to identify our movement," Sharon said. "Save Our Shores is a great name for whatever plan might be under way." In exhaustion, they agreed. SOS it would be. Someone suggested that Sharon should be president, but immediately she said, "No! Nancy should be president." Without further discussion, the group agreed. Nancy was too stunned to say anything.

When she got home, Mal was in bed. She woke him and told him what happened at the meeting. It took him a few moments to process her words, but when she concluded by noting that she was now the president of SOS, he grinned at her. "Now you've gone and done it!"

What, actually, had she gone and done? She realized she was just a housewife and had no experience with anything like SOS, whatever it might turn out to be. The thought terrified her. She looked at Mal wordlessly, and perhaps it was the expression on her face that caused him to reconsider his reaction. He quickly added, "Don't worry, honey. You'll do great!" But Nancy wasn't so sure.

2

EARLY ALERT

It was early October when Phyllis Bennett thought, not for the first time, that this whole venture she and Steve had of starting their own local newspaper might fail after all. She had just left their six-year-old twins, Patrick and Meredith, at school in Brentwood, and was making the half-hour drive to Newmarket, to the top floor

of the old mill building, where the six-member staff of *Publick Occurrences* was preparing the fledgling weekly for its seventh edition. It was a cloudy fall day, chilly and threatening rain, but still dry so far. She drove quickly. If all went well, today *someone*—and that was the key problem, she didn't know who—would feed all the articles for tomorrow's publication into the compugraphic machine, which in turn would produce galleys for the paper, which she in turn would drive down to Plaistow to be printed for next day's publication. The story they had for the paper this time would be dynamite. And none of the other news organizations had it—not the daily newspapers, nor the radio stations, not even New Hampshire's one TV station. It would shock not only Durham residents, but the whole seacoast—if not the whole state. But there was no assurance that all would go well.

The problem was that no one currently on staff had any idea

how to work the compugraphic machine. It was a complicated device requiring a lot of technical skill. Their first operator, an experienced printer who had been laid off from his previous job several months before *Publick Occurrences* began its run (one of the many victims of the recession), suddenly announced two weeks ago that he had another job. He would be leaving the following week. Which was last week. As publisher, Steve had immediately put ads in the local newspapers and at the University of New Hampshire for a replacement, but got only one response, from a Shaunna McDuffee. They interviewed her and found that she was a very capable, somewhat older UNH student, who had already learned the intricacies of operating the complicated machine. Phyllis thought the girl would be ideal for the job. Besides, as she pointed out many times to Steve in increasingly frantic tones, they had no one else, and today was the deadline for getting the layout down to the printer. Unfortunately, Shaunna had the fatal flaw—at least in Steve's eyes—of being the daughter of Jay McDuffee, administrative assistant to GOP Governor Meldrim Thomson. Steve detested Thomson, a displaced, ultra-conservative Georgian who had won the governorship primarily, Steve argued, because of the blatantly distorted coverage of New Hampshire's only statewide daily newspaper, the *Manchester Union Leader*.

"Give me a break! You can't punish someone because of their father," Phyllis said, but Steve was adamant. It was a matter of principle. "Well, it's either her or nobody," Phyllis said. If they missed their deadline, it would be the first time since they had started publishing the previous August. "You can't run a newspaper if you suddenly decide not to publish one week." Steve said he would think about it. Think about it! What was there to think about? Almost screaming at him, Phyllis said, "We've got twenty-four hours to get out the next issue. We're not hiring Shaunna's father. We're hiring Shaunna. Nobody else has responded. And no one else in this building knows how to run this fucking machine!" He walked away. She had no idea what he would do.

This flap over a compugraphic operator was just the latest in a long list of disagreements Phyllis had with Steve over how to run *Publick Occurrences*. When they cashed in their investment last year and decided to follow their dream of starting a local newspaper, she knew then, of course, that Steve had rigid standards. In fact, it was his principled stand on issues that had attracted her to him when they first worked together at the *Baltimore Sun* eleven years earlier, and what had eventually led to their marriage. But his insistence that it was his way or no way when it came to running the newspaper no longer seemed principled, but simply bullheaded.

The disagreements began right at the start, even before they got to New Hampshire. Should they bring Dick Levine with them as their editor-in-chief? Steve insisted that Dick was crucial to the operation—he was a brilliant journalist, and just what they needed. But everyone they knew down in Maryland had warned them against bringing Levine. Yes, he was brilliant, and had even been nominated for a Pulitzer for his exposé of police corruption in Baltimore. But the nomination had been withdrawn by the publisher himself after the two had gotten into some kind of stupid argument. Besides that, Levine seemed congenitally unable to meet a deadline. He was always late and disorganized and was hardly the role model as chief editor for others on staff. Phyllis was strongly opposed to hiring him. "Okay," Steve told her, "you take your half of the money and do what you want, and I'll take my half and do what I want." It was a ludicrous idea. They had children. She couldn't just go off with her half of the money. Besides, when Levine heard that Phyllis might not be part of the project, he said he wouldn't go, either. What a weird and ironic triangle they made, Phyllis thought. But all the warnings they had received about Levine had come true. He and Steve were constantly arguing, often yelling at each other in that small office, each with his own unbending way of doing things, each unwilling to compromise, the whole effort exacerbated by Levine's constant pattern of coming in late, usually with a hangover, and sometimes not coming in at all. Though this was the hardest day of the week as they made their last-minute preparations for tomorrow's publication, Phyllis had no idea if Levine would even be at work by the time she got there.

As she drove through Newfields on the way to the Newmarket office, she passed the town grocery store, reminding her once again, as though she needed reminding, that another of her fierce arguments with Steve had been over the timing of publication. He wanted it on Friday, but she pointed out to him that weeklies thrive on ads from supermarkets, and they typically offer their discount specials every Thursday. *Publick Occurrences* would be coming out a day later. Why not publish a day earlier to maximize their opportunity to get the supermarket ads? "I don't want super-market ads," he told her. "I don't want any ads!" That, of course, was ridiculous. All papers needed ads. Two-thirds of newspaper revenues came from ads. He knew that, but liked to pretend it wasn't so. He acceded to publishing them, of course, as long as he didn't have to solicit them. That was Phyllis's job. But he refused to change the publication day. It was a matter of principle. So, they almost never got any of the ad money from supermarkets, which she knew was the lifeblood of most weekly publications.

Nor would Steve let her seek funding from other people or charitable organizations. "We'll do this by ourselves," he told her. "This is our project, our dream. We don't need others to help us. If we run into trouble, then we'll think about it." But she knew that if you want to raise money, you have to do it when you already have money. No one wants to invest in a losing cause. Now was the time, when they were starting out and had plenty of money. But he would not budge. It was a matter of principle.

She backed off from pressing her point of view. They were joint partners in this venture, but it was Steve's name on the masthead as publisher. And he used that fact to settle their arguments. He would run the newspaper. She would help edit and write articles, and of course take care of the children. She would also do her best to obtain ads for the paper, which he allowed her to do, despite his aversion to them. She left the business part of the publishing to him—he was the one who managed the finances, the salaries, and the expenses of publishing. And the hiring.

When she arrived at the old mill building, she could feel the anxiety rise in her. This could be a turning point. Perhaps the end of a dream. She climbed the stairs and pushed open the door. It was a moderately sized room, with windows that overlooked the Lamprey River. Two desks facing each other belonged to the two major reporters, Jay McManus and Jay Smith. Other desks in the room were for a temporary reporter, Ron Lewis; the Advertising Manager, Bill Hansen; the General Manager, Peter Fagley; and Bob Nilson, the cartoonist and illustrator. The editor-in-chief, Dick Levine, had a small cubbyhole off the main room, and Steve had his own office. An alcove on the far side of the room included the compugraphic machine, and immediately Phyllis looked over there, taking in the cute, young coed sitting behind the computer, typing away. Steve stood behind her, smiling, looking pleased. Phyllis was so relieved, it didn't register with her at the time how attentive Steve was to Shaunna, how close he was standing to her, how he bent down to look at what she was doing, his face close to hers, his soft voice murmuring approval. They turned to look at Phyllis, who greeted Shaunna with genuine delight. This meant that their investigation over the past two weeks, their shocking scoop, would actually go live tomorrow.

• • •

The previous week, George Findel, a local attorney, had called the *Publick Occurrences* office and told Staff Reporter Ron Lewis that several of his clients, each individually, had been approached by the same man wanting to buy some of their property. The clients wondered if the offer was legitimate and a good deal. The attorney told Lewis he was convinced that the effort to buy property on Durham Point was related to the governor's desire to get an oil refinery built in the state. "I tried to get *Fosters* [the daily paper in Dover] and the *Herald* [the daily paper in Portsmouth], and even the *Concord Monitor* and *Manchester Union Leader* to cover this. But they all said it was too speculative," he told Lewis. "The radio stations wouldn't bite, either."

This situation was exactly the reason Phyllis and Steve had founded their paper in the first place—a lack of meaningful news coverage for local towns. That was the core of their dream, their belief that local papers provided the lifeblood of communities. That was also why they had named the paper *Publick Occurrences*—a reminder of the very first edition of the paper with that name, intended to inform the people of the truth of what the government was doing, but which saw just one edition, published on September 25, 1690, after which the Governor and Council of Massachusetts closed down the paper and jailed its publisher. The new *Publick Occurrences*, Steve wrote in the premier edition, would continue in the same tradition of telling the truth, though "we hope to keep our publisher out of jail, even beyond this issue." And now here was the perfect manifestation of the paper's purpose. If the attorney's speculation was true, it would cause a shock wave in the small towns along the Seacoast, and especially in Durham. Eventually, of course, it would become a big story for the state as well. That these other newspapers didn't see the importance of this story was a godsend to *Publick Occurrences*—which would get the biggest scoop of its fledgling existence.

Phyllis had worked with Lewis in writing the article. The attorney did not want to be quoted about his belief that an oil refinery was behind the purchases, and she and Lewis could find no hard evidence of the link. But she wanted to get that information out to the readers. Journalistically, they should only report the facts. But Lewis could ask the land developer about the possible link to the oil refinery, and then—regardless of his answer—they could legitimately mention the oil refinery. She was excited about the final shape of the story.

REAL ESTATE BLITZ ON DURHAM POINT[19]

This paper called at random a dozen Durham Point area land

owners, and found that every one had been approached within the last month to sell their property.

A single real estate dealer, George Pappademus of Hampton and Nashua, made all the offers—for parcels of 20 to 500 acres.

Most of the people we contacted refused to do business with Pappademus, who often persisted despite four or five flat refusals.

[Landowners contacted by the newspaper and by Pappademus were Alex Cochrane, Malcolm Chase, Edith Wilcox, Norman Stiles, Ken Moore, Connie Kitfield, Mrs. Harold Langley, Roland LaRoche, William Woodward, Robert Congdon, Sherwood Rollins, and Evelyn Brown.]

Most were aware that Pappademus was inquiring up and down the road for real estate, offering from $1,000 to $1,400 per acre.

How to explain this blitz? Why is Pappademus acting as though he wants to buy up Durham Point? And for whom?

This is what Pappademus says:

At first he answered "no comment" to all questions.

After much prodding he said, "It is not going to be a development and whatever I do with the land will conform to the zoning of Durham."

Who does he represent?

His answer: "I'd be breaching my trust...."

Why was he sewing up options on Durham Point?

"So far we've only bought up 7. We don't even know if we are going to buy any of the other options."

Why did he give different reasons to different people for wanting to purchase their property?

"Because I have no single reason for purchasing. I want 500 acres for myself as an investment, and I'm representing other people, as well, who have their own interests."

What about the game preserve?

"I'm representing 4 men from Hollis, N.H. who are interested in that."

Why this saturation approach?

"I wouldn't buy a new suit after only looking at a couple, and I wouldn't decide on real estate without doing my best to get a good deal."

What about the widespread rumor that he is acting on behalf of an oil company in search of a refinery site?

"Completely unfounded!"

It is true that oil companies recently have shown much interest in building refineries in New Hampshire.

Governor Meldrim Thomson is the only major official on the East Coast who has indicated a positive attitude toward refineries. New Hampshire's coastal protection laws are lax. New England has an acute fuel shortage problem.

However, many of the people we talked to tend to discount the rumor because Durham Point seems to them an unlikely site. Durham has strict zoning laws and plenty of environmentalists who would fight a refinery.

—Ron Lewis

Pappademus's answers were so patently false, only an idiot couldn't see what was really going on. Phyllis wanted the story on the front page, but Steve argued against it. They had other stories with hard facts that merited front-page coverage. Their lead story was the plan by the University of New Hampshire to ease its shortage of student housing by building a one-hundred-unit mobile home park in the town. The other front-page story was about the Newmarket Day Care Center, a six-year-old undertaking that had become a model for the state. The Durham Point real estate blitz would be relegated to page three.

Still, she felt the story should be given greater prominence. Finally, she arrived at a compromise with Steve. At the top of the page for the October 5, 1973 issue, on the left side opposite the lead story's headline, would be a teaser:

AN OIL REFINERY ON DURHAM POINT?
An attempted land grab causes a week of rumors.
Story, page 3

Now, *that* should get Durham's attention.

3

DEVISING A STRATEGY

When State Representative Dudley Webster Dudley saw the article in *Publick Occurrences* suggesting that someone might be thinking of building an oil refinery on Durham Point, she felt a jolt of anxiety. She had heard rumors of some possible development, related to her by several people in the town. They had been keeping her informed because she was one of Durham's four representatives to the four-hundred-member New Hampshire House of

Representatives, and they thought she might be able to find more information about what was going on. But the idea of an oil refinery in the area was so outlandish, she had never seriously considered the possibility. Even now, she wasn't sure she should take it seriously, though seeing the rumor in print gave it a force that made her pause. She was even more disturbed when, a couple of days later, Barbara Underwood called her and expressed concern about the story. Barbara was one of the few "good" Republicans in the

legislature, a representative from Concord who seemed genuinely worried that someone might indeed be planning to site a refinery on the New Hampshire seacoast.

"Let me know if there is anything I can do to help," she told Dudley. "An oil refinery would be a disaster for New Hampshire."

Well, if Barbara Underwood, a rep who didn't even live in

the Seacoast area, was taking the rumor seriously, Dudley thought, maybe she should, too. Dudley thought of herself as "a real bozo" when it came to state politics, "so unsophisticated, so unknowledgeable," she would later admit. By contrast, maybe Barbara had some sources of information that Dudley did not. Maybe the Concord rep knew specifically what plans were being made, but was obligated not to reveal them. Or maybe she recognized that this was the type of development that would immediately appeal to the business mentality of the GOP leaders in the state. Dudley had no clue as to why Barbara had taken the rumor so seriously, but the fact that she had was more than a little disquieting.

Despite Dudley's diffidence in the state legislature, she was no newcomer to state politics. She had been born in New Hampshire and lived in Durham most of her life, where her father taught English at the University of New Hampshire. After two years of high school in Dover, a small city just six miles from her home, she attended Robinson Seminary in Exeter, a public high school for girls just twelve miles away, and graduated in 1954. That summer, her parents, Bob and Polly Webster, managed the Lake Sunapee Yacht Club, while Dudley taught swimming. There she met Tom Dudley, a Dartmouth College graduate who had completed one year of law school, and was tending bar. He found the young woman with a ready smile and shoulder-length blond hair "intriguing" and "beautiful," writing later that "Our first meeting was a life-altering moment for me."[20] It was for Dudley as well.

She went ahead with her plans the following fall to attend Tufts University, just outside Boston, but before the academic year was out, she and Tom were engaged. She was a competitive diver and had chosen Tufts for its excellent indoor pool (which she later reflected wryly was "hardly the best criterion for selecting a college"), but now that she and Tom had plans to get married, she transferred to UNH for her sophomore year. "Why on earth," she would later explain with a droll smile, "would I spend my parents' money to go away to school when you know the purpose was to find a husband?" Which she clearly had done. In 1956, Dudley

Webster married Tom Dudley, giving her a rare and unforgettable double appellation. (Later, when running for re-election to political office, her bumper sticker would read: Dudley Dudley, Worth Repeating.) Then, after nine years of living in various abodes just across the border in Maine, she and Tom and their two daughters, Morgan and Becky, moved back to New Hampshire, eventually buying a house across the street from where Dudley had been raised, and where her parents still lived.

Dudley's political experience began early. At the age of four, in 1940, she accompanied her parents to the town's Grange Hall to stuff envelopes for President Franklin Delano Roosevelt's re-election effort. Her parents, of course, were Republicans. Who in the town wasn't? But for some odd reason, Bob and Polly were great fans of FDR.

As an adult, Dudley's first major foray into campaign politics came in 1968, when she supported anti-war candidate Senator Eugene McCarthy, who was running against President Lyndon Johnson in the New Hampshire primary. McCarthy did not win, but his showing led to Johnson's refusal to run for re-election, reaffirming Dudley's belief that positive goals could be achieved through politics.

The following year Dudley learned that two African-American Marines, William Harvey and George Daniels, were incarcerated at the Portsmouth Naval Prison solely because they had been overheard saying that Vietnam was "a white man's war."[21] As Tom Dudley would later write,[22] "They did not propose to go AWOL to avoid service there, nor did they encourage anyone else to do so. Their sentences were for 6 or 10 years, just for opening their mouths." While there were already protest efforts by the ACLU, Harvard Law School, and the American Servicemen's Union, there was little activity near the prison itself. Dudley decided to protest publicly and rounded up some activist friends of hers who were sympathetic to the Marines' cause. The prison was actually in Kittery, Maine, just across the Piscataqua River from Portsmouth, facing the Atlantic Ocean. As a longtime sailor, Tom had his own idea of how to protest. When Dudley came home a couple of days later "to the acrid odor of aerosol in the air," she found her husband in the basement, spray-painting a bed sheet with the words, FREE HARVEY AND DANIELS. Dudley later wrote, "That afternoon was the first of many when we sailed back and forth in front of the Portsmouth Naval Prison on our boat, the aptly named 'Right On,' with the bed sheet pinned to the sail."[23]

• • •

Eventually, with Dudley's help, the local protest movement garnered national attention, and finally, in the fall, perhaps embarrassed with its gestapo-like tactics, or at least pressured by the legal community and congressional investigations, the military released the two men. The following year, their convictions were officially overturned for lack of evidence of any real wrongdoing. After the release in September, Tom and Dudley held a victory reception. As Tom later wrote, "The Marines came, as did a large marching contingent of Black Panthers, singing, with signs, dreadlocks, and dancing. All on Woodman Road, in a neighborhood of old white Republicans. The dancing went on late and shook our house; then it was all over. Dudley became political. I signed up to do some draft counseling."[24]

• • •

Spurred on by her strong anti-war views, in 1972 Dudley worked for Senator George McGovern's presidential campaign in the state, helping to set up small meetings with voters, prepare news releases, and organize a get-out-the-vote effort. After McGovern came close to beating Senator Edmund Muskie in the New Hampshire primary, she was rewarded for her diligent efforts by being selected as one of McGovern's delegates to attend the party's national nominating convention in Miami that summer. That was the first convention held under the new, reformed party rules, ensuring a diverse composition of delegates, without which she never would have hoped to have been included.

Inspired by her experience with presidential politics, she decided to run for the state legislature. Four years earlier, she had run unopposed in the Democratic primary, simply to win the Democratic Party's nomination, knowing how unlikely it was that she could actually win in the general election. The last time a Democrat from Durham had won a house seat was in 1918, and since then the party often could not field even a full slate of candidates from the town. Thus, the primaries were always uncontested. That had been fine with Dudley in 1968, since her objective was to attend the state party convention in late summer, frequented by all nominated Democrats. Just to be part of that democratic process was inspiring to her. But now, four years later, with two presidential campaigns to her credit, as well as a satisfying protest effort against the federal government's maltreatment of the two Marines, she was determined to win not just the nomination, but the general election as well. She campaigned hard, going to people's homes to address small gatherings, sending out flyers, putting up signs. All of her efforts paid off. In the contested general election, she came in fourth behind three Republicans, getting 1,686 votes, beating the fourth Republican candidate by eighty-one votes, and the three Democrats by much larger margins. She was the first Democrat to be elected from Durham in over half a century, and the first female Democrat elected from Durham ever.

• • •

It was now, as a state legislator, that she would face her biggest challenge—preventing the state from forcing a refinery on the town. Assuming, of course, that someone did indeed intend to make that effort. If that was the case, there was another problem— the 1973 legislative session, scheduled from January to June, had already ended. According to the state constitution, there could be no additional session in the current two-year term, unless the GOP leaders called for a special session to deal with emergency matters. In her view, the possible siting of an oil refinery in Durham did represent an emergency situation, but convincing the GOP leaders of that might be difficult.

But first things first. How credible was the rumor?

Over the next couple of weeks, Dudley spent long hours on the telephone, talking to her fellow legislators, to businessmen, to local leaders, to anyone who might have some idea of what the land purchases on Durham Point might be. She knew, of course, that Meldrim Thomson, the first-term ultra-conservative governor from the small town of Orford, was obsessed with locating an oil refinery in the state. Given the shortage of oil and the poor economic times, he argued that an oil refinery was just what the state needed to stimulate its economy. So far, he had been unsuccessful in his quest, in part, it seemed, because New Hampshire was hardly an ideal location for such an enterprise. Still, he was actively searching for some company to come to New Hampshire, and it was at least theoretically possible that the land sales on Durham Point meant that he had been successful.

She came away from her conversations distressed by the widespread sentiment that such a refinery would be a boon to the state. While she expected the most business-oriented reps to take that position, she was stunned when she heard even the more environmentally oriented leaders say that they would have to wait and see what an oil refinery proposal might entail.

She didn't need to see any proposal to know that it would be a disaster—not just for Durham, but for the whole Piscataqua region. She and Tom had sailed all over the area, and had studied and seen for themselves the fragile ecosystems that the region contained. It had existed for thousands of years, some 120 square miles of water and land, which included the great Piscataqua River, a fast-moving tidal inlet formed by the confluence of the Cocheco and Salmon Falls rivers. The region also included Great Bay and Little Bay, two larger bodies of water that were fed by five additional freshwater rivers, and which both flowed into the Piscataqua River. The Great

Bay estuary, comprised of a comingling of saltwater and freshwater, produced five different types of habitats, which were home to hundreds of bird, fish, and plant species. She and Tom had tried naming some of them, but couldn't possibly master them all. It was inconceivable to Dudley that anyone would seriously consider risking that unique ecological system by dumping an oil refinery into its midst. It was never a question of whether there would be an oil spill, but when and how big. Surely, if someone were going to pick New Hampshire as a site for an oil refinery, Durham Point should be the very last place to do it.

During her phone conversations, she learned that a local movement, called SOS, had been formed to rally the town against the possibility of an oil refinery. That was certainly an important step, but she feared that even if the town opposed such a facility, the state could force the town to accept it anyway. The other three GOP state reps from Durham were hardly likely to actively oppose a project so dearly desired by their party's governor, so it would be up to her to find the political support at the state level to prevent state intervention. She and Tom discussed what she could do. An environmental argument, they agreed, would surely not work with the GOP legislative leaders, nor with many Democrats, and especially not with Thomson and his close advisers, who seemed oblivious to any such concerns.

And then she remembered. Earlier in the year, during the legislative session, Chris Spirou, a young and dynamic state representative from Manchester, had met with her in her Durham home, along with attorney Marty Gross. Although Gross had served as legal counsel to Walter Peterson, a three-term progressive GOP governor who lost to Thomson in the 1972 state primary, the attorney was a Democrat and was advising Spirou on legal matters. The three of them sat around the breakfast table in her kitchen, drinking coffee and talking strategy, when Gross said, "You know, if you ever really want to get something done in Concord, you have to claim Home Rule. It's sacrosanct. No one doesn't support Home Rule."

And he was right. No income tax, no statewide sales tax. Why? Home Rule. The property tax lets communities collect their own taxes and use them as they see fit.

Little or no money from the state for education. The explanation: Home Rule. That it was unfair to poorer communities, which meant their quality of education would suffer, had little persuasive value.

Few or no state environmental regulations. Let each town deal with its own problems. Home Rule.

"Live Free or Die," the state motto adopted in 1945, reflected the same sentiment as Home Rule—individual independence for people, local independence for cities and towns.

Of course, there were exceptions, such as drivers' licenses, traffic regulations, and selective taxes and fees, which were all necessarily regulated at the state level. More importantly, there were exceptions when the ideology didn't give conservatives the outcome they wanted. They had no qualms about violating the principle of Home Rule when they voted to prevent towns and cities from levying their own income or sales taxes (only property taxes were allowed), and Dudley feared that Thomson and his supporters would be equally willing to violate Home Rule to force a refinery on a town. Still, the Home Rule ideology was strong, and it represented the best chance to thwart a state-imposed refinery.

So, that was the argument: no town should be forced to accept an oil refinery unless the people wanted it.

Dudley recognized that de-emphasizing the much stronger environmental argument—that a refinery would be an environmental disaster for the whole Piscataqua region—could result in a pyrrhic victory. She might help prevent a refinery in Durham on the grounds of Home Rule, but just down the road was Newmarket, with very weak zoning regulations, where a refinery could be just as, or even more, devastating to the whole Piscataqua region as a refinery on Durham Point. And a bit farther south were Newfields and Stratham, which both bordered the Squamscott River that flowed into Great Bay. What if either of those towns wanted the refinery? Home Rule works both ways.

On the other hand, it seemed to Dudley there was little choice. It would be up to SOS to persuade Durham and other seacoast towns that a refinery was not in their interests. Her job was to get a bill passed respecting Home Rule—in a GOP-dominated legislature that was mostly pro-business and anti-environment, in a state suffering from a severe recession and an acute energy shortage.

Good luck with that!

4

SOS EMERGES

It was early Friday morning, October 5, barely two weeks after the meeting of Durham Point neighbors at the UNH library, when Nancy got an excited phone call from Sharon Meeker, her neighbor down the road. Had Nancy seen the latest issue of *Publick Occurrences*? She didn't get a chance to respond, as Sharon kept on talking, informing her that according to the paper, the big secret behind all the land options was probably an oil refinery. Nancy was stunned.

She knew Thomson had been looking to locate an oil refinery in the state, but no one thought he would be successful. New Hampshire hardly seemed the ideal location for such an industrial enterprise. No other New England governors supported an oil refinery in the six states of their region, at least not without serious planning. And even if some company did want to come to the state, it was beyond comprehension that anyone would want to locate an oil refinery in the Piscataqua area. That would have to be the worst possible site, given its fragile ecosystem. Nancy and her fellow SOS board members could hardly believe that the worst possible scenario seemed to be the one that was looming before them.

The newspaper article galvanized the group into action. Nancy knew of Rep. Dudley Dudley, but had never met her and was a bit trepidatious about calling her out of the blue to invite her to a meeting with SOS supporters. But as the only Democrat in the state legislature from Durham, Dudley would be the most likely to help. And indeed that was the case. Nancy called her and found Dudley to be quite friendly and eager to attend. The meeting included some forty concerned citizens and was held at the home of Bob and Jeannette Congdon, who lived in the historic John Mighell house—a Georgian style, two-story, clapboarded wood frame, with a gable roof and a center chimney, built in the 1690s. Located just south of the Oyster River Bridge at 25 Newmarket Road, barely a stone's throw from the start of Durham Point Road, it seemed appropriate to hold this meeting in such a historically important house—the residents of the twentieth century deliberating how to protect the town that had been founded in the seventeenth century.

The attendees confirmed Nancy as chairman of SOS, and Cass Curtis as vice chairman. The attendees also set up four special committees. Sharon Meeker was most interested in community relations. She was the recent transplant from New Jersey who had insisted that Nancy be the president of SOS. She was the tallest, the most imposing, and also the most verbally aggressive in the group in wanting to take action, who had been convinced even before the *Publick Occurrences* article that the clandestine acquisition of property on Durham Point would be catastrophic. "I didn't know what forces were arrayed against us," Sharon would later recount. "But I knew they were big. And I thought there was no way we were going to win. But we sure couldn't give up without a fight." She felt her experience in New Jersey confronting Housing and Urban Development (HUD) on behalf of housing tenants would be beneficial in this confrontation, and volunteered to work on the Outreach Committee. This group would engage the public in the fight against an oil refinery by scheduling small home meetings throughout the town to discuss the issue; getting petitions signed; designing anti-refinery buttons, posters, and flyers; recruiting people to work on the committees; encouraging citizens to write their own letters to the newspapers; boosting large turnouts for committee hearings and for town meetings; and engaging in any other activities they would think of later that might help. After some discussion, Sharon agreed to head the committee, but, recognizing her newcomer status, insisted that Celeste DiMambro, who certainly knew the people in the town better than she did, work closely with her. Celeste was a 1964 graduate of UNH who lived in town with her physician husband, Arthur, and two daughters, Thea and Arna.

Karen Mower, an older woman in her mid-forties with three children—Amy, Robin, and Todd—suggested a technology committee, which she would gladly coordinate. As a longtime Durham resident and an active member of the local chapter of the League of Women Voters, Karen seemed to know everyone in town. Since her husband was a physicist at UNH, and she had long been a member of the Faculty Wives Club, she had met many of the technical experts at UNH who could help evaluate the impact of an oil refinery in the state. She and her committee would figure out whose contribution might be most relevant, and prevail upon the professors to lend their support.

Jeannette Congdon agreed to head up the Legal and Regulatory Committee, which would work closely with lawyers and help prepare for the various town committee hearings that would inevitably be scheduled. An oil refinery would require changes in the town's zoning laws. It was essential that the opponents be well-versed in the legal ramifications of any proposals.

Roger Wilson was designated recording secretary.

Finally, as a man with considerable means himself, Alex Cochrane said he would be willing to chair the Financial Committee to raise funds that would pay for outreach items, such as buttons, posters, petitions, flyers, and related postage. Also, they might need to pay for ads in the local newspapers.

Then, Dudley addressed the group. She commended everyone present on this new and vital organization, and stressed the importance of unifying the town against any effort to locate a refinery in their community. "That will not be enough," she told them. "Even if the town says no, the state could still force a refinery on us." She shared her strategy at the state level, calling for the state legislature to recognize the right of a town to set its own zoning regulations. "But even if Home Rule works," she warned them, "they might just move the refinery down the road...or down the coast." The town's outreach should include efforts to encourage other towns in the Piscataqua region to recognize the disaster that a refinery would mean—not just for their water, air, and land, but for their whole way of life. They would become like northern New Jersey. And nobody wanted that.

• • •

While the women of Durham were organizing their resources against an unknown force, events at the international, national, and state levels were conspiring against them. Already the country was suffering from a prolonged recession. Then, in October, just as Durham was learning about a proposed oil refinery, a war broke out in the Middle East that would lead to a quadrupling of oil prices.

On Saturday, October 6, 1973, the Day of Atonement (Yom Kippur), the holiest day of the Jewish calendar, Egypt and Syrian military forces launched an attack against Israel in the Suez and Golan Heights, respectively. Within six days, the United States responded by sending arms and supplies to Israel. A week later, President Nixon requested $2.2 billion in aid for Israel. The Arab oil countries and Iran respond by raising the price of oil, cutting production, and imposing an oil embargo against the United States and several of its allies. These actions led to an oil crisis worldwide, but especially in the United States, with Nixon's top energy adviser suggesting that gas rationing would probably be imposed the following spring, for the first time since World War II. Governor Thomson was already calling for gas rationing in the state, as service stations with limited supplies were experiencing long lines of cars.

• • •

In Durham, Smitty's Sunoco imposed its own rationing system, allowing no more than ten gallons of gas per vehicle, and only once every other day (determined by whether the plates ended with an odd or even number). The Oyster River district schools had been operating at reduced heat for some time, but in a November school board meeting, the superintendent, John Powers, said more needed to be done to deal with the fuel crisis: "The schools will have to be closed for some period of time." He suggested the possibility of a four-day week. In the meantime, the town selectmen took steps to make sure there were sufficient supplies of gas for town vehicles during the winter by purchasing a ten-thousand-gallon gasoline storage tank, which would provide a three-month reserve.

On Sunday, November 25, in a nationwide television address from the Oval Office of the White House, President Nixon announced several steps to attend to the oil crisis in the coming months, proposing top speed limits on the nation's highways of fifty-five miles per hour; requesting that all gas stations close down every Sunday in order to discourage drivers from making long trips on the weekend; curtailing "ornamental outdoor lighting for homes" and eliminating of all commercial lighting not directly related to the operation of the business; lowering indoor heating to a national average of sixty-eight degrees; cutting heating oil for homes by fifteen percent and for businesses by twenty-five percent; and announcing his "Project Independence—1980" plan, designed to free the US from dependence on foreign oil, with a promise that by the end of the decade, "Americans will not have to rely on any source of energy beyond their own."

Two days after Nixon's announcement, Governor Thomson officially unveiled his plan to locate a refinery on Durham Point.

• • •

When she saw the news on WMUR-TV, Sharon Meeker felt physically ill. Of course, she and everyone else within SOS anticipated that the governor intended to build a refinery on Durham Point.

It was no big surprise by that time. A couple of weeks earlier, he had revealed to the press that he was about to announce a project to establish an oil refinery on the state's seacoast, though he coyly refused to say exactly where. Unlike its neighbor Maine, which enjoys hundreds of miles bordering the sea, New Hampshire has only an eighteen-mile-long seacoast. It didn't take a genius to figure out where a refinery might be located. Almost simultaneously with the governor's announcement that he would be making an announcement, *Publick Occurrences* had discovered that just one man, George Pappademus, had now purchased over 1,000 acres of land on Durham Point. Although the real estate broker continued to insist that he had no intentions to develop it for commercial purposes, only a fool would believe him.

No, it wasn't where the governor's refinery would be located that made Sharon sick to her stomach. It was the size of the refinery itself—400,000 barrels of oil a day! *Publick Occurrences* had recently reported that a relatively new refinery in Benicia, California, just four years old, considered to be quite large at the time it was first proposed in 1966, processed seventy-two thousand barrels of oil a day. The refinery for Durham Point would be more than five times larger. In fact, at a cost of $600 million [$3.2 billion in today's currency], it would be the largest "grass roots" oil refinery in the world.

The company in charge was called "Olympic Refineries," but Sharon couldn't find it listed in any business directory. Though the *Union Leader* had pretended not to know for certain, WMUR had been quite clear: Olympic Refineries was a company newly formed by Aristotle Onassis, who was reputed to be the richest man in the world, a man who could get anything he wanted, who had even—somehow, despite his revolting public persona—been able to woo and marry the late President Kennedy's widow, Jackie Kennedy, now referred to in the press as Jackie O. How could the tiny town of Durham fight a man of such immense resources?

At the press conference with the governor, several representatives spoke on behalf of the refinery, thanking Governor Thomson

"IS THAT YOU, UNCLE MEL?"

for his foresight in welcoming them to New Hampshire. Thomson himself characterized the oil refinery proposal, coming in the days leading up to Christmas, as a gift from Santa to the state of New Hampshire.

But the bottom line was that whatever this company claimed to be, it had never built any refinery before. Calling itself Olympic "Refineries," as though it had constructed and operated more than one such facility, was more than a misrepresentation. It was an intentional deception. Pappademus, it turns out, had obtained options on 3,000 acres of land on Durham Point, about a fourth of the whole land area that constituted the town of Durham. This was going to be one gigantic operation that would transform the town's laid-back, bucolic personality into an industrial monster.

Sharon called Nancy Sandberg to commiserate. But Nancy seemed surprisingly upbeat. "Don't worry," she told Sharon. "It's not going to happen."

"I wish I could believe that," Sharon said. "But you heard

Nixon Sunday night. National energy shortage. The governor already calling for gas rationing. Possible fuel oil shortages this winter. People afraid of being cold and without power. Olympic promising Durham will get all the fuel it needs first. And the refinery will bring jobs. Reduce property taxes. How do we fight that?"

Nancy laughed. "Just what we're doing," she said. "The people just need the truth. And that's what we're giving them. How's the phone calling going?"

She was referring to the phone bank operation that SOS started Monday evening to alert residents to the perils of an oil refinery—and to invite everyone in town to an open, informational SOS meeting the following week. With Karen Mower's help in identifying UNH professors and other experts, the board had prepared an extensive agenda to educate the public about the nature and impact of an oil refinery. It was essential to get as large a turnout as possible.

"Great response," Sharon said. "The actual announcement has finally wakened a lot of people."

"So the news is good," Nancy said.

Sharon laughed. "The eternal optimist. So explain how such a monstrosity is good news."

"What if Olympic had proposed only a moderate-sized or small refinery?" Nancy said. "A lot of people would think, 'Oh, that's not so bad.' Much tougher for us to persuade people how disastrous it really would be. But with this gargantuan project, no one can ignore its impact."

Sharon nodded, though she knew Nancy couldn't see her. "The other side of the coin is that if we fail, the town is shit out of luck." There was a short silence, and Sharon wondered if her earthy language had offended Nancy, who always spoke with precise English.

"It's up to us to make the case," Nancy said. "Trust me. People will listen."

After they terminated the conversation, Sharon felt reassured that Nancy was the perfect person to head SOS. Yes, there was a certain naiveté to her unfailing optimism about the rationality of people, including those who seemed bent on a refinery regardless of consequences. But her good cheer was also inspiring, especially coupled with her steadfast resolve. Deep in her bones, though, Sharon was not optimistic. In New Jersey, she had seen that political power and money overwhelmed those without. And now here was the town of Durham up against the power of money, politics, and the press—represented by Onassis, the governor and the state's political establishment, and the *Union Leader* respectively. This wasn't David versus Goliath. This was David against Goliath and his two giant friends. Durham's odds did not look good.

5

ABANDONING THE DREAM

The mood in the *Publick Occurrences* office was surprisingly subdued when Phyllis returned on Thursday, November 29, to help finish producing the paper for the next day's publication. The governor had finally made his big announcement about a proposed oil refinery on Durham Point just two days before, and the paper had plenty of great stories for its readers. Earlier in the day she had left the noisy office, where her husband, Steve, and the managing editor, Dick Levine, were arguing vociferously over some goddamn trivial point about the layout. It was a weekly ritual that was driving her, and everyone else in the office, crazy. She didn't want to think about how many times Dick had quit in a rage, only to be persuaded by her to resume his duties, or how many times Steve had walked out seething with anger. It was a relief for Phyllis to go pick up Patrick and Meredith from first grade, take them home, spend some time with them before dinner, get them fed, bathed, and into bed, and then—once the babysitter had arrived—return to the office to finish the night's work.

The unexpected calm, she realized, was the result of Steve's absence. There was, of course, the usual hum of activity, the reporters typing in their last-minute changes to their stories and talking in normal tones while Dick worked with Shaunna as she inputted other stories into the compugraphic machine. But no yelling or screaming. No Steve. It was odd. Typically, he and she would both stay until Dick and Shaunna had finished getting the paper ready for printing, and then Phyllis would drive down to Plaistow to the printer while Steve went home to the kids.

Dick came over to her. She tilted her head toward Steve's office. Dick shrugged. He didn't know where Steve was. Phyllis wondered if her husband had stormed out of the office once again. When she got home, she wondered, would he be in a terrible mood? But she didn't want to get into that now. There was a lot of last-minute work that had to be done.

Bob Nilson was finishing a cartoon that would accompany Olympic Refineries' official news release, which was to run as follows:[25]

PRESS RELEASE
FOR RELEASE:
NOVEMBER 27, 1973
10:00 AM

At a press conference in Concord today, Olympic Refineries outlined plans for constructing a clean fuels-refinery in the Durham-Portsmouth area of New Hampshire.

Proposed site for the refinery itself is Durham Point, bordered by the Lamprey and Oyster Rivers, and Great Bay.

Several thousand acres of sparsely settled land have recently been optioned here—sufficient to locate the facilities so that people will hardly be aware of its presence.

A pipeline will extend underground and under water to the vicinity of the Isles of Shoals, connecting with facilities for unloading large super tankers. Extra precautions are being added to the design for protection against disturbing the environment during construction and later when in operation.

More detailed plans will be released during the weeks ahead to assure all citizens of Olympic's genuine concern to build a model refinery here....

Representatives of Olympic have been meeting with Governor Thomson and other state officials for several months. The governor's sincerity and cooperation have been instrumental in their decision to undertake such an enormous project.

Plans are also underway to meet with local officials of Durham, Portsmouth and Rye, in order to provide full details.

Local cooperation is considered vital to the project. Olympic plans to demonstrate that it can be a responsible part of the community—aware of its needs and concerns—and desirous of doing its part to make the area an even better place to live.

More detailed plans and studies will be presented to the governing agencies by mid-January.

Construction is then scheduled to begin as soon as the necessary permits are granted. For extra protection, supplemental long-range environmental studies will continue during construction so as to incorporate all desirable requirements into the design.

She saw Nilson's cartoon of a Trojan horse, opening to let out camels carrying barrels of oil, and laughed. "That's fantastic! It's perfect!"

He smiled. He was used to her compliments—Phyllis was perhaps his strongest fan—but he never tired of hearing them.

Phyllis wondered how anyone could be fooled by the reassurances in the press release. Local cooperation was considered "vital to the project," and Olympic wanted to show "it can be a responsible member of the community"? What a crock. For months, Olympic representatives had been meeting secretly with Thomson and state officials at the same time that Olympic was having Booras and Pappademus buy up land on Durham Point under false pretenses. That's how Olympic intended to demonstrate it could be a responsible member of the community?

The paean to their concern for the environment rang especially hollow, Phyllis thought. "*Supplemental* long-range environmental studies"? A supplement is an addition, but as the lead article for tomorrow's edition would report, there had been no environmental studies about an oil refinery in the area. None. Not long-range. Not short-range. Not by any governmental agency. Not by Olympic, despite what the press release implied. In fact, neither Olympic nor the governor wanted such a study. Last week, when Ron Lewis asked Jay McDuffee, the governor's assistant (and Shaunna's father), if the state shouldn't undertake an in-depth impact study to get some idea of what a major oil refinery would do to the surrounding community, McDuffee was dismissive: "You mean one of those studies that would take months and cost the taxpayers thousands of dollars?" Instead, the governor demanded that UNH undertake a ninety-day examination to assess the desirability of an oil refinery in the state—but with no specific site in mind. UNH would not be evaluating a refinery in Durham, where it would actually be located, but in some hypothetical location somewhere in the state. The task was clearly for show, with no real results expected. Robert Faiman, the vice provost for research, essentially acknowledged that point when he admitted, "We don't have the resources to do an in-depth study." And the governor was providing absolutely no funds for it.[26]

The truth, of course, was that Olympic really didn't care about the environment or about local cooperation. Its strategy was top-down: get all the important people in New Hampshire behind the project, and the town would buckle under the pressure. And, surprisingly, Phyllis thought, that approach might be working. At least, that was the implication of Ron Lewis's article about the town selectmen's reaction to the oil refinery proposal. She set herself to copyediting it before giving it to Shaunna.

She didn't know exactly on which page it would be published, though not on pages one through three, where Jay Smith's lead story was going. That article focused on the negative reactions of regional planners, who were upset that they had not been given any information about any refinery, despite the fact that it would transform the seacoast region. "I couldn't think of a worse place to put it," said Michael Koulkas, Director of the Strafford Regional

Planning Commission.[27] Phyllis thought Jay had done a terrific job with the piece.

And Lewis's article wouldn't be published on page four, which was always the editorial page, nor on page five, where the Olympic news release would be located. In all likelihood, it would be slotted onto page six, with the headline, "Durham selectmen still in the dark."[28] No rush to judgment. Wait for more information. Think about it. Chew on it. No matter how outrageous the proposal might be, be respectful. And keep an open mind. The process revealed the Yankee temperament in spades, Phyllis thought, so different from what she had experienced growing up in New Jersey.

The board chairman, Alden Winn, typified this response. He said he hadn't made a decision yet about the refinery, and at first sounded a bit defiant: "I have to hear a heck of a lot more about what is planned before I draw any conclusions. I'm not about to approve the kind of refinery you see in the Midwest or New Jersey and, notwithstanding company statements that the refinery will be non-polluting, I still need to be convinced that it is possible to build a clean refinery and that they will do it. There are loads and loads of question to be answered." But his bravado wilted when he was asked about the governor's tactics in secretly arranging for a refinery in a town that had contrary zoning ordinances. "Well, I wouldn't have operated that way if I were governor," he said. "However, I hesitate to fault him on that score. I suppose he was considering the greater good for all the people, figuring that outweighed the possible negative effects on Durham."

Selectman James Chamberlin also reflected initial steadfastness. "The board's first obligation is to support our zoning ordinances," he said, but then added that "I would consider—but not advocate—changing the zoning to permit an oil refinery on Durham Point." Many residents, he said, consider the refinery to be a tax boon.

Malcolm Chase lived on Durham Point and admitted he had been approached about selling some of his property, but refused to say what his response had been. "Whether I choose to sell or not is my own private business." He said he had not made a decision about whether or not he would support the refinery. Did he see any conflict of interest between being a selectman representing the town and his personal interest in an offer from Olympic? "If that occurs, I'll be the first to recognize it, and you can be sure I'll take appropriate action."

Only Selectman Larry O'Connell, a young political science professor at UNH who had been born and raised in New Hampshire and had graduated from UNH about a decade and a half earlier, took a flat-out position: "I do not want to see a refinery in Durham. And I will try to move the board in that direction." Phyllis wondered what personality mutation had caused him to be so forthright.

That Durham and the board might eventually have to buckle under the weight of the governor and state leaders was acknowledged by the last selectman, Owen Durgin. He, too, was keeping an open mind. He had "no solid position" on the refinery. But he saw the reality of the forces aligned against the town: "If you array the power of the town against the power of the State and big business, the result may be that the town will have to make the best of a bad situation." He worried that if the town "adopts an attitude that we can stop it—and we are unable to—we may be in a bad position to deal with the refinery's impact." He felt it would be best to plan as though the refinery was definitely going to be built, so they would be in a better position to influence regulations that would lessen its detrimental impact.

● ● ●

Phyllis finished editing the article and took a look at the other lead story, "Durham rallies against refinery."[29] It was mostly about Rep. Dudley Dudley's intention to draft two bills for the special session of the state legislature, which was scheduled shortly after the New Year. The bills were intended to prevent the state from locating a refinery in a town without the support of the town's residents. Phyllis would not have given the story such a broad headline—"Durham rallies"—when the actual information was so narrowly focused on just one person. But she was not going to second guess Dick right now. Everything was working smoothly for once. She wanted to keep it that way.

It was close to midnight when the galleys were finally ready for Phyllis to take down to the printer in Plaistow. That was good. She could avoid getting another parking ticket from Patrolman Lester Heath, the Newmarket cop who would wait near the cars of the *Publick Occurrences* staff and immediately, at the stroke of one, write tickets for everyone still inside. The ban on parking from 1 a.m. to 6 a.m., November through March, was to clear the streets for snow ploughs—when it was *snowing*! But rather than add that qualification, the law simply specified the hours and the months of the ban. And Lester, for some perverse reason, seemed delighted to enforce the letter of the law. Given his first name, the staff couldn't resist adding an epithet. But tonight, unbelievably, they had finished putting the news to bed early. And Lester the Arrester, looking to write his parking tickets, would be sadly disappointed.

• • •

When she got home and walked in the door, Steve was standing in the living room with a suitcase. She looked at him, then at the suitcase, then back to him.

"I'm moving in with Shaunna," he said. At first she didn't grasp what he was saying. Moving in with Shaunna? The college student? Why? Did she even know about this? "I'm in love with her."

Phyllis dropped into a chair. She couldn't speak. She had no idea anything had been going on between the two of them. God, how long had Shaunna even been working for them? It seemed like they had just hired her. But no, it must have been last month. Or maybe two months ago. She couldn't begin to imagine how they had found time together. Her own life was a blur, taking care of the kids before they left for school and after school was over, and in between those times driving into the Newmarket office, and if not there, then to the many businesses in the seacoast area that were willing to advertise in their paper, never knowing exactly where Steve was at any given time, but always trusting, trusting that he was doing what needed to be done to keep their joint venture going, trusting—did she really need to think this?—that he still loved her.

"And I'm leaving the paper," he said. "We should sell it if we can. Or just fold it up. We've lost half our investment, and we'll run out of the other half in a couple of months."

Running out of money? He had never said anything about running out of money before. How could that be? They had started with $1 million. Their nest egg. They had saved it together from their investment in the Maryland paper. And now, three months later, it was almost gone? She was barely able to murmur: "Where'd it all go?"

"Things were more expensive than I expected. The office, the salaries, typewriters, compugraphic machine—it all adds up. We can sell some of it. Get some of the money back."

She couldn't believe he was giving up everything he had said he ever wanted. Giving up his dream of running his own newspaper, of being a voice for the people. Giving up his children. Giving up her.

"I'm not quitting," she said, her voice more firm now. "If you want to give everything up for her—for Shaunna—go ahead. But I'm no quitter."

He shrugged. "Fine! I don't care what you do. Keep the whole thing. Run it into the ground. I don't want any part of it."

He picked up his suitcase and walked to the door. "I'll come back later to pick up the rest of my stuff."

Phyllis didn't move from the chair. She sat there for a very long time, unable to make sense of what had just happened, her mind a blur of memories and feelings and colors, her only concrete thought: who's going to run the compugraphic machine?

6

THE MAN BEHIND THE THRONE

On November 28, the *Manchester Union Leader* trumpeted the Olympic Refineries announcement, with the story and full-page headline focusing on the governor: "Thomson Unveils Refinery Plans." The lead: "An oil refinery believed to be bankrolled by the Greek shipping magnate, Aristotle Onassis, may be located

in the New Hampshire seacoast area, it was disclosed yesterday at the state house." In addition to a long story that carried over to an inside page, the paper provided the full text of the press conference. The next day the publisher, William Loeb, devoted his daily front-page editorial to his support of the refinery, giving a pat on the head to the governor for his work in bringing the facility to the state and enumerating the many incredible benefits the refinery would bring. He warned his readers that without the refinery, they would suffer terribly, and denounced the refinery's opponents:

GREAT GOOD NEWS

The news announced by Governor Thomson that Greek interests will establish a $600 million oil facility on the seacoast of New Hampshire is incredibly good news to every New

Hampshire home now worrying about whether they are going to get through the winter without freezing.

While other governors have been sitting around wringing their hands, Governor Thomson in typical, practical, down-to-earth fashion, did something about it and now New Hampshire citizens can see the possibility of some warm homes, shops, and offices ahead....

Of course, unfortunately, none of this can happen tomorrow, so none of us can start turning up our thermostats as yet. It will take time to build these facilities....

The news that came out of the Governor's Office yesterday is some of the most important and the happiest news that any of us have heard in a long, long time.

There will be, of course, the usual uproar from the environmentalists who apparently want to huddle by their smoking wood stoves and don't care how cold the rest of us are in home, office, or factory...

The State of New Hampshire and the people of the Granite State are in no mood to have further suffering forced on them by irrational and hysterical conservationists.

If these misguided people don't want to do their cause irreparable harm, they won't try to block this refinery with all that it means for the future of the comfort and industrial growth of the State of New Hampshire.

—William Loeb

The editorial was printed on the upper half and right side of the paper, under a booming headline, "Oil Price Went Up 11.5¢ Last Night." The headline fed into the narrative of Loeb's editorial—that Granite Staters would certainly freeze to death, later if not sooner, unless they came to their senses and agreed to the Olympic proposal. But the headline, like Loeb's fearmongering about the upcoming cold winter, was, at best, misleading. The increase in the price of heating oil did not, as the article acknowledged in the fourth paragraph, apply to domestic heating oil from sources like Mobil, Gulf, and Texaco. In fact, it was not at all clear that any New Hampshire residents would be affected. Such sleight-of-hand was similar to Loeb's editorial, proclaiming the good news of the oil refinery to everyone "now worrying about whether they are going to get through the winter without freezing." Yet, as Loeb admitted later in the piece, it would "take time to build these facilities," leaving residents to freeze that coming winter even if they did embrace the oil refinery proposal.

The announcement by Olympic Refineries of its intention to build an oil refinery on Durham Point marked the culmination of months of negotiations by Governor Meldrim Thomson and his staff, with representatives of the Greek shipping magnate, Aristotle Onassis. Officially, Olympic Refineries declined to mention Onassis's name in its press release, and even Loeb and the *Union Leader* pretended they didn't know for sure about Onassis's involvement, the reporter saying the refinery was "believed" to be financed by the shipping magnate, and Loeb referring to "Greek interests," rather than to Onassis himself. It was never clear why the announcement was shrouded in such pseudo-secrecy, but whatever the reason, the lack of candor added to the skepticism of the Durham residents.

To outward appearances, it was the governor who had triumphed with his acquisition of an oil refinery for the state, a goal he had pursued since being elected the previous year. The *Union Leader* articles merely reported on the governor's success, and Loeb's editorial merely commented on this "news" with the publisher's own expressions of support. But behind the scenes, to the state's business and political leaders who had inside information about the relationship between the newspaper and the governor, the oil refinery announcement reflected a very different dynamic. The real power in the state was clearly the newspaper publisher, who had been terrifying local politicians for decades, and who now—with his puppet, or at the very least his ideological doppelganger, in the state house—could impose his own public policy.

• • •

Loeb's purchase of the Union-Leader Publishing Company occurred on November 21, 1946, two and a half years after both of its partner-owners died within ten days of each other, and the widow who inherited the paper decided to retire to Florida.[30] Loeb also owned other newspapers in Vermont and Connecticut, but these were not especially successful because of strong local competition. By contrast, the new purchase was a well-established, successful enterprise, publishing both morning and evening editions, and it was the only statewide daily newspaper in New Hampshire.

Loeb's motivation for acquiring newspapers was not the same as the one that led Phyllis Bennett and her husband to found *Publick Occurrences*. They were passionately committed to the idea of a local newspaper that would provide people with the information they needed to be informed citizens. Loeb entertained no such lofty goals. He was less interested in telling readers what was happening than in telling them what to think. His ambition, as he told many of his friends and acquaintances, was to be a publisher so he could be the "power behind the throne." When he bought his first newspaper, he acted immediately to achieve that goal—writing front-page editorials to ensure that readers would see what he thought about the day's events. It wasn't sufficient for him to have an editorial section inside the pages of the paper, as was the common journalistic standard of the day. The new publisher's views on current events were as important, if not more so, than the events themselves. His front-page editorials and control of the newsroom would give him the political power he desired.

There were other strategies he might have followed, of course. Running for office is one example whereby he could be on the throne, rather than be the power behind it. But Kevin Cash, a reporter who wrote a critical biography of Loeb in 1975 entitled *Who the hell is William Loeb?*, speculated that the publisher feared that his personal life, if made public, would doom him to failure. Equally plausible is that Loeb learned early on in life that he was not one whom others viewed with fondness, and that he would have a difficult time winning any popularity contest. Thus was he forced to choose the role of kingmaker rather than king.

• • •

He was born the day after Christmas, 1905, when his father, William Loeb, Jr. (now, with the birth of a son bearing the same name, transformed into William Loeb II), was executive secretary to President Theodore Roosevelt. William Loeb III was christened a short while later at an Episcopalian baptism, with the Roosevelts participating as his godparents. This would prove to be an important occasion in the young Loeb's life, as he would later tout with pride his christening and his godfather, the former president of the United States, as proof he was not Jewish. Called a "Jew-boy" in elementary school, and later in life demeaned as Jewish, he always sought to separate himself from any association with Jews.

The young Loeb, often referred to as III, would grow up in a rarified political environment, seeing and meeting many of the most powerful men and women of the times. The senior Loeb remained close with the Roosevelts even after the president declined to run for re-election in 1908. Though out of office, Roosevelt remained a political force to be reckoned with, and he often consulted the senior Loeb about political strategy. They lived only a few miles apart on Long Island, Roosevelt at Sagamore Hill, Loeb in Mill Neck. Guests who visited the ex-president would often visit Loeb as well. Young William got used to the visits, and was often encouraged to demonstrate his brilliance by participating in the discussions.

In school, among his peers, however, his views on life were not so welcome, much to his discomfort. After being privately tutored in his early years, he was sent to a private school in New York City, The Allen-Stevenson School, which he hated. He transferred to The Hotchkiss School in Lakeview, CT, as a sophomore, but again found it difficult to get along with his classmates. He later admitted he was "sort of an 'aginner' who didn't always fit in."[31]

While some of his school mates would taunt him as "the Jew kid," which he loathed, they called him other nicknames as well, "snake" being one of them. Nevertheless, he apparently considered himself quite attractive to the fairer sex, writing in the Hotchkiss yearbook, "It's my eyes that makes [sic] the girls fall for me!"[32]

On graduation, he attended Williams College in Williamstown, Massachusetts, then a men's college. He was no more popular in the fraternity he joined at Williams than he had been in prep school at Hotchkiss. In their spare time, the Williams men sought female companionship at the prominent women's colleges of the day, the closest being Smith College in Northampton, Massachusetts, about fifty miles away. There, William met and eventually married—at age twenty, just before the end of his junior year—his first of three wives, a Smith College philosophy professor, Elizabeth Nagy, eight years his senior. His parents objected to the marriage, though they continued to pay his bills. When he visited them a year later after graduation, Mrs. Elizabeth Loeb spent the night in a nearby lodging house while her husband spent the night with his mother and father. He started law school at Harvard, but again did not fare well, and quit in his second year, moving back home to his parents' house in Mill Neck, where he filed for annulment. Elizabeth Nagy Loeb in turn filed an alienation of affection suit for $100,000 against the parents, but eventually settled for just $5,000.

In the next several years, Loeb engaged in an assortment of enterprises, but never gained traction in any one area, all the time being supported by his parents. His father died in 1937, when Loeb was thirty-one, but Loeb, Sr., left no money to his son, despite his considerable fortune—all of which went to his wife, except for a small amount to each of his three sisters. Mrs. Loeb, however, felt determined to support her son, and made him responsible for the investment of the estate's portfolio, giving him half of the profits he was able to make. He continued to dabble in various ventures without much success, including a failed effort to become a journalist. Finally, in 1941, he and a friend from Oyster

Bay, Charles Graham Weaver, the editor of the city's weekly newspaper, agreed they would look to buy a newspaper. After much searching in Vermont, Loeb discovered the *St. Alban's Daily* was for sale for $40,000. With his mother's money, he purchased the paper and hired Weaver to work for him. In February 1942, he bought another Vermont newspaper, the *Burlington Daily News*, this time with money from a recently separated woman who was receiving a generous settlement from her wealthy husband. At the time she invested in the project, she didn't realize that her contribution was virtually the whole cost of the purchase, with the remainder coming once again from Loeb's mother.

In the meantime, he had begun courting Eleanore McAllister, an equestrian instructor at the Foxcroft School in Middleburg, Virginia, whom he had met at a tea dance of the social set on the Long Island North Shore. She worked at a horse farm in Londonderry, Vermont, in the summer of 1942, where Loeb visited her frequently. In late September of that year, before returning to Foxcroft School, she and Loeb got married. Loeb told her he had only forty-seven dollars in his bank account at the time. "I felt sorry for him," she later told Loeb's biographer, Kevin Cash. For over a year, she had been sending him the money she earned—$5,000 a year—and she continued to do so after the wedding.

Then, in 1946, came an exciting possibility. A very profitable newspaper corporation in New Hampshire was up for sale. The owner was Annie Reid Knox, widow of Colonel Frank Knox, Secretary of the Navy and one of President Teddy Roosevelt's Rough Riders—the cavalry unit led by Roosevelt in the Spanish-American War. Annie Reid Knox was a close acquaintance of Loeb's mother. They had met at the annual reunions of the Rough Riders, which the senior Loeb and his wife also attended because of the senior Loeb's continuing friendship with the former president. Mrs. Knox had inherited the paper from her husband, but had no inclination to run it. Instead, she wanted to retire with her sister to Florida, and let it be known the paper was for sale. Several potential buyers expressed interest, but in the end her choice came down to a man with an outstanding journalistic record, John McLane Clark, whom she did not know, and William Loeb, son of a friend, and owner of two other apparently successful newspapers. Friendship prevailed. She accepted Loeb's purchase offer for one and a quarter million dollars.[33]

In the ensuing years, Loeb distinguished himself as a man whose private and public lives were equally contentious. When he first entered the social scene in New Hampshire, he was inevitably polite and well-dressed, but there were quirks that did not sit well. It was disconcerting, for example, that when he went to dinner at the Manchester Country Club, he would take a loaded pistol from his holster and lay it on an empty place setting. Also perplexing to people who had invited him to dinner, given his editorial condemnation of divorce and sexual immorality, was his habit of escorting a woman with him whom he would introduce as his wife, though everyone knew he was married to the former Eleanore McAllister, who was still living in Vermont, and pregnant. Nor were the women he claimed to be his wife always the same—it was as though he either thought that everyone was too dense to realize what he was doing, or that he simply wanted to insult their sensibilities. Eventually, his favorite escort was a woman named Nancy Scripps Gallowhur, member of the founding family of the Scripps-Howard newspaper chain, still married to her husband George, and heir to a substantial fortune. It wasn't long before the members of the Manchester Country Club decided they could exist without Loeb's charm. The publisher was banned.

Loeb and Mrs. Gallowhur soon decided they would divorce their spouses and marry each other. Loeb got his divorce in Nevada. In so doing, he avoided having to pay any alimony to Eleanore, but a Vermont court still required him to pay child support for his daughter, Penelope—but he never did. He avoided jail for non-payment of child support by staying out of the state.

His personal troubles did not end there. His mother sued him for $1 million after she discovered that he had used her money without her permission to help purchase the *Manchester*

Union Leader. Eventually, she relented, but continued to support Eleanore and Penelope until she died. She left $1 million to her granddaughter, explicitly excluding her son from any inheritance. But Loeb went to court and tied up the inheritance for close to five years, claiming he should get three-fourths of the money, finally settling for less than ten percent of that amount. In the meantime, he had forced Eleanore to spend more than half the inheritance on legal costs, and caused much stress to his own daughter.

His chip-on-the-shoulder approach to his personal life paralleled his take-no-prisoners approach to his front-page editorials. He was a Donald Trump before there was a Donald Trump, coming up with less-than-flattering nicknames for people with whom he disagreed. Dopey Dwight. Snake Oil Lyndon. Kissinger the Kike. Kennedy, the No. 1 Liar in America. Senator Eugene McCarthy, the Skunk's Skunk's Skunk. Nelson Rockefeller, a wife-swapper (for divorcing his first wife and marrying again). Apparently he had never heard, or at least had paid no attention to, the warning about stone-throwing in a glass house.

Besides his political opponents, Loeb seemed especially antagonistic toward the University of New Hampshire, a bastion of communism and immorality and all sorts of other threats to American values. His relentless attacks scared many politicians into silence, fearing that if they spoke out, they would become a target of Loeb's vitriol.

His front-page denunciations were not limited to the politicians themselves, but landed on their wives and children, as well. Perhaps the most egregious case was his denunciation of the fifteen-year-old daughter of Governor Peterson after she had naively said to an Associated Press reporter, who had come up to her at a school function in Washington, DC, that she didn't think smoking marijuana was so bad. Loeb and the paper kept up the assault against the girl, with headlines claiming a school head said she had lied about marijuana use, although a subsequent investigation concluded that no school official had made such a claim. Loeb had already entered a post-truth world, where it mattered not what the facts were, but what people believed them to be—based on what he and his paper decreed. To people in New Hampshire, the newspaper's motto, taken from Daniel Webster, "There is nothing so powerful as truth," was the height of irony. Clearly, Loeb's notion of truth was not fact-based. The governor, of course, was irate about the attack on his daughter, and sent a protest letter to Loeb, who nevertheless doubled down on the governor, calling him a bad parent and continuing to demean the daughter. She spent most of her senior year hospitalized because of stress from the sudden national notoriety she had received, but Loeb didn't let go of the incident for another several years.

So toxic was the environment that in 1957, a state senator, James Cleveland, sponsored a resolution to censure Loeb. Then in 1962, while running for the Congress, Cleveland gave a speech in his hometown: "Mr. Loeb, I did not crawl out of a foxhole in the Pacific Theater to come back home and crawl on my belly before a junior-grade Goebbels whose combat experience has been chiefly confined to lawsuits and character assassinations....Far too long, New Hampshire has suffered the blighting, corroding and malignant influence of the Loeb papers...."

Just over a decade later, Tom Bonner, the recently resigned president of UNH who had been excoriated by Loeb from the time Bonner had arrived at the university three years earlier, had this to say about his experience with the paper:[34]

> Such grotesque journalism, I learned, had been common since Loeb's coming to New Hampshire in 1946. But my worst jolt on arriving in the state was to find that a number of otherwise thoughtful people took it seriously....Almost no one spoke out in my defense. Faculty members and students, awed by the fury of the attacks and lacking specific information were largely silent. The burden of proof that I was innocent of the gross calumnies of my character and record had fallen on me.
>
> It was then I learned that New Hampshire was afraid. Leading politicians, churchmen, professional leaders, University trustees alike condemn in private the newspaper's frightening

influence on New Hampshire, but few try to organize and fight openly its oppressive weight on life in the Granite State....

As I sat with his [Loeb's] top executives and reporters in that first summer of 1971, the words that occurred to me over and over again was Hannah Arendt's phrase, 'The banality of evil.' Surrounded by these well-mannered and friendly men—they might well have been a group of Baptist clergymen—I realized that so commonplace, so banal had become the monstrous evil they do daily to hundreds of human beings that they regard it as of no more moral consequence than studying a dinner menu or driving to work each day.

Kevin Cash did not defend the silence of most political, religious, business, and academic leaders in the state when Bonner was so roundly attacked by Loeb and his paper. Everyone knew that Bonner's main transgressions were that he had at one time worked for George McGovern, a liberal senator from South Dakota, and that he was an educator with a liberal arts orientation—open to the free flow of ideas in a university. But Cash did note that most people felt powerless to do anything.

"Such attacks," he wrote, "and particularly the attacks on Dr. Bonner, were absolutely nauseating to thousands of those in New Hampshire, but at best, they had no way to counter the offensive. Had they made public orations, they knew they would become Loeb's prime targets, and, in many instances, they knew that was all Loeb wanted."

It would be incorrect to assume, however, that Loeb wanted only to vent his anger at people he didn't like. While he clearly enjoyed that pastime, what he really wanted was to exert control over the political process. Yes, he wanted to be the kingmaker. But not just of any king. Certainly not one who might get into office and then act on his own. Loeb wanted a king who showed proper deference, who would act only with the express permission and direct guidance of the kingmaker.

It took a quarter of a century before Loeb finally achieved that goal. In 1972, Meldrim Thomson was elected governor.

7

THE MAN ON THE THRONE

By New Hampshire standards, the man who became governor in 1972 was a carpetbagger.[35] In a state in which the political leaders were mostly born and bred, or were, at the very least, longtime residents, Meldrim Thomson was hardly more than a foreigner, having arrived only eighteen years earlier at the age of 42. Born near Pittsburgh, Pennsylvania, in 1912, but raised in Georgia, he sported a southern accent and a courtly manner, which belied his distinctively combative personality. In that style, he and William Loeb were closely aligned.

Thomson attended Mercer University in Macon, Georgia, where his grandfather had once served as mayor and had equipped a Confederate rebel group called "Thomson's Raiders." After graduation, Thomson moved on to the University of Georgia School of Law and was admitted to the practice of law in Florida in 1936. Two years later, after moving to Brooklyn to work for the Edward Thompson Law Book Company, he married Anne Gale Kelly, who worked there as a secretary. In 1952, he started his own law book business, Equity Publishing Co., and in the fall of 1954, he and Anne and their six children moved to Mt. Cube Farm in Orford, New Hampshire.

It wasn't until 1966, however, that the southern gentleman came to the attention of William Loeb. As chairman of the Orford

School Board, Thomson had formed a group called the Taxfighters, which included nine other towns. They all agreed to reject federal funds for remedial reading on the grounds that the federal government had no business meddling in education. Such defiance of authority appealed to the newspaper publisher, who thought that this man might be the one to help him in his war against the "old guard" Republicans, whom Loeb had been fighting almost since he arrived in New Hampshire. But he had to be careful. He had once before groomed and elevated a local attorney to the governorship, only to be humiliated when his impassioned request for a small favor, a favor which he knew was really in the best interests of the state, had been publicly rejected. He did not want another Judas in the governor's mansion who would betray him like that.

• • •

The Judas Loeb had in mind was Wesley Powell, an attorney from Hampton Falls, who—as the administrative assistant of Senator Styles Bridges—had helped Loeb obtain some needed financing in 1949 so that Loeb could buy out his business partner and obtain full ownership of the *Union Leader*. The next year, Powell decided to run for the US Senate against the GOP incumbent, Charles Tobey, and Loeb, obviously feeling grateful for the help he had received from Powell the year before and delighted that he had a candidate who would challenge the entrenched elites, enthusiastically supported the candidacy. This would be Loeb's first political campaign. And, indeed, unlike the coverage provided by most newspapers at the time, "campaign" accurately describes how the Loeb newspaper reported on the contest. As Kevin Cash, Loeb's biographer, noted, it was typical of the day that newspapers would endorse a candidate at some point during the campaign, laying out reasons for the support. And that had been the case in New Hampshire as well, before Loeb arrived on the scene. However, as Cash wrote, "during the primary campaign of 1950, the readers of the *Union Leader* were given their first taste of what it is like when William

Loeb backs a candidate. It was Powell, Powell, Powell throughout the newspaper, no matter what day, no matter what edition. The news stories and editorials lionizing Powell, his wife, his family, everything about him, got to the point where the *Union Leader* could be considered the daily Powell campaign newspaper."[36]

Powell lost by 1,400 votes out of 72,000 cast, and Loeb was furious. He wrote scathing editorials about the "bunglers and appeasers" who had caused Powell to lose. Loeb called for a new election, a recount of the primary election, and a write-in campaign for Powell in the general election. Another vigorous campaign by Loeb on behalf of Powell's independent bid during the general election, however, produced only 12,000 votes for the attorney out of 190,000 cast, a reality check for the publisher about the extent of his influence.

Loeb and Powell tried again in 1956, this time Powell running for governor instead of the Senate. And, again, Powell lost. Two years later, they tried again. And this time, they were successful. Powell beat former Governor Hugh Gregg in the primary by 396 votes out of eighty-four thousand cast and went on to win in the general election by about three percentage points. This was Loeb's first victory, and he couldn't have been happier. He was also pleased in 1960, when Powell once again edged out former Governor Hugh Gregg by about one percentage point in the GOP primary, and went on to win re-election.

In the fall of 1961, however, the symbiotic relationship between the governor and the publisher dissolved. Senator Bridges died of a heart attack in November, leaving the governor to appoint someone to fill the unexpired term. There was some thought that, given Powell's previous campaigns for senator, he might decide to step down as governor and have himself appointed as senator instead. However, Loeb made a public plea in a front-page editorial that Powell appoint Bridges's widow as "the best possible tribute to the late senator, to whom New Hampshire owes so much.... If Governor Powell can put aside his own personal ambitions, it would be a magnificent act for him to name Mrs. Bridges."

But Powell didn't obey. On December 6, he called a news conference to announce that he would not have himself appointed for Bridges's seat, nor would he run for the seat in 1962. However, he would not appoint Mrs. Bridges, either. The next day he announced his choice—the recently confirmed State Attorney General, Maurice Murphy.

Loeb had a hissy-fit, calling the governor "vindictive" and "egotistical" and "an ingrate." He had much more to say in his front-page editorial:[37]

> As everyone knows we have devoted, over the years, much effort to Governor Powell's career. We have risked unpopularity with many people in the state through our support of him....
>
> IT IS NOT EASY TO CONFESS A MISTAKE OR TO SAY THAT ONE IS WRONG, BUT THIS NEWSPAPER FRANKLY SAYS THIS MORNING THAT WE HAVE WASTED ELEVEN YEARS OF EFFORT ON BEHALF OF GOVERNOR POWELL.
>
> FOR A BRILLIANT MIND, A GOLDEN TONGUE, OR A GREAT AMBITION AVAILS A MAN NOTHING, AND SERVES NEITHER THE STATE NOR THE NATION, IF IT IS NOT WEDDED TO GREATNESS OF CHARACTER AND HUMILITY OF SPIRIT...WE QUOTE FROM ST. MATTHEW: 'WHAT DOES IT PROFIT A MAN IF HE SHALL GAIN THE WHOLE WORLD, AND LOSE HIS SOUL?'
>
> —William Loeb

For the next six years, Loeb had no winning candidate. When Powell ran for a third term in 1962, Loeb turned his fire on the governor, supporting John Pillsbury, a local businessman and member of the state legislature. The businessman won the primary, but lost in the general election to John King, the first Democrat to win the governorship in forty years. The same scenario played out in 1964. Then, two years later, former Governor Hugh Gregg, a member of the "old guard," won the gubernatorial primary, leaving Loeb with no GOP candidate to support. He then did the unthinkable: he endorsed the Democrat King for a third term, revealing that his conservative ideology was less important than his personal grudges against the establishment Republicans.

But that was also the year Loeb first heard about the southern gentleman from Orford with the strongest anti-tax stance of any politician Loeb had yet seen in the Granite State. Over the next two years, he began grooming Thomson for statewide office, as Loeb had done for Powell all those years ago, publishing numerous stories touting one good action or another by the farmer from Orford. In 1968, with Loeb's support, Thomson declared his candidacy for the GOP gubernatorial nomination. He would be opposed by the House Speaker Walter Peterson, one of the "old guard" Republicans—and, it turns out, by the perennial candidate, former Governor Wesley Powell. Loeb waged his campaign on behalf of Thomson, but fell short—Thomson came in third, but only 1,200 votes behind Powell and 4,000 votes behind the much better known Peterson. Once again, Loeb could not support the establishment GOP candidate, and campaigned on behalf of the Democrat. This time, Peterson won. Loeb had lost twice—both in the primary and in the general election.

A similar outcome occurred in 1970, only this time it was Thomson versus Peterson in the primary, with no third candidate. A vigorous campaign by Loeb cut Peterson's 1968 margin almost in half, with Thomson losing this time by just over two thousand votes.

Then came the magical year, 1972. This would be the third time that Loeb and Thomson had tried to defeat the "old guard" Governor Peterson. Thomson hammered the governor on his support for a sales tax while Loeb echoed that theme, adding to it his relentless criticism of Peterson for the governor's permissiveness with respect to drugs, bringing up his daughter's name from the controversy Loeb had created about her three years earlier. In the primary election, Thomson edged out the incumbent by 1,400 votes. In the general election, he beat the Democrat by more than 7,000 votes.

Loeb had finally attained his second gubernatorial victory. Only this time, it turned out, the man on the throne and the man behind the throne were, as one newspaper competitor observed, "virtually indistinguishable."[38]

As governor, Thomson exhibited a number of quirks that flaunted the accepted norms of the day, some of which were in fact against the law.[39] He had an assistant examine the tax returns of his political opponents, an action that the State Supreme Court later ruled was illegal—although at that point, nothing could be done about it. Thomson's response was that the Supreme Court was entitled to its opinion, and he was entitled to his own. Thomson also personally went to Wellesley, Massachusetts, to the New England Organized Crime Intelligence System center to request any files it might have on New Hampshire politicians. There were none, he was told, and he never justified his actions. He cancelled an agreement with Maine over fishing boundaries without consulting anyone, prompting an altercation with the governor of Maine over fishing rights that almost led to "a lobster war," with each governor sending out patrol boats into disputed waters. When his limousine passed a motorist who gave him the finger, he had the State Patrol stop the car and arrest the driver. Later, as United Press International reported, he "had a penchant for lowering state flags to express his conservative sentiments. He lowered them to protest amnesty for Vietnam-era draft-evaders and tried to mark the death of Jesus on Good Friday by flying state flags at half-staff."[40]

Apart from those quirks, he was following a decidedly arch-conservative agenda, vetoing twenty-nine bills passed by the House and the Senate that he claimed were not fiscally responsible. Also high on his agenda was an attempt to locate an oil refinery in the state, dismissing any concerns raised by environmentalists or by the other New England governors who were working on a regional plan to bring refineries into the area. "If we wait until they finish their studies," Thomson said, "we'll never get a refinery. The other governors know I feel that way....They talk, they study, and then they go home and forget about it."[41]

Loeb echoed Thomson's disregard of regional planning and antipathy toward environmentalists, who—they both claimed—were stalling progress for the state. But that wasn't their only area of agreement. In fact, the governor and the publisher seemed to be on the same wavelength with respect to every other issue as well—the paper constantly showcasing every action and utterance of the governor about policy, personnel appointments, concerns about the legislature, and the state of morality in western civilization.

And there was a reason for such congruity between the two men.

In his investigative reporting, Rod Paul, a reporter from the *Concord Monitor*, discovered that from January 1973, when Thomson first took office, to the fall of 1974, near the end of his first term in office, Thomson had personally called Loeb on the telephone literally hundreds of times—as many as nine calls in one day—all at state expense. Whenever there were several calls in the same day, always the next day Thomson would make some major policy or personnel announcement, or take some other significant action. Invariably, the day after that, either Loeb or his editorial writer would heap praise on Thomson for his action.[42]

To some, the revelation of the phone calls proved that publisher William Loeb was, for all practical purposes, the Governor of New Hampshire. To others, who shied away from classifying Thomson as a mere puppet, the information showed only that there were two men who simply thought alike.

To the citizens of Durham, however, the latter clarification was a distinction without a difference. What they knew, even before confirmation by the *Monitor* reporter, was that the two most powerful men in New Hampshire were working in tandem, the power of the press reinforcing (if not guiding) the power of government to favor one of the most powerful men in the world.

8

MEETING OLYMPIC

Dudley Dudley was horrified when she saw the governor's announcement about the refinery on WMUR-TV and read about it more thoroughly the next morning in the *Union Leader*. She simply could not get her mind around such a massive facility. *Four hundred thousand barrels of oil each day*! Piped in from tankers on the Isles of Shoals, nine miles off the coast, to the town of Rye. Then piped over land another twelve miles from Rye to Durham. Four hundred thousand barrels of oil *every day*. How large would those pipes have to be? And what would happen to the four hundred thousand barrels of oil after it was refined? Would it be sent back to tankers even as new oil was coming in? Would there be two different, massive pipelines, one with oil coming in, the other with oil going out? Or would the refined oil be loaded on oil trucks and shipped out from Durham to the northeast region? That seemed more likely, but how many oil trucks would be needed to transport four hundred thousand barrels of oil *every day* from Durham to points elsewhere? The roads on Durham Point, as well as in town and the surrounding area, were narrow, barely two lanes wide. There would have to be a massive restructuring of the road system. Traffic would be horrendous. And there would be additional facilities, Olympic Refineries said. What exactly would those be? She had driven by oil refineries in New Jersey and Louisiana, and they stank of rotten eggs, an odor attributable to hydrogen sulfide, she had been told, one of many chemicals associated with refineries and their attendant chemical plants. Apart from the traffic and smell, there was always the problem of oil spills—not whether they occurred, but how often, and how large they would be. Great Bay would die. The fragile ecosystem, part freshwater and part saltwater, could not survive small oil spills, much less the humongous oil spills that would inevitably occur. *Four hundred thousand barrels of oil every day!*

If that wasn't scary enough, another paper, the *Concord Monitor*, reported that Thomson's legal counsel, Chuck Douglas, said the proposed oil refinery was not subject to Durham's zoning laws. In the 1973 legislative session, which had ended only four months earlier, Douglas had crafted, and the House and Senate had enacted, a power plant siting law. "That law provides that all state agencies concerned with aspects of a power plant shall hold a joint set of hearings," he said, but "the ultimate decision on whether to allow the plant shall be made by the Site Evaluation Committee."

So, Dudley thought, this meant that Thomson, with legal support from his counsel, would try to ride roughshod over Home Rule. That was exactly what she feared.

And then she read the paper's editorial, and she could not believe it. This, after all, was the *Concord Monitor*, the paper that competed with the *Union Leader* for coverage of state House news, not a liberal paper as such, and not conservative either, but at least a partial antidote to the lies spewed forth by William Loeb and his lackey reporters and editors in Manchester. For Democrats and moderate Republicans who might want a more objective rendering of the days' events, and a more rational assessment of their meaning, than what the *Manchester Union Leader* provided, the *Monitor,* located in the state's capital city, was their go-to source. After Dudley read all the way through the Nov. 28 editorial, she felt physically ill.

EDITORIAL
THE PROSPECT OF A N.H. OIL REFINERY

The prospect that New England's first major oil refinery will be situated in New Hampshire, with the state's residents getting priority in its production, is a tremendous coup for Gov. Thomson.

It should be emphasized at the outset that the proposal of Olympic Refineries, Inc., which is owned by the Greek shipping mogul Aristotle Onassis, is not a fly-by-night proposition. It involves the investment of $600 million or more.

Gov. Thomson set out more than six months ago to try to persuade various oil companies to build a refinery in the Granite State, and though several of his early leads fizzled, he kept at it....

Olympic Refineries, though a comparative neophyte in the construction of oil processing plants, hired some of the nation's leading experts to conduct feasibility studies in the Durham-Newmarket area. It also employed a widely-respected marine engineering firm to study the ocean aspects of the proposed operation....

All this does not mean that construction of the oil refinery is assured. There are still many tedious steps to be taken and serious questions to be answered to the satisfaction of skeptical environmentalists and residents in the area before approval is won.

The Great Bay estuary, for example, still is a comparatively unspoiled wildlife habitat. The impact of an oil refinery on this refuge must be weighed in light of the oil crisis confronting all of New England.

Officials of Olympic Refineries have assured that the proposed facility will be as clean, as unobtrusive and as non-polluting as modern science can make it.

Dudley quit reading. The editorial read more like an Olympic Refineries press release than a thoughtful assessment of the project. Why, she wondered, did the paper so quickly accept that the refinery had to be located on Great Bay? If a refinery absolutely had to be located in New Hampshire, why not farther south in Rye, where the pipeline would initially bring the oil to the mainland, or in North Hampton or Greenland, which were closer to Rye than was Durham Point and had no large estuary that could be polluted? Besides, where were those alleged "feasibility studies" that "the nation's leading experts" had conducted? How could they have concluded that it was better to have the oil piped twelve miles from Rye to Durham Point than from Rye to closer locations?

If even the *Concord Monitor* was so willing to accept the refinery proposal, what chance did Durham have against the Loeb-Thomson-Onassis juggernaut?

"You have to do something," Tom told her at breakfast the next morning.

"I know." But she felt overwhelmed. Weeks earlier, when *Publick Occurrences* had first warned residents of the possibility of an oil refinery, her calls to many state legislators had been less than promising. In fact, downright discouraging. Of course, an oil refinery in the state was a good idea, most all agreed. And now with an implicit endorsement from the *Concord Monitor*, that sentiment would be even more widespread. It was easy for her husband to say she should do something, but what? She had researched the laws dealing with oil refineries, and of course was already aware of the recent power plant siting law, which she wanted to amend, but as a first-term rep, and a female in a legislature amid an old-boy culture where there were no female leaders, she hardly had much clout. She shared these feelings with Tom.

"You'll figure something out," he said. "I have confidence in you."

"I was thinking about calling Chris," she said.

He smiled. "See. I knew you'd think of something."

• • •

Chris Spirou had just turned thirty. Born in Porti, Greece, he had come with his parents and siblings to America in 1956 at the age of 13, and lived in Manchester ever since. He had been elected to the State House in 1970, only two years before Dudley, but he was already part of the Democratic Party's legislative leadership, as assistant minority leader. He was tall and swarthy, with dark hair that came down over his ears, and a mustache that made him look older than his years. When he spoke to someone one-on-one, he leaned in as though confiding something special to his companion. Once he started talking, he was like a runaway train. He could monopolize a conversation like no one Dudley knew. Still, if anyone could help, it would be Chris. She called his number.

"It's terrible," he said in a strong voice with a distinctive Greek accent. "It would destroy our state. Not just the refinery itself. Everything that goes along with it. We're not New Jersey!"

"I was thinking of introducing a bill that would strengthen regulations to make it safer."

"If we could do that, would you be willing to have a refinery in Durham?"

"No. Of course not."

"Then why propose a bill that assumes a refinery will be built. You just weaken your argument against it."

"That wasn't my only idea…"

"You must not go down that path," he said. "Fight it all the way."

"I was thinking of our meeting with Marty Gross…"

"It's gotta be Home Rule," Spirou said. "You can't argue environment."

"I know," she said quickly. "That's why…."

"It won't work. Nobody will listen. Not the Republicans anyway. Not even a lot of Democrats. You know that. Right?"

"Yes. That's why…."

"We've got to argue Home Rule. Amend the laws to protect the towns and cities. We'll work together. Me behind the scenes. You're the one from Durham."

"I think there are two RSAs…"

"Whatever the number. You offer an amendment…."

"Chris. I know. I know." She quickly told him she had thought about amending RSA 162 F, the power plant siting law that had been enacted only a few months earlier. Her amendment would prohibit locating a refinery in any town or city unless the residents had first voted their approval. The governor's legal counsel, Chuck

Douglas, who had crafted the RSA, claimed it specifically allowed the Site Committee the final authority over where to locate a refinery. She also wanted to amend RSA 362.2, which defined the term "public utilities," to explicitly exclude oil refineries and related terminals. "But will O'Neil let me do it?" she said. "The governor says he wants a strictly limited agenda. He won't like what I've got. And O'Neil does what the governor wants."

"Don't worry about the speaker," Spirou said. "He and I understand each other. Just prepare the amendments."

"Do you think they'll pass?"

"You never know until you try."

"That's dangerous. Especially if we don't have a backup."

"That's politics," he said. "We have to fight, even if we lose. And set up a tour of the area. Get as many reps as you can to come see Durham Point. They need to know what the area is like. Why it shouldn't have a refinery." He gave her a list of names and legislative leader positions. "Put me at the top."

• • •

That night, representatives from Olympic Refineries came to Durham to meet with citizens and town leaders in an open forum.[43] The town had no large meeting room, depending typically on using the high school gymnasium when there was sufficient time to plan. The last-minute request from Olympic made the town leaders scramble to find a suitable location, which they finally did—room 217 of Hamilton Smith, which housed the university's English Department. When Dudley arrived, the lecture hall was bulging with people, everyone talking at once, the noise reverberating down the hallway. She worked her way into the room, smiling and waving to several people she knew. She found a place where she could lean against the wall, about halfway back in the room. On the stage in front, standing behind a lectern, was Alden Winn, a white-haired university professor and chairman of the town's Board of Selectmen. Three chairs on stage were occupied by men in suits and ties, presumably the representatives of Olympic Refineries, who had come to explain to the seacoast residents what the proposed refinery might mean for their neighborhoods. In the lecture hall's front row of seats were the other four selectmen. Larry O'Connell and Owen Durgin were, like Winn, UNH professors. The other two, Jim Chamberlin and Malcolm Chase, were local businessmen.

Winn banged a gavel on the lectern and whistled to get the crowd to quiet down. When the noise petered down to a dull roar, Winn started speaking in a loud voice, and soon the noise abated altogether. "…come to talk with us about the project. We welcome this opportunity. We have a lot of questions." The crowd growled its consent. Winn smiled. "From left to right on the stage," he said, turning to his right, "are Joseph J. Bonasis, engineer for the Frederic R. Harris, Inc., engineering firm; Robert L. Greene, vice president of Purvin and Gertz, Inc., consulting engineers; and Peter Booras of Keene, spokesman for Olympic." Scattered boos greeted the mention of Booras, one of the men who had obtained options on Durham Point under false pretenses. Winn banged his gavel on the table several times. "We will all be respectful here! These men have voluntarily come here to Durham to help us understand the nature of this proposed project. Let us hope we all come away from the meeting better informed and much wiser than when we came in."

Peter Booras stepped to the front of the stage. Despite Winn's admonition, several boos rang out over the crowd. Booras welcomed everyone to the meeting and said how pleased he was at the large turnout despite such short notice. He gave a quick overview of the project, "which probably all of you have already heard." He talked about the gas shortage, the rising price of heating oil, and the need for New England to have its own source of oil. And he lauded Governor Thomson's efforts to bring an oil refinery to New Hampshire, a pronouncement that was met with a new chorus of boos. But he was undeterred. "Tonight, we are making an honest effort to explain the project in the greatest possible way. The people at Olympic Refineries want to exchange ideas with people in the community. The objective is to have the refinery beneficial to everyone. We want to help make New Hampshire as self-sufficient as possible. So, I welcome the opportunity to work with everyone. New Hampshire is uniquely situated to have an off-shore unloading facility because of the Isles of Shoals, and to have a refinery in the seacoast because of the water from Great Bay." When he was finished, there was a smattering of applause, along with jeering whistles and boos.

Sitting in the front row next to Councilman Jim Chamberlin was the town's attorney, Joseph Millimet, a slight, balding man with large spectacles, highly regarded in the state. He raised his hand and Winn pointed to him. The crowd became quiet.

"These comments are meant for you, Mr. Booras, and for Mr. Greene and Mr. Bonasis, and to whomever else they might apply," Millimet said. His voice was surprisingly strong, given his slight stature. "I am unable to determine on what basis you feel this facility can be built anywhere in the town. You are not authorized to construct this under the ordinances. You have to deal with the whole town in a town meeting. You may be spinning your wheels."

"We expect to receive permission," Booras replied.

So Booras says now, thought Dudley, but that contradicts what Thomson's legal counsel claims—that permission is not necessary. Olympic and state officials may appear to seek approval as long as the town seems willing to grant it, but if they don't get it, they are apparently prepared to force the refinery on the town anyway.

"Maybe yes. Maybe no. The concern is that these people," he turned around and gestured toward the crowd, "are now living in a town that over the years has decided not to allow industry in the town. Many towns welcome industry. This happens to be one that hasn't. And the proposed refinery is a rather large industry." He paused as the crowd reacted with caustic laughter and vocal affirmations of this obvious point. "The people want to know exactly where the refinery would be built, what it will produce, and everything about it. Whether all that is acceptable has to be decided in a town meeting, and as you know, that is a very inquiring body. And we don't have ready information that will give answers to our questions. Also, we want assurances that the project will not destroy our way of life. And if you make such assurances, the people want to know how you can guarantee that you will actually live up to them."

"Thank you very much, Mr. Millimet," Booras said. "As you know, this is very early in the planning stages. We are anxious to give assurances to you. To all of you. The main reason for this meeting was to assure you of our sincerity to work with the community."

Millimet sat down as a loud voice rang out: "What did Thomson promise Olympic? What kind of tax breaks do they get? What do you get?"

"No inducements were offered to Olympic. No special considerations. No tax deductions. The proposed facility is many times the tax base of property in Durham. It should be a real boon to the town's taxpayers. And I get nothing. I only thought the citizens of New Hampshire wanted to be self-sufficient."

Someone yelled out, "What citizens?" Another raised voice asked, "Why did you and George Pappademus lie about why you wanted to buy options on Durham Point? Why not tell the truth?"

"There needs to be a certain procedure followed," Booras said. "We bought the land and asked to pay a fair price, and in many cases paid more than a fair price."

Boos erupted from the crowd, people yelling to be heard. Winn banged his gavel again. "Order! Order! We can't learn anything if everyone is yelling at the same time." He pointed to a woman with her hand raised.

The woman stood up. "Will the people who were duped into selling options, when you and Pappademus lied to them about why you wanted them, be allowed to change their minds, now that they know what they're really for?"

"Officials of Olympic will meet with Governor Thomson and town officials to seek their cooperation and explain all the details."

More booing, the crowd boisterous now, many people who were sitting jumping to their feet and yelling.

"That's not an answer!"

"That's bullshit!"

"Liar!"

Again Winn banged on the lectern, but now the crowd would not be tamed.

A voice rose over the noise. "What happens to the oil once it's refined?"

Robert Greene got up from his chair, and a quiet descended on the crowd. He walked forward on the stage as though he wanted to bring the audience into his confidence. "Look, we're going to do everything possible to minimize the disruption of your daily lives. There are many hideous refineries, and I have been to a large number of them. This is not going to be one of them. Major improvements have been made in the design and operation of modern refineries. As for what happens to the refined product—most of it will be piped back to the tankers off the Isles of Shoals for distribution elsewhere. Some of it will be piped to storage tanks along the Piscataqua River in Newington and Portsmouth. There is also a 'possibility' of a truck terminal being constructed along I-95 at the Portsmouth line. But no major truck transportation of oil from Durham. You'll hardly know the refinery is here."

Several voices rang out.

"Yeah! So you say!"

"But you'll be gone!"

"Did you conduct any feasibility studies?"

Greene responded to the last question. "Our firm's only involvement so far has been to select the site."

"So you didn't conduct any studies?"

"Enough to determine that Durham Point is the best site."

"Are you aware that the Durham Point area is all stone and marsh?"

Greene looked backed to Bonasis and Booras, then faced the crowd again. "No. I was not aware of that. I confess, we have not yet made tests of the soil on Durham Point."

"What about big tankers coming up the Piscataqua to Great Bay?"

"No tankers. All oil will be piped in from an off-shore terminal, and most of it, as I said, piped back for distribution elsewhere." Greene described how the incoming oil would be off-loaded from tankers off Lunging Island and piped underwater to Rye, then piped overland across Pease Air Force Base, then under Great Bay to Adams Point, and overland to the refinery on Durham Point. "The shorter the pipe, the least disruption of Great Bay." Then, to reassure the citizens, he added, "The processed water used to cool the refinery will not be emptied into Great Bay, but into the Atlantic Ocean. All EPA requirements will be met."

The last sentence about meeting EPA requirements could hardly be heard over the crowd's angry outburst triggered by the promise to empty processed water into the Atlantic Ocean. A middle-aged man standing next to Dudley shouted out, "Are you fucking kidding me? It'll destroy the fishing industry!" Dudley doubted, however, that his words could be heard over the din. Finally, Alden Winn was able to bang the crowd back into an acceptable level of order.

"Look," Greene said, "if New Hampshire is to use oil, it has to be shipped in somehow. A refinery is required somewhere. It will provide jobs. And heating oil. And gas. One estimate is that the revenue coming to Durham would be ten times the taxable value of the town." Vigorous applause broke out from some residents, while others looked on in angry silence. "This is *good* for Durham. And for the seacoast. And, really, for all of New Hampshire." A substantial part of the crowd stood and applauded.

Then, simultaneously, many of those who had not stood shouted out questions, so many that Greene just stood there. Winn had given up on banging his gavel.

"What about oil spills?

"Can you guarantee there won't be any oil trucks transporting refined oil out of Durham?"

"Who is Olympic?"

"What experience has Olympic had in building refineries?"

"What other industries will Olympic bring?"

"How can you prevent Durham from being a stinking cesspool?"

"What assurances can you give that oil won't simply be refined here and then sent elsewhere?"

A sudden silence followed the last question, as though the audience had collectively lost its breath. Booras stepped forward. "I can't make any such assurances, but I hope that won't be the case."

Another round of boos.

"Look," Booras said, his voice rising, "if this becomes a big problem, I don't think Olympic will build here. One of their representatives said that if Olympic receives any hassle, they'll pull up and leave. They have other sites they can consider in Maine and Massachusetts." Many in the crowd booed the specter of losing the refinery, many others clapped and shouted encouragement.

Dudley remembered the local news broadcast on WMUR that she had seen just before coming to the meeting, in which a reporter had interviewed Constantine Gratsos, the "face" of Olympic Refineries. Like Booras was doing now, Gratsos threatened to have Olympic pull out of the project if the state didn't immediately go along with the company's demands. "If opponents give us any hassle," he said, "we'll just pull up and leave. We'll kiss them good-bye in twenty-four hours." If only that were true, she thought. But she knew better. This was a threat, a bluff to rile up Loeb and Thomson and the GOP establishment, who all desperately wanted the refinery and would do anything to accommodate Olympic. And now here was a threat to residents who supported the project—that this goodie bag might be taken away before it was even opened.

It was clear to Dudley that Booras and company had little specifics to share with the crowd. She worked her way to the door and left the assembly, angry voices still reverberating down the hallway. It was scary to see how incompetent Olympic had been in running the meeting. How unprepared. Their incompetence should have given her hope that the company wouldn't be able to persuade Durham and other seacoast residents to accept the refinery. But she feared that it wouldn't matter what the people thought. It all depended on what the legislature would do. Given the forces behind the refinery, it seemed almost hopeless that opponents could prevail. And if Olympic was so bad with its public relations, how really bad would it be in building the largest oil refinery in the world?

Even more distressing was the positive reaction of many of the residents who had attended the meeting. She had to admit that it was difficult to counter the promises of more jobs, a plentiful supply of gas and heating oil, and a large increase in the tax base—a significant reduction in property taxes. But it would be a Faustian bargain. *Four hundred thousand barrels of oil a day!*

Following her out of the room was Dave Meeker, another university professor whom Dudley had met at the SOS meeting with Nancy Sandberg earlier that month at the Congdon's house. His wife, Sharon, Dudley remembered, was the outreach coordinator for the group. After she and Dave greeted each other, he gave her a broad smile and said in a drawl: "Quite a show in there. Don't think Olympic had any idea. What a bunch of boobs!"

Dudley laughed. But she still didn't feel reassured.

9

TOURING DURHAM POINT

Two days later, some thirty legislators and neighborhood town officials met at Dudley's house on Woodman Road, just a short distance from the center of Durham, their cars lined up and down the short street.[44] It was cold, the temperature at seventeen degrees in the early morning, though it had warmed up somewhat by early afternoon. The cold front had brought with it plenty of sunshine, and Dudley saw it as a glorious winter day, perfect for the tour of Durham Point that she had scheduled. At first, there were just a few people gathered outside, but little by little, as more cars arrived, the group increased in size. Everyone greeted each other in their parkas and boots and heavy mittens, their cold breaths rising from their faces as though they were all smoking. The smell of burning wood hung over the neighborhood as they stood outside Dudley's house, shifting their weight from one foot to another and clapping their gloves together to keep warm. Finally, the last car arrived with the charismatic Chris Spirou, all smiles and enthusiasm, greeting everyone and shaking hands as though he were running for office and these were his potential constituents rather than his colleagues. The group got back into a few of the cars in parties of four and five, following Dudley and Spirou out of town on Route 108 toward Durham Point Road. In just a few minutes, they turned left, heading southeast on the narrow, twisting road that led through the wilderness that was Durham Point. At the junction of Langley Road, Durham Point Road turned south and several minutes later reached an intersection: To the right was

Bay Road leading to Newmarket; to the left, Adams Point Road down to the Bay. They turned left down the road that narrowed to one lane, crossed an isthmus with water lapping on either side, drove up a wooded hill, and shortly after arrived at Adams Point Wildlife Management Area. It was at this location, or very close to it, depending on what Olympic Refineries finally decided, that the proposed pipeline would deliver four hundred thousand barrels of oil every day for processing.

They parked their cars in a paved area overlooking a building with a sign on it that read "Jackson Estuarine Laboratory." As they assembled, a short, solid man in ski jacket and knit cap pulled down over his ears emerged from the building and bounced up the steps to the parking lot. He greeted everyone, telling them he was Art Mathieson, the director of the lab, and that he was delighted to have them visit the site. Before going into the lab itself, he wanted them to get a feel for the beauty and importance of Great Bay. He led them across the road a short distance up to a viewing platform, and encouraged everyone to take a look. Under a cloudless sky, the water was unusually blue, the sun glittering off the gentle waves. "Feel that breeze," he said with a big grin. "Doesn't it just invigorate you?" Some nodded in enthusiasm, while others groaned good-naturedly.

He climbed up to the top of the platform so he could address the group. He gestured toward the water. "As you probably already know," he said, "Great Bay is one of the largest estuaries on the Atlantic Coast, fed by the tidal waters of the Piscataqua River coming from the Atlantic Ocean through Portsmouth Harbor some twelve miles away. The Piscataqua, of course, marks the boundary between New Hampshire and Maine. It flows inland and comingles with fresh water from seven additional rivers: the Winnicut, Squamscott, Salmon Falls, Cocheco, Lamprey, Bellamy, and Oyster rivers.

"On your way here, just as you left town, you had to drive on the bridge over the Oyster River, where it flows over the Mill Pond Dam and meets up with the tidal waters coming in from the Atlantic. Did you notice?" He waited as some of the group acknowledged they had seen it. "Well, when the tide flows out, the Oyster River flows southeast parallel to the road you took to get here, and empties into Little Bay. Which is just opposite the lab building and off to the left—the north." He pointed over the lab building and swept his arm to the left. "Great Bay is way off to our right, and is linked to Little Bay by the Furber Strait, which is in front of us, a bit to our right, just offshore from Adams Point." He waited while the group absorbed this information. "Most boats and ships can't make it through the strait because it's too shallow, but they can make it from Portsmouth up to Durham Point. Olympic says it won't send any oil tankers of any size into Portsmouth and beyond, and that they'll only use the big supertankers that will be docked at the Isles of Shoals, nine miles off the coast. But, if Olympic decides to send some normal size tankers up to Durham Point, they could."

After everyone had taken some time to orient themselves, Mathieson led them into the lab, where they crowded inside a small lunch room, taking a few minutes to enjoy the warmth and shed their outer clothing.[45] Mathieson then gave them some background about the long history of Great Bay and the Piscataqua Region, where various peoples had populated the area for more than ten thousand years—the Paleo, Archaic, and Abenaki natives, followed centuries later by European settlers and their descendants. Overall, he noted, the region encompasses an area of 120 square miles, ranging from York, Maine, in the north to Seabrook, New Hampshire, in the south, and west to Durham and Newmarket, including in between Hampton, Rye, New Castle, Portsmouth Newington, Greenland, Stratham, Exeter, Dover, and Rollinsford in New Hampshire and South Berwick, Elliot, and Kittery in Maine. The Bay itself has a rich variety of habitats: eelgrass meadows, mudflats, salt marsh, channel bottom, rocky intertidal, and upland forest and fields. Each one serves a different function, but all together, they provide homes for some 160 species of birds, fish, and plants.

The estuary, he said, is part of the North Atlantic flyway, and twenty species of waterfowl, twenty-seven species of shorebirds, and thirteen species of wading birds use the bay as a wintering area or migratory stopover. Winter waterfowl counts at Great Bay average five thousand birds annually, with black ducks being the most prominent species. Over eighty percent of all winter waterfowl native to New Hampshire's coastal areas are found in Great Bay. Home to several endangered and threatened bird species, the Bay also supports a large winter population of bald eagles.

"So what do we study here at the Jackson Lab? Everything!" Mathieson told them UNH had been studying marine biology and the Great Bay estuary since 1908, when Zoology Professor C. Floyd Jackson initiated the effort. Twenty years later, Jackson established a Marine Zoological Laboratory on Appledore Island, one of the Isles of Shoals. In 1963, UNH leased the site from the state and began plans for a laboratory that would study the unique properties of the Great Bay estuary, and seven years later, the Jackson Lab was completed.

"Today we have over twenty scientists affiliated with this program, who are conducting field-based and experimental research on the physical and biological components of coastal ecosystems. We're especially interested in mapping the human influences on such ecosystems, information that is useful not just here in New Hampshire, but in the Gulf of Maine region more generally, with applications to ecosystems around the world."

He paused, then started a slide show. "Let me show you the effect one of the potential human influences, specifically an oil refinery, would have on this ecosystem. We know there would be oil spills. They are inevitable. What damage would such a spill, even a small one, do to the habitats in Great Bay? Let's take a look." For the next hour or so, he showed pictures of devastation to wildlife caused by oil seeping into coastal waters, and discussed how those pictures related to the wildlife in Great Bay. He pointed out that because of shallowness, the waters from Great Bay and Little Bay never fully flush when the tide goes out. It's commonly believed that oil is lighter than water, that oil floats on water, and that is partially true, he said. But there are certain oil components that do not float and instead sink to the bottom. "That would wreak havoc," he said, "on, among other things, oysters. I don't know about you, but for me that would be terrible!" Everyone laughed. "Oysters live only in estuaries like Great Bay. But an oil spill would devastate many other animals as well, animals that are essential to maintaining an ecological balance in the Bay: worms, soft-shelled snails, green crabs, and horseshoe crabs, among many others. Wading birds, such as snowy egrets and great blue herons, could be wiped out."[46]

• • •

An hour later, the group headed back toward Durham. A couple of miles up Durham Point Road, they turned off to the right onto Colony Cove Road, which ran north, parallel to Little Bay. After a short distance they came to the top of a hill and then moved down the other side, a magnificent vista in front of them. They had arrived at "Salty," Evelyn Browne's property, just south of where the waters of the Oyster River and Little Bay met and together flowed north to the Piscataqua River. At the end of the one-lane dirt road was a small cabin, smoke shimmering up from the chimney. The group parked in a clearing and were immediately greeted by Browne and her partner, Marion Beckwith, both of whom invited them inside. The two women had prepared warm mulled apple cider with orange slices, and the cinnamon-tinged aroma filled the small room. As the guests sipped their drinks and munched on cookies, Browne told the group: "You're standing on the very wide boards that George Pappademus said he would buy right from under me. So be careful!" Everyone laughed. Later, she gave them a walking tour of Salty, ending back at the cabin overlooking Little Bay and the Piscataqua River. Browne asked, "Can you imagine an ugly oil refinery right here?"

They returned to Dudley's house, where Tom, her husband and

acting attorney for SOS, had ordered pizza. They talked politics, some of the reps saying the tour had changed their minds—they had no idea of how pristine, nor how important to wildlife, the area was, and they couldn't understand why Olympic had chosen that location, rather some other area farther away from the Bay. Spirou announced that he had to leave, but before he did, he gave a pep talk about the importance of everyone sharing their experience of this tour with others, to help persuade enough reps to oppose the refinery.

Those who stayed were joined shortly thereafter by a special guest. The event captured in a report from *Publick Occurrences*, dated December 7, 1973:[47]

> The scene in Rep. Dudley Dudley's living room last Sunday seemed to have been set with an eye toward heightening the antagonism that was about to take place.
>
> The focus of the room was a recently installed school-house-type wood stove. It was sitting on the hearth in front of the closed-up fireplace with its pipe running through the shield up the chimney flue.
>
> The principal invited guest, about to arrive, was the man who's planning to bring the benefits of an oil refinery to Durham Point....
>
> Into this setting came Peter Booras of Keene, a man whose interests range from greeting cards to land speculation, to set everyone's mind at ease that his friends at Olympic Refineries intend only good for Durham and the state of New Hampshire.
>
> One of the legislators who'd been waiting noticed a large, expensive sports coupe pull up outside. "That looks like the kind of car Booras would drive," he said. It was.
>
> Booras entered, remarking that he hadn't been sure whether he'd be able to get there with most of the gas stations closed on Sunday. He said he'd finally found one open in Durham.
>
> "I asked the guy if he'd give me some gas if I paid him double," Booras said. "He finally took pity on me."

After seeing how badly Olympic representatives and Booras had answered the questions of the attendees at Friday's presentation at UNH just two days earlier, Dudley had asked her guests before Booras arrived to press him on the environmental issues. She introduced him to the group, and then stepped back. He said that his work with Olympic Refineries was as a friend, but not an employee, of the company. "I'm a lifelong resident of New Hampshire. My primary interest is, and always has been, the interests of the state."

He reaffirmed that he was getting no pay from anyone associated with the proposal, and that he was just "representing my very close friends at Olympic Refineries who want to come to New Hampshire." He was a lifelong friend of Constantine Gratsos, who managed the affairs for Aristotle Onassis. Booras knew they were looking for a location for an oil refinery and thought New Hampshire would gladly welcome such a facility. "I can't see anything but good coming from this proposal. I don't understand why Durham wouldn't want it. Look at all the benefits—available gas and heating oil; reduced property taxes by up to ninety percent; thousands of jobs; a modern, clean-as-a-clinic refinery."

One of the legislators challenged Booras: "Yes. You claim clean as a clinic. In the company hand-out, it also claims 'no adverse effects on surrounding land or waters should result from this project.' What evidence do you have for that?"

"Olympic has already looked into all of the environmental aspects and came to that conclusion."

"Have you seen any environmental impact studies from Olympic about a refinery in Durham?"

"That's not my specialty."

"But you can get a study for me?"

"I'm not sure."

"So, you have no concrete information about any study that would support that Olympic claim about no adverse effects on surrounding land or water?"

"I wouldn't know," Booras admitted.

"What about environmental consultants? Do you know of any who have been hired by Olympic?"

"I'm sure they have. I just don't know any offhand."

"Can you get the names of any that have been hired?"

"I really can't say. Look: we've done some studies, talked with some consultants. But nothing elaborate. Olympic intends to have some substantive impact studies done in the future."

"But there's nothing you have now."

"This thing is still in the early stages. We can't answer all your questions now."

"So that statement in the proposal is simply false."

The questions and answers continued in that vein, with Booras giving vague or non-answers to specific questions of concern—such as where Olympic would get enough cooling water for the plant, how the company could assure a supply of oil given the worldwide shortage, whether it was true that New Hampshire's needs for heating oil and gas could really be taken care of first, and how much truck traffic would there be for transporting the oil out of Durham. Then one last exchange set the group on edge.

"According to the Olympic report, 'The refinery will form the core necessary to develop petrochemical plants and further downstream processing to serve New England markets for additional products.' How extensive will these additional industrial activities actually be?"

Booras said, "I can assure you, we are only concerned with a refinery. We have no plans to operate petrochemical or other industries using refinery by-products."

"Then why did the report say there would be additional industries?"

"I really don't know. I didn't write the report."

"But you're saying there won't be any additional industries."

"Yes. We have no plans to operate other petrochemical industries."

"Can you state for sure there will be none?"

"All I can say is that there are no plans for such industries."

"So that *could* happen. You just don't know of any plans right now to operate them? Even though the report explicitly says there will be other petrochemical plants?"

"Well, we'll see how things go," Booras said. "It depends on the demand and the disposition of the people."

"It sounds to me like we should believe what the report says."

"I don't know. Maybe."

"So Durham will become the Newark, New Jersey, of New England."

• • •

Later, after everyone had left, Tom and Dudley discussed the day's events. She was pleased with the tour and the Q&A with Booras, but she wondered how much influence the thirty or so legislators who attended would have on the other 370 House members who had not made the visit.

"It's a mixed bag," she said. "The perception among many reps will be that today was less about Home Rule than about NIMBY."

"Towns should have a right to say 'not in my back yard' if they don't want the refinery," Tom said.

"Of course," she said. "But apart from the Bay, we're just like any other town saying we don't want petrochemical plants or big industry in our town. If not here, where? Let other people suffer the consequences? That's not a strong argument."

"But some towns are willing," Tom said. "Newmarket seems to want the refinery."

Dudley shook her head. "We'd be almost as bad off if Olympic builds there. The Bay would still get polluted. We'd have chemical plants and heavy truck traffic all around us."

"The limits of the Home Rule approach," Tom said. "But what other option do we have?"

10

TOWN MEETING

When the governor confirmed that he was working with Olympic to establish an oil refinery in Durham, Nancy Sandberg's life dramatically changed. She had been busy before then, organizing SOS and filling her roles as a mother and wife and part-time farmer, but after the governor's official announcement, and for the next four months until Town Meeting Day, the second Tuesday in March, her days and evenings were consumed with matters related to the refinery. The vast majority of her time was spent on the phone, talking with reporters and coordinating activities among the SOS volunteers. So frequently did she have a phone receiver against one ear or the other that both became painfully swollen. Finally, a month later, she and Mal got a second phone line and a speaker phone.

The pressure on her as head of SOS sometimes seemed enormous, pushing her almost to the breaking point. It was exhilarating, too, finding herself in a position she had never thought possible—she, Nancy Sandberg, whose only aspirations had been to be a good mother and wife and caretaker of her father and grandmother's homestead, now leading her town in a struggle for its very existence. At first she had felt apprehensive that she wouldn't be up to the task, but she had had little time to think about that as she became immersed in confronting the Onassis proposal. Her husband, Mal, and Sharon's husband, Dave, often exchanged babysitting duties after they got home from work, while she and Sharon connected with each other every day.

The first item on Nancy's agenda after Thomson's announcement was to prepare a news release that would counter the supposed advantages of the proposed refinery. She consulted with Sharon, and with her neighbors, Dan and Sally Ford, who said they had experience in their business with press releases. They all met at Nancy's house and moved to the kitchen with its large table. Together they crafted a statement that criticized the governor for proposing a refinery when there had been no comprehensive planning to address the economic and environmental implications.

> The planning board and the Durham Board of Selectmen were never consulted in the selection of the site, and the proposed use of the land violates the town zoning ordinances of both Durham and Rye.
> "The refinery would spell doom for the seacoast area's rural character, since it would occupy the last large undeveloped area bordering Great Bay. Because satellite industries follow refineries, SOS expects that the various economic activities of the area would give way to heavy industry.

They had no SOS stationery, so Nancy typed out the statement on standard typewriter paper, putting SOS on the top, along with her phone number in case the press wanted more information. Dan and Sally said they would get the statement Xeroxed and mailed out to the newspapers and broadcast media. From that time forward, her phone was busy most hours of the day and evening. Later, with a grant from Marion Beckwith, Evelyn Browne's partner who had been duped into selling an option to Olympic by Chris Booras (Peter Booras's brother), Nancy hired a public relations professional to handle her constant stream of correspondence about the refinery.

Once the news release had been prepared and sent, the most significant and pressing project for SOS was the upcoming Town Meeting, scheduled for Tuesday evening, December 4. For weeks, Karen Mower of the technology committee had been lining up UNH experts to come before town residents and outline some of the problems that the refinery would bring to the state. At the same time, Sharon Meeker, working with several other women on the outreach committee, had prepared a flyer inviting all residents to come to a town meeting where they could learn more about what a refinery would mean to the town. One of the women on the committee had a mimeograph machine at her house, and she and several of the committee members gathered there to stuff and address envelopes, while others posted flyers all over town. Because they weren't conducting an official town meeting, they couldn't schedule it in the high school or at the university, but instead worked with the priest at St. Thomas More Church, which had a basketball gym next to the rectory. The gym had no bleachers, so volunteers helped set up hundreds of chairs facing a makeshift stage.

• • •

By 7 p.m. on the designated Tuesday, the SOS volunteers had set out all the chairs and placed a standing microphone in the middle of the floor. Another microphone was installed on stage for the presenters. Nancy had no idea how many people would actually show up, but already, scores had arrived. People kept coming, and coming, and coming. Earlier she and the SOS executive committee had worried that not enough people would attend; now they were worried that all the people who came couldn't fit in the small gym. It had looked big when they first checked with Father Michael about using it, but now....

It wasn't until almost a quarter to eight when Tom Marshall, the moderator, was able to start the meeting. All the chairs were taken, and many people stood along the side and back walls. Marshall spoke into the microphone, "Ladies and gentlemen..." and the murmuring quickly subsided.

• • •

700 meet in Durham; explore the problem

By the end of the meeting, Nancy was satisfied with what SOS had accomplished in such a short time. Three days later, she was pleased to read an account of the meeting in *Publick Occurrences*. The paper gave a three-page spread to the event, complimenting SOS for its preparation, and including a short summary of each speaker's major points. Also in the story were photos of Nancy talking from the floor mic and Dudley addressing the audience, as well as photos of UNH professors Galen Jones, Gail Ulrich, and Jim Horrigan. Nancy was particularly pleased with the compliment the reporter gave to SOS:[48]

> It was clear that a lot of homework had been done by the people rounded up by Save Our Shores. In contrast to the almost total lack of specifics and documentation from the

proposing company, Olympic Refineries, whose very existence was called into doubt, the panelists cited chapter and verse on the laws governing refineries and land use; the pollution hazards, and what they considered the meretricious nature of the "tax boom" promises; the dangers of catastrophic failure and enormity of the disruption such a facility would have on the way of life of the whole region.

Nancy thought that Gail Ulrich had perhaps best summarized the Olympic proposal when he said: "As a chemical engineer, it's not my business to go around knocking oil refineries. In fact, it is my opinion that if allowances are made for transportation, aesthetics, community acceptance, and land use, somewhere in New Hampshire there may be a suitable location for an oil refinery. However, on the basis of any one of these criteria, I think this refinery is preposterous." There had followed the loudest and most prolonged applause of the evening.

Though the meeting had been an unmitigated success, with the large turnout, the several sober assessments and criticisms of the refinery by the invited experts, and now the positive press reaction, Nancy knew that the fight against Olympic was still heavily weighted against them. And she was put off by the reluctance of the town leaders to take a strong stand against the refinery. In his presentation at the meeting, Alden Winn, Chairman of the Board of Selectmen, had warned residents that the situation was precarious. "My advice to you," he said, "is that whatever action any one of us takes in the town, let us not take any action that can precipitate any state action to intervene."

She had no idea what that meant in practical terms. The state was already going to intervene. The governor was trying to force a refinery down the town's throat. Should the residents now keep quiet for fear of offending the governor and inciting him into doing...what? He was already doing the worst thing possible. The chairman of the planning board was no more helpful, reiterating the obvious—that the board itself couldn't stop the refinery, but could only ask questions. What a passive response! What town officials could do was send strong messages to the legislature and the governor that the town didn't want the refinery—but none of them seemed inclined toward this particular course of action.

Dudley Dudley's presentation stood in stark contrast to Winn's. As *Publick Occurrences* noted, she had come to the meeting "laced with facts and figures about state and federal laws." She had researched all the statutes pertaining to all the commissions and agencies that they could "rely on to help keep out, or at the very least control, the operation of an oil refinery." It was an upbeat presentation, giving people hope and inspiring them to join with her and others in a common cause. Nancy admired the older woman's poise and confidence, her ability to project herself as a leader. She felt good that they were working together.

At the end of the meeting, Nancy informed all in attendance that they could sign a petition against the refinery, if they hadn't done so already. Sharon and her outreach committee had been knocking on doors and holding small gatherings in homes throughout the town to discuss the ramifications of the refinery and encourage people to sign petitions. At the meeting in the gymnasium, they got several hundred more signatures. Dudley had suggested that she could take the petitions to the governor once SOS finished collecting them. Nancy thought that was a great suggestion. The town needed to send a clear message: No Refinery in Durham.

11

PURSUING THE DREAM

The Friday morning after Steve left with his suitcase in hand, Phyllis had no choice but, as she would later describe it, *to keep moving, keep breathing.* She had cried most of the night, and in the morning, exhausted by lack of sleep and self-recrimination for having driven him out, she had somehow managed to get Meredith and Patrick off to school, delaying explaining anything to the twins when they asked where Daddy was. She then drove down to Plaistow to pick up the batch of five thousand newspapers, drove back up to the post office in Newmarket where she left half the batch for mailing to subscribers, took the other half of the batch to the old mill building office where the staff divided the papers among themselves and set out to deliver their apportioned number to some thirty-five different locations all up and down the seacoast, and finally, after completing her assignment, arrived back home in the early afternoon and collapsed on the living room sofa.

After a while, she called her parents. Her mother answered, which was good, because she was always so supportive. And she was this time, too, not berating Phyllis for having married such a loser in the first place, though that is exactly what her mother had said about Steve before they got married. Her mother promised to fly up from New Jersey to help in any way she could, assuring Phyllis that she would go pack now and take a flight out the next day.

Her father got on the phone, which Phyllis half-dreaded, because she knew that he had *really never* liked Steve, and she did not want to hear any "I told you so" comments. While her mother had come to accept her daughter's decision, her father never had. "You are twenty-four and you have never done anything as terrible as you are doing now," he berated her right before the wedding. And he had never wavered in his opinion, not even when they had the twins, nor when they had started their own newspaper. "You just can't trust him," was his common refrain. When her father got on the phone, he was surprisingly sympathetic, telling her how bad he felt that Steve had left, and how much he would like to help. Phyllis wondered if her mother had warned him to be nice before he got on the phone. That would be like her. He asked Phyllis about the paper, and she told him what Steve had told her—that half their investment had already been spent, and that the paper was hemorrhaging money, though she had yet to look at the books to see what the exact numbers were. All she knew was that she had to pay a substantial sum each week to get the papers printed, and another couple of hundred dollars for postage to mail them to subscribers. She knew that the salaries they paid their staff compared favorably with other local newspapers—she and Steve had agreed that they would never shortchange the people who worked for them—but she had a lot more to learn.

"Well, I want you to know," he said, "I'll help you and the children. Whatever you need. But I will *not*," and here his voice got louder, "give you a penny for that newspaper. It would just be good money after bad. I told you then it was a terrible idea. A crazy idea. You should have kept working for a good newspaper. You're a great writer. But going into business with Steve…I told you, you just couldn't trust him. And I guess I was right."

Phyllis hardly knew how to react. She was mortified he had interpreted her telling him about her financial difficulties as asking for money. "I would never, never, ever, ever ask him for a dime," she would later recount. "I would have died on the street corner with my kids holding cups in their hands before asking him for anything."

"Yes, you told me you couldn't trust him," Phyllis told her father. "But you never gave any substantial reason why. All you ever said was 'He's skinny and he's from Oklahoma.' That wasn't exactly something I could hang my hat on."

"Well," he said, "everybody knows you can't trust anyone from Oklahoma."

• • •

When she picked her kids up from school that afternoon and they arrived home, she finally had to answer the question, "Where's Daddy?" She told them he had left and was going to live with another woman, and when Patrick said, "Does that mean we're orphans?" her heart stopped. No, she told him, orphans are children who have no parents. And I'm here. "Does that mean we're half-orphans?" She hugged them both and cried.

Her mother arrived the next day as promised. Phyllis did not want to discuss with her mother what might have caused Steve to leave, but surprisingly the topic never came up. Her mother commiserated with her daughter, gave her moral support, promised any financial help she might need—though Phyllis immediately declined the offer—and took care of her grandchildren. Phyllis spent the weekend going over the bills and checking account. Neither she nor Steve had been business majors in college. One of them thought it was important to consult with a business expert before launching their newspaper enterprise. The other did not, and would not allow it. But now that the business skeptic was gone, Phyllis knew what needed to be done. As soon as she could, she would go to the UNH business school and ask for help.

The next Monday, her mother took the kids to school and dropped off Phyllis at the Newmarket office. Phyllis wondered what Dick Levine and the other reporters and staff knew, and whether they would be willing to continue to work at the newspaper now that Steve had left. She could feel her heart thudding against her chest as she walked up the steps of the old mill building to the *Publick Occurrences* office. When she walked in the door, she saw that Dick was already there, something that almost never occurred.

He was a notorious late sleeper, and would constantly come in late, usually with a hangover—but today he was in the office before she was. As were the reporters and editors. Shaunna, she noted, was not at the compugraphic machine, though that was not surprising. Her work wasn't needed until later in the week, once some of the stories had been written and Dick and Steve were beginning to prepare the layout for that week's edition. She had barely come in the door and taken stock of those present when Dick and everyone stood and started clapping. She was stunned. Somehow they knew. She felt herself flush as Dick announced, "Our new publisher! Congratulations!" The others echoed Dick's words. She shook her head, embarrassed but pleased, saying she didn't know whether she could do this, whether she could really replace Steve, but immediately they reassured her that things would be better now with her as sole publisher. Dick reminded her, as though she even needed reminding, that she already was doing more for the paper than most publishers (he didn't specifically mention Steve), writing and editing, and at the same time soliciting ads for the paper, and getting no official credit. Starting in the upcoming issue, he said, we will list you as publisher. But Phyllis said no. They argued a bit, Dick insisting that she deserved to be listed, should have been listed as co-publisher right from the beginning, and certainly now that she was sole publisher. But Phyllis was adamant. She didn't want to telegraph to the readers that there was some turmoil at the paper, and that maybe it wasn't something they should subscribe to. It was a pure business decision. She didn't need the official recognition. It was the work that counted. Besides, she said, people would probably have less confidence in the paper if the publisher were a woman instead of a man. Dick disagreed but acquiesced, saying he would respect her decision as the publisher. It was a startling moment, Dick not absolutely insisting that he get his way, as both he and Steve had done almost every day. Now that Steve was gone, she wondered how well she could work with Dick, but this willingness on his part to go along with her decision gave her hope.

And her hope was realized. Over the next several weeks, the

atmosphere in the office was a complete reversal from what it had been for the previous five months. And Dick, whom she had not wanted Steve to bring with them because she felt that while Dick was an excellent editor, he was also highly irresponsible, now became her trusted colleague. Their professional judgment on what stories needed to be included and emphasized seemed almost always to agree, and when they had differences, they were able to work them out without rancor. Hardly a week went by when one or another of the staff didn't mention how much more pleasant it was working at the paper now that Dick and Steve weren't screaming at each other every day.

Dick admitted to her that on Steve's last day, the two of them had argued fiercely, even more so than usual, and that Steve had walked out saying he was never coming back. Dick hadn't told Phyllis about it that Thursday, when Phyllis asked where Steve was, because he genuinely didn't know where Steve had gone and thought she should hear about his quitting from Steve himself, not from Dick.

"What did you argue about that was so bad?" she said.

"Steve complained that we were obsessing with the oil refinery. We shouldn't be spending so much time on a storyline that affected just one town. I told him the refinery affected all the thirty-two towns we cover in the paper. Then the argument got personal."

"Personal?"

"Yeah. We said some things to each other I don't want to repeat. It was ugly. From both of us."

Phyllis couldn't imagine what could be so bad that Dick refused to talk about it. She had heard them yelling at each other for weeks, and it always seemed to devolve into personal insults. She could never figure out why Dick didn't quit. She never expected that it would be Steve who would quit instead. She said, "What about Shaunna? Who's going to replace her?"

"Don't worry. She said she'll continue to work with us until we get a replacement. She knows someone who she says knows the compugraphic machine. She'll bring him in later today or tomorrow." He watched her reaction. "It's okay, Phyllis. I'll take care of it. You don't have to deal with her. That's my job. I'm the editor. You're the publisher."

Phyllis felt a sense of relief that she had not thought possible since Steve announced he was leaving the previous Thursday. The acceptance by Dick and the staff, and the knowledge that without Steve, the paper would continue to operate, set her at ease. But still hanging heavy in her mind was her fear that the paper might soon go bankrupt.

12

PETITIONS AND THE GOVERNOR

On Monday, December 17, Dudley drove to Concord, some thirty-five miles away on the two-lane road that was Route 4, to meet with Governor Thomson at 2 p.m. and give him the petitions that Nancy and her SOS colleagues had gathered over the past several weeks.[49] This was her third appointment, the first canceled, after she had waited an hour, because the governor was behind schedule and had to leave. The second appointment was canceled because Thomson was going to New York City to negotiate for extra fuel for snowmobiles. She could hardly believe her ears when the secretary told her that. Here we are, she thought, with long gas lines for cars and trucks, and he's worried about…snowmobiles?!

In the meantime, more petitions had been added since the SOS presentation to the town. The total was now up to four thousand, though Dudley wasn't sure any number would be sufficient to influence Thomson. She arrived at the State House about a half hour before the appointed time and went upstairs to the governor's outer office. The secretary said Governor Thomson would be with her shortly, and in the meantime Dudley could go into the adjacent Governor and Council Chambers. Unlike other states, New Hampshire has a Governor's Executive Council, which consists of five councilors elected from roughly equal districts across the state. The Council meets every two to three weeks with the governor to pass on all substantial government contracts, approve appointments, and conduct other oversight on the chief executive. The door to the Chambers was left open, and soon some reporters, waiting to see the chief executive, noticed Dudley with her pile of papers. They wandered into the Chambers and talked with her, Dudley explaining why she was there. The reporters began looking at the petitions, which she had laid on the table. After a while, she looked at her watch and noticed it was almost half an hour past the appointed time, and thought that the governor might have dragged her up to Concord once again only to cancel the meeting. She said to the reporters, "Hey, why don't you take a photo of me holding the petitions in front of my ancestor by marriage?"

Hanging on the wall was a painting of Joseph Dudley, the Governor of Massachusetts and New Hampshire from 1702 until 1716, a period in which the two colonies were combined into one governing unit. He was the son of Thomas Dudley, also a governor of New Hampshire for two one-year terms, 1640 to 1641 and 1650 to 1651. Dudley explained that her husband, Tom, was a direct descendant of these two men. She stood in front of the painting, holding the top petitions while letting the rest dangle onto the floor. Just as the cameras began flashing, Thomson's secretary came in the room. "The governor will see you now," she said.

It was 2:30.

Dudley quickly tried to fold all the petitions back together, but the reporters wanted to continue examining them. She cut loose about a third of them and rushed into the governor's office, the papers spilling out of her arms. "I'm sorry for the disarray," she said. "These are petitions from Durham residents against the refinery." She placed them on a nearby table.

He was sitting behind a big oak desk and did not get up when Dudley entered. Instead he glowered at her. "Why are they so untidy?" he said.

"Because photographers were taking my picture, and I was showing them the petitions," she said. "They just slipped out of my arms. The reporters have the rest."

"Did you do this to get your picture in the paper?"

"No. I thought…"

"Well, why did you bring these to me?"

"Well, Governor, I thought you might want to know how four thousand of your constituents are feeling about this issue."

"How do I know they're my constituents?"

"There's a place on each petition to indicate where they live."

"How do I know they're even voters?"

"You know, Governor, if they live in New Hampshire, they're your constituents whether or not they're voters."

"Don't be impertinent! I've heard many of the signers are students, just in the state temporarily. They're not really my constituents."

"There's a place on the petition to indicate whether they are registered or not."

"I don't understand the opposition to this refinery," Thomson said. "It ensures Durham will not run out of gasoline and home heating oil."

"I think you're mistaken, Governor," Dudley said. "The energy shortage isn't caused by a lack of refined oil. It's caused by a lack of crude oil. So, it's not clear how a refinery would help us get more crude oil."

"What do *you* know about an oil shortage, Mrs. Dudley? The fact is Durham should welcome this development."

"But it doesn't, Governor. And I'd like to draw your attention to a letter you wrote to Alden Winn, Chairman of the Board of Selectmen, where you said that if the town didn't want the refinery...."

Thomson stood up and pointed a finger at her. "You don't need to point my attention to anything! Get off your high horse. And get out!"

It was 2:35.

The reporters were still in the Chambers and wanted to know what had occurred in such a short time. "He was very discourteous," Dudley said, elaborating on the exchanges between her and Thomson. "I was very badly treated and very badly used."[50]

Two hours later, the governor's office issued a statement saying Governor Thomson found Mrs. Dudley's demeanor to be "provocative and belligerent."[51]

13

THE OIL REFINERY—
NINETEEN ARTICLES AND REPORTS

On Thursday, December 13, the eve of the second publication of *Publick Occurrences* under her leadership, Phyllis was a bit worried. She had come into the Newmarket office in the mill building right after taking the kids to school, and Dick Levine was not in yet. That wasn't what was worrying her, however. His on-time attendance record had improved considerably, and she felt confident he would be coming in shortly. What concerned her was his insistence that the paper provide some kind of coverage of the ongoing impeachment proceedings against President Nixon. Dick's behavior on this matter seemed more in line with the out-of-control manner he exhibited towards Steve, rather than the new conciliatory persona he had assumed in the past ten days since Steve's departure, and Phyllis wasn't sure how to deal with it. The day before, she had reminded Dick that *Publick Occurrences* was never intended to cover national events, and it wasn't going to start now. Yes, in early November it had covered Minnie Mae Murray's impeachment drive in Durham, the local resident's campaign to get signatures demanding that the US House of Representatives impeach President Nixon. Minnie Mae had started the drive, she said, after the "Saturday Night Massacre" on October 20, when Nixon's refusal to comply with a request for information from the special Watergate prosecutor, Archibald Cox, had led to the firing of both Cox and the Attorney General, Elliot Richardson, and had also led to the resignation of Deputy Attorney General, William Ruckelshaus. But her impeachment drive was local news. What Dick wanted to cover had no local element to it.

And this week's publication, Phyllis was proud to note, was particularly bursting with local news about the oil refinery, some nineteen articles in all. She felt passionately that the refinery, more than any other concern, was the issue that needed to be thoroughly covered. It confronted all of the seacoast towns with significant consequences no matter which way it was settled, and no other paper was giving the citizens of these towns the in-depth information that *Publick Occurrences* was. This was exactly the role that she and Steve had envisioned for their paper, and she simply couldn't understand why he had abandoned that dream.

As Ron Lewis wrote in the lead article, "Supertankers will be off-loading Arabian crude oil around the clock, day in and day out, at Isles of Shoals if Olympic Refineries completes its present plans for a refinery on Durham Point." The implications of that fact needed to be presented to the public. Perhaps the most cynical view was found in a letter that Constantine Gratsos, Onassis's close associate and spokesman for Olympic Refineries, had written in response to a letter sent by a well-known Durham resident, Katie Wheeler:[52]

> November 29, 1973
> Dear Mr. Gratsos:
>   Please, come to Durham, walk around the town, visit a town meeting, see the beauties of Durham Point and talk to the people before you continue with your plans to build a refinery, which would irrevocably destroy one of the last lovely places to live… Would you put a refinery next to your house?

We are a small cohesive town, which has consistently voted against even *light industry*, feeling that the promised tax-advantages were overshadowed by the possible environmental destruction. Even if one disregards for a moment the environmental impact of a refinery, imagine the chaos created in a town of 7,500 inhabitants by the influx of 2,500 to 1,000 [sic][53] new people all wanting town services and a place to live. Surely, the place for a refinery is in an industrial park or at least in an area already zoned for industry.

We in Durham will fight to the end to prevent the destruction of Durham Point and our tiny bay, but we wish that you would come to visit us so that you will understand and perhaps sympathize with our opposition.

Sincerely,
Katherine W. Wheeler

December 4th, 1973
Dear Mrs. Wheeler:

I wish to acknowledge receipt of your letter of November 29th, for which I thank you.

I had the opportunity both in the past and this summer to visit New Hampshire and, particularly, the Durham Peninsula and I cannot agree more with you as to the loveliness of the place...

Unfortunately, the evolution of the world since the industrial revolution, [and] the universal population explosion[,] will inevitably result in the elimination of all that you and I and many other people cherish....In other words, today and in the future, we will have to choose between existence and beauty...

Aesthetically, a modern refinery when illuminated, looks more like a Christmas tree than anything else and is not uglier than the modern sculptural masterpieces adorning the streets of the major capitals of the world...

Very truly yours,
Constantine Gratsos

Even as she reviewed the exchange, Phyllis could not believe how anyone, even someone representing the oil industry, could be so tone-deaf. To suggest that modern industry would "inevitably result in the elimination of all that you and I and many other people cherish" seemed so extreme, she wondered how he could possibly think it would do anything but create more resistance. And she questioned his aesthetic sensibilities that would equate a sprawling, ugly, smelly refinery with a Christmas tree, or with sculptural masterpieces. If that was the aesthetic view of the Onassis men, the citizens really needed to know what they would be in for if Olympic were to succeed.

Another article provided even more questions about the company that was making the refinery proposal. It was hardly a company at all, she had discovered, certainly not one with substantial experience in constructing and operating a giant facility that its plans called for. She still acted as a reporter,[54] had personally called Gratsos to find out more about Olympic, and had been frustrated in obtaining the information she sought. The company was hardly the kind of organization in which people could have much confidence. Galvanized, she wrote the story:[55]

OLYMPIC NOT YET A COMPANY

Olympic does not yet exist as a United States company, according to Constantine Gratsos, the man who has been most prominently named as an official of the non-existent company.

In an interview with this paper this week, Gratsos said that Olympic Refineries will be incorporated "as soon as we have an okay from the United States about the refinery. We need the authority to build the refinery. You know, we have to go through a lot of pain to get it."

In the initial press release announcing a proposal to construct an oil refinery on Durham Point, Olympic Refineries was named as the initiating corporation....

Gratsos would answer no questions about the proposed corporation's officers, assets, or structure. "Olympic Refineries is a private company," he said.

• • •

Phyllis was reviewing the layout of the paper when Dick arrived with his usual hangover, needing some time to get all his pistons running. After he had settled in and consumed a cup of coffee, she went over to his desk and sat down next to him. "We need to talk," she said. He was surprisingly cordial, not obdurate as she had expected. All he really wanted to do, he said, was write an editorial about the impeachment proceedings, not a regular news story. He pulled out an earlier issue of *Publick Occurrences*, published on November 9, and turned to an editorial written by Stephen Bennett, "How easily we forget." It reflected on the assassination of Martin Luther King, Jr., and how the passage of time had made the event hazy in the country's collective memory. The editorial was mostly a philosophical musing, with no specific reference to current events, either nationally or locally.

She remembered it, of course. Even at the time, she thought it was a bit out of line with her and Steve's publishing philosophy, but given the many conflicts she had with Steve over the paper, she was not going to initiate another one over such a relatively trivial matter. And she immediately recognized Dick's point: After all, there was this precedent. The previous publisher had written a one-page editorial about a national event, albeit one that happened years earlier. Shouldn't the newspaper's editor be allowed the same prerogative?

"Okay," she said. "Nothing less than impeachment…" was set for page five.

There was yet another exchange of letters Phyllis wanted to include. Representative Dudley Dudley had met with the governor a couple of days earlier, and had been kicked out of his office, apparently—according to an Associated Press story—because she had called his attention to a letter the governor himself had sent to Alden Winn, of the Durham Board of Selectmen, in which he supported Home Rule. Phyllis had tracked down Winn and gotten the letter. She wrote the piece:[56]

Alden Winn, Chairman of the Board of Selectmen, wrote to

Gov. Thomson on Nov. 21, asking if there was a link between the options being purchased on Durham Point and the governor's plans for an oil refinery. He did not respond until Dec. 7, saying he could not do so earlier because "I had been asked by the Olympic group to treat their plans in confidence, and I felt it in the best interest of the State to do exactly that." He reassured Winn that:

"Neither the Olympic group nor this office have any desire to impose an oil refinery on a town that would be reluctant to accept the benefits that could flow from such an economic addition to a community.

"If in a proper, orderly and legal manner, the Town of Durham should reject the proposed Olympic Refinery, it would certainly be your town's loss and a great loss to the state, but this office has no intention of trying to force such a benefit on any community."

That was a promise he could not deny. Whether he would actually abide by it was a different story. But at least there was a public record of it.

• • •

The next day, Friday, after she had picked the papers up from the printer and delivered the appropriate stacks to the post office and the people on her staff so they could deliver them to the other thirty-five locations, she returned home to find that her mother had gone off someplace, probably grocery shopping. She retrieved her copies of *Publick Occurrences* and re-read the editorial Steve wrote that Dick had referenced. It was a bleak commentary on American life, how people forget the important events that shape the nation as they go about their daily business. It was also a personal reminiscence of his reporter days when, in the aftermath of the assassination of Martin Luther King, "I had covered the Baltimore ghetto, knew most of the black leaders, was comfortable there." But now? Did Steve feel comfortable here in New Hampshire?

Whether you move to a small town in Maryland or a town on the New Hampshire seacoast, you somehow learn not to remember or think about those wrenching days....You look out at the ocean or across a country field and these problems seem so far away....how easy it is to forget, or ignore, that national disgrace....And even worse, and part of that disgrace, you watch your children grow up in a world apart from those black brothers and you must sometimes worry about the barriers that keep your children and the black children apart, and the resulting damage fed by mindless prejudice and the natural fear of the unknown. Mustn't you?

Did Steve actually feel disgraced for living in New Hampshire with his wife and children? Or did he just pine for the action of a reporter covering big stories?

His last editorial, which he titled, "Fuel and self-reliance," was in the November 23 issue. Another personal musing about the importance of people showing concern not just for their own plight, but for the plight of others. It was the opening paragraph, however, that clenched at her heart. She had not understood it when it was published. Only now did the words signal what was to come. "The fuel shortage is doing strange things to people. I found myself in the woods on Sunday chopping firewood. My six-year-old son at my side, I saw myself as a man with a mission. It took me about an hour to realize that there is just so much sacrifice a man can make. How do you explain to your six-year-old son that you are only a philosopher?"

The words infuriated her. *How do you explain to your six-year-old son, and your six-year-old daughter, that you are a philosopher who is abandoning them? How do you explain to the woman you promised to love for the rest of your life that you are abandoning her?* She poured herself some wine and, for the umpteenth time in the past two weeks, cried herself to sleep.

14

CAMPAIGNING FOR OIL

While SOS was focused on persuading residents to oppose the oil refinery, the governor and the publisher of the *Manchester Union Leader* continued their campaign to convince the rest of the state that a refinery was essential to the state's very survival. On Friday, December 7, just days after the SOS town meeting, Loeb penned one of his more pointed condemnations of refinery opponents, using—as he usually did—a combination of bolded and capitalized words:

> …**We are dealing here with arrogant know-nothings, educated beyond the capacity of their intelligence …**
>
> Of course, you understand that these people would not do any of this work themselves. They would be the FIRST to scream if their television sets did not work, their electric toothbrushes didn't run, or if they couldn't get warm simply by turning up the thermostat.
>
> **BUT BECAUSE THEY ARE SO STUPID AND SO ARROGANT, THEY DON'T DRAW THE CONNECTION BETWEEN THE OIL REFINERY AND THEIR OWN LIVES OF COMFORT. THEY THINK THEY CAN HAVE ALL THE GOODIES OF LIFE WITHOUT THE REFINERY OR ANY OF THE OTHER INDUSTRIAL WONDERS OF THE MODERN WORLD…**
>
> What these people fear, or profess to fear, is in actuality a very tastefully designed refinery, which would not injure the atmosphere of the Town of Durham, but which would quietly send forth a live-giving stream of oil to take care of the needs

of all the residents of New Hampshire, as well as a good section of New England, while providing immense tax revenues to the Town of Durham.

ALAS, WE HAVE EDUCATED A CERTAIN TYPE OF JACKASS IN THIS COUNTRY TO BE SO ARTICULATE THAT HIS BRAYING OFTEN DROWNS OUT COMMON SENSE AND LOGIC!

—William Loeb

In the meantime, the House and Senate leaders were holding hearings to determine which bills would be considered during the 1974 special session. Since 1879, the General Court, as the legislature is known, had been meeting only on a biennial basis, typically from January to June or July. Elections for all statewide offices were also held biennially, so that the 1972 election was followed in 1973 by the regular session of the General Court. But since the end of the regular session in July of that year, much had happened requiring legislative action. The state could not wait until after the 1974 election to address these issues in 1975. Thus, in accordance with Part 2, Article 50, of the New Hampshire Constitution, the governor, with approval of the Executive Council, called for a special session to commence at 11 a.m., on Tuesday, February 19, 1974. It would be only the sixteenth time since 1800 that the General Court would meet in special session.

The governor let it be known that he wanted a limited agenda, though in fact once he and the Executive Council called the special session, his only ability to shape the agenda was the power of persuasion. The issues that had to be addressed included the capital budget, which had stymied the legislature during the regular session, and a supplemental operating budget to deal with the oil crisis. Everyone recognized that the special session would also have to confront the controversy over the Onassis oil refinery. Despite her initial fears that as a freshman legislator she would face resistance in introducing her bills, Dudley found the House Speaker quite willing to allow her that prerogative. The principle of Home Rule, it turned out, was too ingrained in the state's culture to be treated lightly. Also, she was sure that Chris Spirou had put in a good word to the Speaker on her behalf.

The day after her meeting with the governor, Dudley testified before the Joint Rules Committee in favor of the two bills she wanted to introduce.[57] As she had explained to Durham residents many times, and now argued before the committee, it was essential to amend the energy siting committee regulation to prevent it from forcing an oil refinery on a town that didn't want it. But she also wanted to amend the RSA that specified what constituted a "public utility," so that an oil refinery and its pipelines and related terminal facilities could not be so classified. Instead, she wanted them to be treated as part of the normal operation of a business, so they could be taxed by local governments and subjected to local ordinances. Public utilities, because of their general benefits to the state, were subject only to state regulations and taxes, and could be located wherever state agencies felt they would most benefit the state, regardless of local sentiment.

"These bills," Dudley argued, "represent emergency legislation, required by the unbelievable haste in which the world's largest grassroots oil refinery is being thrust upon the state of New Hampshire. Olympic Refineries is a ghost company owned by a single man, which represents an immediate threat to the seacoast area." She also argued that while some people would disagree with her assessment of the proposed refinery, it was beyond comprehension that the state, which had always valued Home Rule, would force such a gigantic industry on any town or city that did not want it.

While she was pleased that her bills were being considered, she was distressed to learn of a separate bill that was being presented, which would allow the energy siting committee to make the final decision as to where a refinery could be located. It seemed obvious that the governor and his supporters were not deferring to the principle of Home Rule, no matter what Thomson was saying publicly.

• • •

Separately, Thomson continued an aggressive pursuit of Onassis, agreeing to fly down to New York City to meet with him personally. The *Union Leader* was eager to give as much positive coverage to Thomson's efforts as it could. On Thursday, December 13, it gave front-page coverage to the announcement of the visit, with pictures of both men under the headline, *Governor Plans Onassis Parley*. And then two days later, the paper gave top-of-the-front-page coverage to the actual meeting, "Thomson, Onassis Confer," with a sub-headline, "Refinery Could Guarantee Oil for NH Needs." The latter article reported that "Governor Meldrim Thomson, Jr. said last night that he had a lengthy meeting with Greek shipping magnate, Aristotle Onassis, and had come away 'pleased to have found a hard-headed businessman who is prepared to meet all environmental standards' in the construction of a $600 million oil refinery on Durham Point."

But the big news was that Aristotle Onassis himself was coming to the Granite State on Wednesday, December 19, for a "first-hand look at the situation."[58] Constantine Gratsos, a longtime associate of Onassis, said that the visit was "sort of an exploratory thing…. We're moving ahead because we are willing to take the risk we might spend some money and not get anywhere. But that's in the cards of doing business." Were he and Onassis at all discouraged by some opposition expressed in Durham? "Certainly not," he said. "In our long careers, we have met opposition all over the world and I think that when there is an atmosphere of understanding, all problems can be solved."

Loeb could hardly contain his excitement, running a front-page editorial, with his usual pedestrian language:

WELCOME TO THE TWO BIG O'S —OIL AND ONASSIS!

When Mr. Aristotle Onassis arrives in New Hampshire today, he may be missing the white beard and the red suit. However, the season of his coming here is appropriate in the sense that he is the nearest thing to Santa Claus that the State of New Hampshire will ever see.

This is because he is bringing with him the greatest possible gift to the Granite State, namely, an opportunity to engage the fuel and gasoline shortage which is burdening the rest of the region.

Of course, it would take a pretty good effort by the reindeer to carry an oil refinery to our shores, but they could do it in about two or three years—and then many of our fuel problems would be over....

So, let's end all this hysteria about this great gift that the combination of nature and Mr. Onassis is giving New Hampshire....

THE MODERN ONASSIS REFINERY...WOULD BE HARDLY NOTICEABLE BY THE INHABITANTS OF THE SEACOAST AREA, UNLESS THEY WERE TO FLY DIRECTLY OVER IT.

This paper should certainly not need to point out to the taxpayers of the Town of Durham what this huge addition to their tax rolls will do to reduce their own property taxes. Obviously, it will reduce them considerably—as anyone should be able to figure out....

—William Loeb

The announced schedule for the Onassis visit included a helicopter flyover of the proposed site on Durham Point in the morning, then lunch in Concord with Governor Thomson and William Loeb, among others. At 4 p.m., Thomson would hold a press conference with Onassis at the Sheraton Wayfarer in Bedford, followed immediately afterward by a reception for state and community officials. Thomson, Loeb, and the Onassis men all had high hopes that the visit would spark widespread support for the refinery.

Instead, it was a disaster.

15

THE RICHEST MAN IN THE WORLD

In the winter of 1973, when he was about to visit New Hampshire, Aristotle Onassis should have been thrilled with his new investment in oil tankers, and with the prospect of constructing his own

oil refinery, which he had sought for years. If all worked out well, he would achieve vastly increased levels of wealth. But he wasn't thrilled. "I can't get excited about it," he told his cousin and good friend, Costa Konialidis. "Perhaps I've used up all the excitement, perhaps I don't need it as much as I thought I did." To his cousin, this was almost heresy. Onassis had always exuded energy and confidence, had always calculated number of ships in terms of millions in profits, but now lamented: "Millions do not always add up to what a man needs out of his life."[59]

• • •

When he was young, what Onassis felt he needed out of his life was, most importantly, to be rich. And also famous. And, of course, successful with women. That he achieved all three goals is without question, though his beginnings did not presage his accomplishments.

Born in 1900, in Smyrna, a town (now Izmir) currently

in Turkey, Onassis and his family lived in a prosperous Greek community, his father, Socrates, in the tobacco business. In the aftermath of World War I and the break-up of the Ottoman Empire, the Greco-Turkish War erupted, leaving the Greek community vulnerable to massacre. Many of Onassis's extended family were killed, but Onassis helped his stepmother and sisters to escape to Greece. And he went back to Turkey to bribe officials to let his father escape as well. Once in Athens, however, Ari, as he was later known, found little opportunity, and, at the age of 22, decided to emigrate to Argentina, where he had distant relatives. Once in Buenos Aires, he finally found steady employment as a nighttime telephone operator for a central switchboard. He saved his money and could live comfortably, but wanted to be part of Argentinian high society. He was short, but well built, with broad shoulders and a muscular torso. He bought some nice clothes and joined a rowing club, where he pretended to be a successful businessman, though he was intentionally vague about what exactly he did. There he met some of the wealthiest and most influential people in Buenos Aires. As he later explained to a biographer, "At 7 a.m., I'd finish at the [switchboard], have coffee and a bizcocho, or biscuit, at a little café just off the Avenida de Mayo where the waitresses knew me and treated me swell; I'd sleep for a few hours, then bathe, get dressed and do the rounds, looking up friends, a pretty girl or two, anyone who might be useful."[60]

In listening to conversations as a switchboard operator, he came up with the idea of manufacturing cigarettes that would appeal to women. Most of the cigarettes at that time were made with Cuban tobacco, which many women found too strong. Onassis's idea was to use a milder Turkish leaf. He consulted with his father, who was still back in Greece, although his own tobacco business had been destroyed in the Greco-Turkish war. After some false starts, the young Onassis finally found a niche for his new cigarettes. He was aided in this venture by Claudia Muzio, a famous opera star, whom he had deliberately seduced, after seeing her in a performance in *La Boheme*. She agreed to smoke his cigarettes in public, which—

given her celebrity—made her a role model for other women. "She liked my survival strength," he told the biographer, "but she thought I was a conner. And I was, I suppose; I needed to be."[61] His cavalier treatment of women continued unabated. Later, when a ballerina, with whom he claimed to be deeply in love, left him after one of their violent quarrels, he seemed clueless as to why she had gone. His new friend, Costa Gratsos, told the biographer, "I reminded [Onassis] that he hadn't been very kind to her. Ari said that he couldn't afford to be kind. 'First, I have to be rich,' he said. He was already a very rich young fellow, but he knew that he was still at the pupal stage of his fortune."[62]

In pursuit of greater fortune, Onassis decided to invest in the shipping business. He had observed that the transport of his tobacco from Greece to Argentina was earning the shippers more money than he was making selling the cigarettes. The decade of the 1930s saw his investments expand into oil tankers, providing him with significant profits. When World War II broke out, some of Onassis's tankers were used by the Allies for war purposes, while others were impounded until the end of the war. Still, Onassis emerged from the war in an ideal position to continue his business. None of his ships had been damaged during the war, nor had any of his workers been killed. And his personal life took a new turn when—in December 1946—he married the seventeen-year-old daughter of Stavros Livanos, a rival shipping magnate. Athina, or Tina, as she was called, first attracted Onassis when she was just fourteen years old, twenty-nine years younger than he. It wasn't until three years later that her father agreed to the union. Two years after the wedding, she gave birth to a son, Alexander, and two years later to a daughter, Christina. After that, the marriage began falling apart as first, Ari, and then later, Tina, engaged in numerous infidelities.

In 1952, Onassis bought a World War II frigate for $50,000 and spent $4 million converting it into what King Farouk called "the last word in opulence,"[63] and what one author called "a floating Xanadu that seduced them all."[64] Named after his daughter, the *Christina* would host many famous men and women over the next two decades.

Apart from launching the *Christina*, Onassis did not find the early 1950s very much to his liking. In the spring of 1953, at a social gathering in New York, he met Bobby Kennedy, brother of the just elected Massachusetts Senator John F. Kennedy. The two men took an instant dislike to each other. Their enmity would last the rest of their lives. More immediately, Bobby was minority counsel to Senator Joseph McCarthy's senate committee, which was investigating the influence of communism in the United States. Bobby's focus was on what McCarthy called "blood money," US allies who were trading with Red China, which was supporting North Korea in its fight against the US and South Korea. Bobby discovered that many Greek shippers had extensive business with Red China, and an investigation led to questions about other Greek shippers—Onassis, for one. At the end of the war, he had somehow acquired several US surplus tankers that had been for sale only to US firms. In October 1953, a federal grand jury handed down a sealed indictment against Onassis, charging him with criminal conspiracy to defraud the US government of millions of dollars. It also came to light that a dozen years earlier, FBI Director J. Edgar Hoover had written a memo about Onassis, saying that the Greek shipper had "expressed sentiments inimical to the United States war effort, and that his activities and movements should be carefully scrutinized."[65] Eventually, Onassis pled guilty to fraud and paid a $7 million fine in exchange for the Justice Department's agreement to drop criminal charges. He spent one night in jail. Onassis was convinced that it was Bobby who had caused all the trouble, telling Gratsos, "Nobody gave a shit about who owned those tankers until Kennedy started shooting off his big Irish mouth."[66]

Onassis had another encounter with the US government, when, in 1954, the CIA was able to disrupt a pending agreement between him and the Saudi government, giving the Greek shipper exclusive rights to transport its oil around the world. Referred to as the Jiddah agreement, it would have brought Onassis untold wealth, but the US threatened King Saud with serious consequences should the proposal be accepted.[67] Onassis believed that Bobby Kennedy was behind the action and was after him personally.

For the next couple of years, Onassis endured a tough struggle. In the wake of his conflicts with the US government, many oil companies canceled regular contracts, leaving his ships without cargo. He expanded his investment into gambling casinos in Monaco, and by buying the Greek national airline, which he renamed Olympic Airways. Finally, in 1956, he found the pot of gold. When the president of Egypt nationalized the Suez Canal, France, Great Britain, and Israel launched an attack against Egypt that temporarily closed down the canal. Now it was necessary for ships to make the long journey around the cape, and Onassis was uniquely situated to respond to that need. Much of his fleet was not under contract, and he had some of the largest tankers in the world. Suddenly, the oil companies that had been trying to force him out of business began jostling for contracts with him, causing the spot price of oil to surge more than fifteen times its pre-war level. "Ari began making money on a scale unimaginable even in his own grandiose dreams."[68]

In 1958, at the request of former British Prime Minister Winston Churchill, Onassis invited Senator John Kennedy and his wife, Jackie, to a visit on the *Christina*. Two years earlier, JFK had come close to winning his party's vice-presidential nomination, and Churchill—who had known Joseph Kennedy—said he was interested in meeting the son who, he had heard, was "presidential timber."[69] Onassis was unimpressed by JFK, but highly impressed with his wife—her style, her beauty, and her intelligence. "There's something *willful* about her, there's something provocative about that lady," he told Gratsos. "She's got a carnal soul." Gratsos told Onassis, "She's too young for you."[70] In fact, she was only four months younger than Tina. Ten years later, Jackie Kennedy would become Jackie O.

In the meantime, however, Onassis began a much publicized

affair with the American-born Greek opera star, Maria Callas. That led in turn to the termination of both of their marriages, though they never got married to each other, much to Callas's distress. On January 20, 1961, the same day JFK was sworn in as president, Onassis celebrated his birthday in Monte Carlo. In attendance, coincidentally, was Jackie Kennedy's younger sister by four years, Lee Radziwill, married just nine months earlier to her second husband, Polish Prince Stanislaw Radziwill.[71] Onassis was immediately drawn to her. Whether the attraction was to Lee herself, or to the status she now represented as sister-in-law to most powerful man in the world, Ari claimed at least that he admired "the way she was at home with wealth, the way she took luxury in her stride."[72] They soon became lovers, which the Kennedy brothers viewed as a political disaster in the making. For both political and personal reasons, the last thing they wanted was the despicable Greek shipping magnate to be part of their family. Over the next several months, the couple's affair drew more public attention, and they seemed intent on getting married. Bobby, now the US Attorney General with potentially significant power over Onassis's ability to dock in US ports, tried to intervene directly by threatening Onassis, but to no avail. Ari let Bobby know he was aware of Jack's and Bobby's own dalliances with Marilyn Monroe, which cut the conversation short.[73]

On August 7, 1963, Patrick Bouvier Kennedy was born prematurely and died two days later. This was Jackie's third tragic pregnancy. Before giving birth to two healthy babies, Caroline and John, Jr., she had suffered a miscarriage and later had given birth to a stillborn baby. Jackie's sister, Lee, flew in from Greece to comfort her sister and to attend the funeral. When Lee returned to Greece and shared the news of the tragedy with Onassis, he immediately told Lee to invite her sister to spend some recuperation time with them on the *Christina*. "Call her now," he said. "Tell her the *Christina* is hers for however long she wants it."[74]

Jackie agreed to spend the first two weeks in October with Lee and Onassis, along with several other guests. JFK was angry about her decision, but could not dissuade her from going. During the trip, Jackie came to appreciate Onassis in a way that she had not thought possible. She was fascinated by his stories and amused by his humor. She was in awe at how he had escaped from Turkey and saved his stepmother and sisters, and then gone back to free his father. She would later tell Artemis, Ari's sister, that Ari had "revealed a depth and a side of himself that surprised and touched her deeply." Ari also was attracted to Jackie, and abandoned any plans to marry her sister, Lee, preferring Jackie instead.[75]

A month after Jackie returned to Washington, JFK was assassinated. For the next several years, Jackie continued to see Onassis in secret, while he gave her large sums of money. They both wanted to get married, Ari impatient with Jackie's procrastination, Jackie feeling constrained by Bobby's fierce opposition for political reasons. She finally agreed with Bobby to put off any public commitment until after the 1968 election. When he was assassinated in June 1968, the last hurdle to a marriage with Onassis was gone. On October 20, 1968, Jackie and Ari were married on the island of Skorpios.[76]

The marriage caused a media uproar. Across the world, newspaper headlines reflected the disappointment and anger that many people felt about the union, especially in the United States. As Onassis's biographer wrote, "Instead of giving him a touch of class and opening doors for him in Washington, the marriage had anathematized him across America."[77] Onassis himself expressed buyer's remorse only two days after the wedding, when Jackie refused to accompany him to Athens to meet the Greek prime minister, where he would announce plans for a major Onassis oil project that included an oil refinery. "I've made some terrible mistakes in my life, but marrying Jackie might take the biscuit," he told his confidant Yannis Georgakis just forty-eight hours after the wedding, when he arrived in Athens without her.[78] His own son, Alexander, told a friend of his that Jackie made his father look like "another sugar daddy."[79]

While the marriage got off to a rocky start, the early months nevertheless seemed to bring some satisfaction to both Jackie and Ari. As Onassis's biographer noted, "there were early signs of domestic tenderness" between the two. "Jackie gave him her own special name, Telis," while Ari seemed concerned about her incessant smoking and tried to get her to stop. Jackie "appeared relaxed and radiant, in almost hoydenish high spirits." Ari was especially generous, giving Jackie free rein to redesign the house in Ithaca, his only request a long sofa by the fire "so I can lie and read and nap and watch the flames."[80]

Such enchantment was short-lived. Within sixteen months, Onassis had gone back to seeing Maria Callas.[81] Ari's business attention was focused on completing the proposed Omega project, a massive investment that he expected would keep his oil tankers fully operative. He was especially interested in constructing his own oil refinery, planned for Athens. His planning included buying oil from the Soviet Union, but the US government was not about to approve such an arrangement. Greece was heavily dependent on US aid, and the Nixon administration made it clear the Greek government should not approve the Omega project with Onassis. The final decision to reject the proposal came in October 1971.[82]

Onassis became more and more agitated with Jackie's behavior, resenting her long absences when she would return to New York, and also what he felt was her extravagant spending. In early January 1973, after having spoken several times with his New York lawyer, Roy Cohn, Onassis had dinner with his son, Alexander, in Paris, and told him he was going to divorce Jackie. Three weeks later, his son was dead from an airplane crash. Onassis was devastated. He refused to believe that it was an accident, blaming the crash instead on the CIA or the Greek junta, out to get him.[83] In the summer of 1973, on Skorpios, still devastated by his son's death six months earlier, it often happened that "he sat up all night beside Alexander's tomb, rocking back and forth on his haunches as he held his head in his hands, sobbing and muttering garbled messages to his departed son for hours at a time." In an interview, Gratsos revealed: "Ari blamed himself. He felt somehow responsible for the crash, for Alexander's death. That destroyed him. He really did not want to live anymore." His longtime lover, Maria Callas, made a similar observation: "It was as if a lifetime of guilt had crystallized around Alexander's death, and that Ari's grief and rage, unchecked and turned against himself, were destroying him."[84]

Compounding his personal and business worries, by December 1973, Onassis's health was failing. He felt tired all the time, and looked it. Right before his visit to New Hampshire, one Olympic executive said of the shipping magnate that "he looked sick as a dog."[85] Only the next March would Onassis learn that he was suffering from myasthenia gravitas—"whose symptoms are aggravated by alcohol, which he consumed in quantity, and fatigue, which now seldom left him."[86] Onassis then learned that "Myasthenia is classed with rheumatoid arthritis as a disease in which the body turns against itself. Its cause is not known, but its symptoms are brought on by stress, by too much alcohol, and by fatigue"[87]—all of which applied to Onassis in spades.

With all of these problems, Onassis was more than a bit irritated with the situation he found in New Hampshire. Gratsos had promised him smooth sailing, given the enthusiastic support of the governor and of the publisher of the state's largest newspaper. Throughout the fall and winter of 1973 to 1974, Onassis and his men dismissed the refinery opponents as "primitive reactionaries." As one of them said, it was "like trying to bring electricity to grandma."[88]

Onassis complained to Gratsos that, "These ecology nuts piss me off. A modern refinery's no worse than a modern apartment block. We're living in an age when people have to make up their minds what they want—survival or pretty picnic scenery."[89] Those were exactly the sentiments that Gratsos would echo in a response, dated December 4, 1973, to Durham resident Katie Wheeler, when he wrote that "a modern refinery when illuminated looks more like a Christmas tree than anything else," and in the future people "will have to choose between existence and beauty."[90] Nothing better illustrated the different world views between the Onassis men and the people of Durham than that exchange.

Whether the opposition was like "grandma" or not, it was real and had to be confronted. Despite poor health and serious business and marital worries, Onassis allowed himself to be cajoled into a visit to New Hampshire by Thomson and Loeb. Ari was known for his ability to deal with the press in a positive and dynamic way. His personal appearance, the governor and publisher argued, might be able to reassure the people that the refinery project was in the best interests of the state. They didn't realize how beleaguered the Greek shipper really was. And it would turn out that he was hardly up to the task. He would look tired and spiritless, and "under questioning, the sure touch and easy affability which generally marked Onassis's dealings with the press" would desert him entirely.[91]

the oil and the ... world where bet you ... Red Oasis men ... people of Durham even though they ...

Whether the explanation was like "grandmother" means, it was not and had to be continued ... prior beliefs and serious ...

16

THE OIL MAN COMETH

The day of Aristotle Onassis's visit was sunny and bitter cold, a low overnight temperature of just two degrees, rising only into the teens by the time of the helicopter flyover. A couple of days earlier, two inches of snow had given the land an icy cover. Sharon Meeker and Celeste DiMambro called their compatriots on Durham Point, reminding them of the plan. At Woody Rollins's house, the kids

were back home on vacation from college. When Woody's daughter, Dale, heard about the flyover, she and her brother and Dan Ford took huge, hand-painted "SOS" signs and planted them in seven fields on Durham Point. Other contingents of the "un-welcome" committee had carved "ARI GO HOME" in the snow. On

Evelyn Browne's property, John and Maryanna Hatch supervised the construction of a message written in twenty-inch red crepe paper letters ten feet high saying "NOT HERE." It would be impossible for the Greek oil magnate in his helicopter to miss the many messages.

Sharon heard on the morning news that Onassis intended not just to fly over the area, but to land at Adams Point and take a personal tour of Durham Point, accompanied by the governor, who was to drive down to Durham in his official limousine. She had signs, "ARI GO HOME" and "NO OIL REFINERY," already prepared, so she got in her car and headed down Durham Point Road. A short time earlier, she had actually seen and heard the helicopter fly over her house, and drove as fast as she could to get there before Onassis would leave on the tour. She wanted to plant the signs so he would be sure to see them. On her car itself, both in the front and back, she had "NO OIL REFINERY" bumper stickers. She was just turning onto Adams Point Road when a large sedan passed her going the other way. She saw the governor in the back seat, a nasty scowl on his face, glowering at her.

When she arrived at Adams Point a few minutes later, she saw no sign of the helicopter. She hadn't heard it fly over her again, but it was clear Onassis had not landed. Later, she would learn, he had seen the signs in the snow and was unwilling to get in a car to tour the area. She couldn't have been more pleased.

• • •

After the announcement of the Onassis visit, several reporters asked Nancy Sandberg if she was attending the reception. She hadn't received an invitation, she told them. The reporters questioned the State House about the lack of an invitation for the Chair of the SOS organization. There was neither confirmation nor denial of Nancy's claim, but on the day of the visit, she received a telegram inviting her to attend.

Dudley had also not received an invitation. After calling the other state reps from Durham and some of her fellow reps around the state, all of whom had received invitations, she called the State House to see if there had been a mistake. She was given a telephone number in New Jersey, where the telegrammed invitations were being coordinated. When she called, the receptionist there told her that she was not on the invitation list. Dudley noted that everyone else from Durham, including all the selectmen and state reps, had been invited, so wasn't it possible a mistake had been made? The answer: no.

The lack of an official invitation, however, did not deter this "provocative and belligerent" state rep. While she had no intention of crashing the reception, Dudley knew the press conference itself was open to the public. She drove to the Sheraton Wayfarer, a familiar place for any politician in New Hampshire, especially those who had ever been involved in the New Hampshire Primary. And Dudley had been active in that revered process, both in 1968, working to help Gene McCarthy, and again in 1972, working for the McGovern campaign. The Wayfarer was the place where national reporters covering the primary elections loved to congregate, to find warmth and comfort after being out on the cold campaign trail, to exchange their weird stories with other national reporters, and to hobnob with local officials to find out more about the strange state that was New Hampshire.

When she walked into the crowded Covered Bridge room of the Wayfarer, many of the reporters recognized her.[92] With little effort, she was able to wend her way through the throng of reporters and cameras, which included the three major networks, until she was standing only a few feet from the podium, where a couple of Olympic consultants were answering questions about the refinery. After a while, Jay McDuffee, the governor's press man, came to the podium and introduced Governor Thomson. The governor noted what everyone already knew—that Onassis had come to New Hampshire "to look over the possibility of establishing a refinery." Thomson went on to say, "This would be a tremendous thing not only for New Hampshire but for all of New England." He mentioned the $600 million cost of the refinery, which he claimed would provide jobs for one thousand workers when completed. "And so it is, Mr. Onassis, with a great deal of warmth that I welcome you to New Hampshire." [93]

After perfunctory applause, Onassis said, "First, I want to make it clear that I am not a Greek bearing presents to New Hampshire." There was a smattering of chuckles. "The last thing I

would like to do is to impose an unpleasant investment onto the inhabitants of New Hampshire. Particularly, if we bear in mind that the inhabitants of New Hampshire are part of the American aristocracy. However, every aristocracy needs a kitchen. All this time, for years now, your supplies were coming from very far away—expensive restaurants. So if we can manage to produce a refinery clean as a clinic, without any smell and without any smoke, and if we can persuade and convince the experts and the officials of the environment and ecology, I hope we are doing something good for everyone. That's all I have to say."

Given that he didn't want to impose anything on New Hampshire, a reporter said, what would Onassis do if the people of Durham didn't want a refinery, but the state did? Thomson interjected, "I think the answer to that has already been given. Because I have assured [the citizens of Durham] there will be no imposition of anything in that way…if they're not smart enough to understand this could be of great advantage to them, there are many others that do want it."

A reporter asked, "Governor, are you saying that people who don't want a refinery aren't very smart?"

"I didn't say anything! That's your question, and that's your answer!"

A new question for Onassis: why did his real estate agents tell people they were buying land on Durham Point for a rest home or a mansion? Wasn't that misrepresentation?

"I have something to make a little joke with you," he said, obviously prepared for the question and a way to avoid answering it. He held up a bottle of maple syrup. "We certainly didn't come to say we are going to build a distillery of maple syrup!" Thomson laughed. "This is made by the governor. It's an exclusive syrup produced by the governor without the distillery." The reporters laughed, among them Anne Gouvalaris, who was standing only a few feet away. Later she would write that Onassis looked dazed, his body floppy. "He was holding that jug of syrup in his hands with a look on his face that seemed to say, 'What in God's name is someone as rich as me doing with this idiotic thing?'"[94]

In between the answers Onassis gave to reporters, Dudley saw Thomson quietly urging his guest to say something else:[95] "Ari, tell them what you're going to give them." Thomson repeated his whispered suggestion several times, and each time, the Greek shook his head as though he was too embarrassed. Once again, Thomson urged, "Tell them, Ari. Tell them what you're going to give." The Greek said, "No, no. You tell them. You tell them."

Thomson turned to the cameras: "Mr. Onassis has authorized me to say that he is considering in general terms establishing an anti-pollution laboratory at the University in connection with the refinery."

Dudley almost laughed out loud. The offer was hysterical! No wonder Onassis was hesitant to say anything. It was a bribe, plain and simple. And a shabby one at that. It was like promising someone a band aid after slitting his throat. *Thanks for the pollution lab, Mr. Onassis, which—by the way—we wouldn't need if there was no refinery in the first place.*

At the end of the press conference, just as Onassis was being escorted out of the press room, Gouvalaris asked him if he thought it was unfair that he could use his wealth to essentially force people to give him what he wanted. "You don't force with money, my dear," he said. "You seduce."[96]

The group moved into the Wayfarer Convention Center, filled with state representatives and senators and many other local officials throughout the state. When Dudley walked by the door to the reception room, a state rep from Salem said, "You didn't get an invitation. Why are you here?" That surprised her. How did he know she wasn't invited? Maybe everyone knew. At least all the Republicans. Clearly, Thomson was getting back at her for going to the press when he kicked her out of his office. "You know," the rep said, "here we have one of the great men of the world offering us a real benefit to the state. You should be thankful for that instead of being so contrary."

What a twit, she thought. She contemplated crashing the reception after all, just brushing right by him, but there were too many Republican reps standing around the door, who no doubt knew she had not received an invitation. She couldn't muster the chutzpa to storm past the barrier. Besides, a couple of reporters she knew invited her to join them for a drink and some food at the bar. Maybe she would try the reception again later.

• • •

After receiving a belated invitation by telegram, Nancy was at first dubious about attending a reception where she knew there would be hundreds of people. She didn't see how being there would lead to any meaningful engagement with Onassis and his men, or with any of the home-grown supporters of the oil refinery, including the governor and *Manchester Union Leader* publisher. Still, she thought it might seem churlish if she didn't go, and if there was any possibility of actually talking with Onassis, she didn't want to pass it up. So she arranged for a babysitter to take care of their daughter, Betsy, and she and Mal drove over to Bedford for the reception. After only a short while in the crowded room, she realized that her skepticism had been fully justified. There was no effort by anyone associated with Onassis to engage her in conversation or to address any of the serious issues of the refinery proposal. A reporter asked how she felt about the reception. "I made arrangements to come here, hoping to tell him our side of the story. Instead, there was nothing. I'm really disappointed."

Later, as she and Mal were leaving, they saw Dudley talking with some reporters outside the reception room. A PR man from Olympic, "Tex" McCrary, came over to the group and apologized to Dudley that she had not received an invitation. He invited her and Nancy to meet with him at breakfast the next day. The town selectmen would also be invited. They both said they couldn't make it because of prior obligations. What about lunch then? Nancy couldn't, because she had commitments the whole day. "Besides," she said, "I want to speak with Onassis personally." McCrary said he would try to arrange for both of them to be flown down to New York City to meet with Onassis in the near future. He then urged Dudley to attend the lunch meeting with him and the Durham officials. This was such a last-minute deal, she had no idea if the selectmen would actually be there, and she had no intention of attending by herself. "I'll think about it," she said.

The next day, Nancy read in the Dover newspaper that Murell "Tommy" Thompson, the Durham leader of the pro-refinery movement, had personally met Onassis at the reception and had given the Greek shipping magnate some 200 petitions in favor of the refinery. But no mention was made of the four thousand anti-refinery petitions that Dudley had delivered to the governor. Nancy also read that the selectmen had declined the invitation to meet with McCrary because the invitation was too short a notice. What kind of a rag-tag operation was Olympic running, anyway?

Later that day, when reporters called to ask Nancy if she was going to accept the invitation to meet with Onassis in New York, she said she would not. If Onassis wanted to meet with her, the meeting would have to fulfill three conditions: it must be in New Hampshire, it must be public, and it must "meet substantive issues head on."[97] She later wrote a letter to Olympic Refineries with a more formal refusal:

> Mr. Onassis had every opportunity to meet with members of SOS and other citizens of the Durham community... Mr. Onassis chose instead to shield himself behind a wall of press agentry and to "meet" the people of Durham only from a helicopter.
>
> My husband and I, being the only members of SOS invited to Mr. Onassis's cocktail party (our invitations being tendered only hours before the event) drove across the state to have the opportunity to talk with Mr. Onassis. We were given no chance to speak with the gentleman whom you represent.
>
> Similarly, when we have attempted to make known the feelings of many of the citizenry of Durham and the New Hampshire Seacoast regarding the proposed refinery to Mr. Onassis's agent, Mr. Gratsos, the response has been polite but meaningless...
>
> It appears that Mr. Onassis is determined to proceed with siting a refinery in Durham on the basis of what must be the poorest investigation, planning, and research ever made in an attempt of this sort.... The efforts of Olympic Refineries to locate a refinery in Durham has reflected...an appetite for profit at the expense of New Hampshire people.
>
> Thus, your offer of a New York meeting with Mr. Onassis is a rather puzzling one, unless one considers it at its face value, as a publicity stunt designed to make Mr. Onassis appear most agreeable of men. It is for this reason, and the reasons stated above, that I must decline your invitation.
>
> SOS members welcome the opportunity of a meaningful meeting with Mr. Onassis if he comes to Durham in the future.

Dudley later confirmed that she too would not accept the invitation. Onassis should meet with all the major representatives of Durham, she said, including the town selectmen, not with just Nancy and her in New York.

Town officials were no more impressed with Onassis's visit and reception than were the two women. One of the selectmen, Jim

Chamberlin, told *Publick Occurrences*[98] he had hoped to get more information by attending the reception and "drove all the way to Manchester [actually Bedford, just outside Manchester] and didn't learn a thing." Another selectman, Owen Durgin, noted, "There was no information there. It was just a big party."

• • •

While sentiment among the anti-refinery activists ranged from disappointment to outrage, for Governor Thomson and William Loeb, the Onassis visit was simply splendiferous, the man himself apparently as close to perfection as any human could be. The *Union Leader* noted in its coverage of the visit the next day:

> The world famous Onassis has strong facial features but is disarmingly soft spoken and displayed a good sense of humor with an infectious smile....
>
> Gov. Thomson told Onassis, 'I hope and pray you'll be coming back to New Hampshire soon for a groundbreaking ceremony,' and Onassis smiled broadly in an unspoken agreement with that sentiment....
>
> The luncheon conversation ran the gamut of politics, the state of the world today, a sympathetic view of the demise of Spiro Agnew and even the Maine-New Hampshire lobster war. Onassis appeared conservative in his views and made constant analogies of current events to Greek history.

On the front page, the headlines shouted the good news that Onassis "Offers Clean Refinery," a picture of the Greek visitor accompanied on either side by the newspaper publisher and Governor Thomson, Onassis holding a copy of the *Union Leader* in his hands. The caption underneath the picture gives the publisher a pat on the back: "'VERY IMPRESSIVE' was the comment of Aristotle Onassis, head of Olympic Refinery of New York, as he views Page One editorial welcome of Publisher William Loeb which appeared in Wednesday's *Union Leader*."

Inside the paper were other stories, plus a whole page devoted to pictures of Onassis—standing next to Governor Meldrim Thomson and *Manchester Union Leader* publisher William Loeb and two of Onassis's men, all with big smiles;[99] receiving the OFFICIAL GREETING of the governor and his aides; being the house guest of Governor and Mrs. Meldrim Thomson at the Bridges Mansion for lunch; CHATTING with Governor Thomson and Major Alexander P. de Seversky, noted aeronautical engineer and anti-pollution researcher; HANDSHAKE with Governor Thomson as he introduces the head of Olympic Refinery to the press at the Sheraton Wayfarer; pondering a question asked of him during the press conference at the Sheraton Wayfarer; DISPLAYING a jug of Mt. Cube Maple Syrup grown by Governor Thomson on his farm; ENJOYING himself at the Sheraton Wayfarer in a chat with Governor Thomson and the Chairman of the State Liquor Commission; another picture of Onassis, this time by himself, once again reflecting on "OIL AND ONASSIS," the headline of *Union Leader* Publisher William Loeb's welcoming editorial; receiving PETITIONS from the Save Our Refinery group of Durham, while Murrell Thompson of the SOR group and Governor Meldrim Thomson look on; and flying off in his HELICOPTER for a visual tour of the proposed refinery site in Durham.

Simultaneously with its fulsome praise of Onassis and his visit to the state, the *Union Leader* also printed numerous attacks on the refinery opponents, Dudley among the most frequently mentioned. Two days after the visit, in an editorial entitled, "Something Good for Everybody," Jim Finnegan (the paper's editorial writer) contrasted "the calm, gentlemanly manner in which Aristotle Onassis conducted himself," with "the hysterical antics of those who are opposing his proposal." Specifically, Finnegan noted the "benighted attitude of the opponents of the oil refinery as demonstrated by one of their most voluble spokesmen, Mrs. Thomas Dudley of Durham." When asked about the possibility that Onassis would establish an anti-pollution lab at UNH, she had responded, "I can think of no other word to use than a bribe." On the other hand, Finnegan wrote, "If Onassis had not indicated that he is thinking along those lines, Mrs. Dudley would have accused him of being disinterested in preserving a clean environment."

When she read the editorial, Dudley could only laugh. She remembered that at the press conference in Bedford, a reporter had asked just that question: "Would the establishment of the anti-pollution set-up be in any way considered a bribe?" Thomson had rejected the characterization: "I wouldn't say so at all. I'd say it was done in the same fine spirit that the Coca-Cola Company, for example, built Emory University. He [Onassis] has not authorized me to give any of the details." Well, it still sounded like a bribe to her, and apparently to at least the reporter as well. In any case, the editorial was correct—if Onassis had not made the offer, she would have criticized him for not caring about the environment. And given that he had made the offer, she would still criticize him for not caring about the environment. The lab offer was irrelevant.

Right below the editorial praising the Onassis visit was another opinion piece, "Apologies to Mr. Onassis." Lamenting the "boorish performance" of the reporters who attended the press conference at the Sheraton Wayfarer (presumably including the question as to whether the Greek shipping magnate was trying to "bribe" the state with his anti-pollution lab), Finnegan despaired that Onassis might come away from his visit "with the impression that the Fourth Estate in this area of the country is composed largely of jackasses." If Onassis had that impression, "he was not far off the mark." The problem, the editorial writer believed, was that the reporters apparently felt they were the center of attraction, "rather than this world-renowned businessman who could have bought the lot of them for what they are worth and turned a handsome profit by selling them for what they think they are worth…." Therefore, "since those responsible for the discourteous performance are probably not bright enough to extend their apologies to Governor Thomson and his eminent guest, we'll do it for them."

And in the process, Dudley thought, they might want to kiss his ass as well.

Only a few days later, on Christmas Eve, another Finnegan

editorial continued the attack, "You Can't Reason With Unreason." In this piece, Finnegan defended Onassis from criticisms that the Greek shipping magnate hadn't met with anyone from Durham, despite promises to the contrary. Of course, he couldn't keep that promise, Finnegan proclaimed, when it was "predicated on the assumption that opponents of the refinery proposal were interested in an open discussion of the refinery questions. But obviously, this was not the case." (Actually, the promise had not been predicated on the assumption that the people in Durham had an open mind, but that the Olympic people might want to hear what exactly townspeople's reservations were.)

Finnegan went on to criticize specifically "opposition leaders Nancy Sandberg and Mrs. Thomas Dudley" for declining a breakfast meeting "where they could get answers to their questions in a quieter setting." He did not mention that Onassis would not attend, nor did he acknowledge that the Durham selectmen had also refused to attend this last-minute invite. But that didn't prevent Finnegan from once again attacking Dudley, continuing to refer to her as Mrs. Thomas Dudley and the Durham housewife, rather than her official title, Representative Dudley Dudley: "The point is that it's impossible to satisfy people who are determined to be unreasonable, or—in the case of Mrs. Thomas Dudley—are motivated primarily by a hunger for personal publicity. If the Onassis PR man had assured her that the TV cameramen would be present, we're sure the Durham housewife would have braved a hurricane to get her picture taken."

Two days after Christmas, the *Union Leader*'s editorial writer pounced again on Dudley for her opposition to the refinery. This time, the paper included a headshot of her, with the surprising gender-sensitive reference, "Spokesperson Dudley's Logic." But even that was fodder for sarcasm:

> Consider the kind of illogic demonstrated earlier this year by Mrs. Thomas Dudley, the Durham legislator who is currently the most voluble spokesman—whoops, spokesperson—against the oil refinery....

The Durham housewife quite seriously contends that the refinery's backers should not have purchased real estate on Durham Point without telling the owners the exact reasons why the purchase was being made, although to have done so obviously would have driven up the price of the real estate and rendered the refinery concept economically unfeasible.

And when informed that Onassis is considering building an anti-pollution laboratory at UNH in connection with the refinery, Mrs. Dudley's brand of logic led her to attack the whole idea and call it a "bribe."

After reading the editorial out loud to her husband Tom, as they relaxed in their wood-stove-heated living room, she said, "Sounds logical to me."

17

NEW YEAR, NEW WOES

It was Thursday, January 3, two weeks after the last publication of *Publick Occurrences*, and the staff was back together again. Phyllis and Dick had contemplated taking two weeks off, but there was simply too much going on to have such a long hiatus. In fact, Phyllis hadn't wanted any break, but finally acquiesced to Dick's feelings that everyone needed some time to relax, and what better time than Christmas, when few people would be paying close attention to the news anyway? Still, the reporters had been working on and off since the last issue.

The weather had been unusually warm for New Hampshire that winter season, she was told, and she had to agree—the temperatures in Christmas week were higher than she would've imagined at that time of year, reaching fifty-four degrees the day after Christmas. And no snow. In fact, only a little rain. This week was colder, more like she expected, with temperatures almost making it to freezing. But the ground, the streets, were clear of snow. And that was a significant fact, because Lester the Arrester had been on a tear from the beginning of November. Yes, Phyllis had read the law. "During Winter Parking Ban, no vehicle may be parked on any Newmarket road or town-owned parking lot between 1 a.m. and 6 a.m., November 1 through April 1. There are no exceptions." And she understood why the law was passed—so snow plows wouldn't be obstructed. But really? If there's no snow, why is Lester so doggedly determined to write tickets on parked cars, which he knows full well belong to people working at *Publick*

Occurrences and will definitely be moved at the latest, maybe, by 1:30 a.m., sometimes earlier, or only a few minutes late? She personally had gotten five tickets since the ban went into effect, and there hadn't been even one scintilla, one iota, one micro-milligram of the white precipitation anywhere in sight.

But she believed—hoped, anyway—that the solution had been found. Two weeks earlier she had left the office a few minutes before the parking ban witching hour, and when she got to her car, there was Lester, a big grin on his face, his ticket pad at the ready. "Officer Heath," she said. "That is one big smile."

"Thank you!" he said, his smile widening even further.

"In fact, it is so captivating, I would like to put your picture in our newspaper. Would you allow me to do that?"

By now his smile was so wide, she thought it might split his face. He folded up his ticket pad. "Yes, ma'am. If you'd like."

Now in her hand was the photo that she had asked George Burke, a few days after the encounter with Lester, to take of the patrol-man. She penned a caption: "Every new year should start with a warm smile. This one, of Patrolman Lester Heath of Newmarket, we saved for just this occasion." There was no news story accompanying the photo, but it would be in the paper, on page eighteen, and she would personally deliver a copy to the town police station, just for Lester.

• • •

She wondered what Steve would think of such blatant manipulation. He was so moralistic, she was sure he would have absolutely refused to print the photo. She could argue that there had been no explicit quid pro quo, but that wouldn't have satisfied him. His standards of integrity were strict and unbending. She recalled one time after they had gotten married when they were both in the grocery store, and she had eaten a single grape to see whether she should buy a bunch of grapes. Okay—she knew it was wrong, and as far as she could remember, there might even have been a sign that said, "NO TASTE TESTING OR YOU'LL GO TO HELL!" But c'mon. If she hadn't tasted it, she definitely wouldn't have bought any more, and she did taste it, and liked it, and put a bunch in their basket for purchase. So, that was good for her. And it was good for the store. But Steve was appalled! He fumed, *You can't do that. It's against the law. It's wrong. You're stealing food.* Well, something like that, though obviously she couldn't remember exactly what he said all those years ago. But she did remember exactly what he did. He saw a grocery store clerk and asked him to get the manager, and when the manager arrived, Steve snitched on her. Of course, that's not how he would describe his actions. He informed the manager that he was honor bound to report that his wife had eaten one of the grapes. Phyllis was shocked. The manager was struck dumb. Nobody said anything, at least as far as she could remember. And then she and Steve continued their shopping as though nothing had happened.

And yet, if his standards of morality were so high, she thought bitterly, why didn't they apply to his marriage? How could he live a lie all that time, keeping his affair secret from her for—how long? She had never asked. Didn't really want to know. He had come to the house over Christmas, driven down from North Conway, where he was working with a local paper. He wanted to see the kids, he said, and he also wanted to return the Irish albums he had borrowed for Shaunna. For Shaunna? Phyllis couldn't believe what he was saying. He had to tell her why he took the records? Did his sense of integrity permit him not even a modicum of sensitivity, but instead compel him to tell his wife how much he wanted to please his mistress? Phyllis told him she didn't even know the god-damned things were missing. Finding time to play records was not high on her agenda, so he needn't have bothered to return them. But, he said, he wouldn't feel comfortable taking them without her knowledge. That would be stealing. Now that was some twisted morality she couldn't quite fathom.

• • •

As usual, Phyllis was pleased the paper had a lot of stories about the refinery for the next issue, but the tenor of the stories, especially three of them, did not bode well for the town. Every night this week, after completing their work for the day, she, Dick Levine, and the reporters had all congregated at the Stone Church to discuss local events. Located high above Newmarket, it was just a short walk from the mill where their office was—down into the main part of town, and then up a steep hill, where they could look over the town and the Lamprey River. They went every week, Phyllis often bringing Meredith and Patrick with her. A young woman who lived near her, Lois Harmon, would often take care of the kids, and lately she had begun writing stories for the paper as well. Between her and Lois, the twins spent a lot of time in the newspaper offices and the Stone Church, which even decades later they would recall with fond feelings. The adults drank cheap cold beer and listened to live music, while the kids ate burgers and played games. For the past several weeks, the staff had been speculating on the likelihood that Onassis, Thomson, and Loeb would prevail. This week, they all agreed, the tide appeared to be turning against the opponents of the refinery.

Jay Smith was perhaps the most vocal on this matter. He was writing a story, "Can the State force an industry on a town?,"[100] and the conclusion was depressing. Of course, both the governor and Onassis continued to reassure the town that neither had any intention of forcing a refinery on Durham. But, Smith said, their actions suggested otherwise. In a recent Boston radio interview, Thomson acknowledged that "Local opposition (to a refinery) in Durham will be a problem." Then he added an ominous qualification: "But not an insuperable one." Was he just predicting the townspeople would ultimately support the refinery, or was he thinking of other stratagems? Everything indicated the latter. Announcements from his office hinted that either recently passed legislation, or newly proposed legislation, could provide the means of overriding local opposition. The governor's own legal counsel, Charles Douglas, had been asked by a reporter, "Do you think the state can take private land against the owner's wishes or the town's wishes for a private use such as an oil refinery?" The counsel's answer was not reassuring. "That's what lawyers are paid for."

Dick Levine agreed that the governor couldn't be trusted. The editor had made just that point in an opinion piece in the last issue, right before Christmas, "Who needs this fight?" The basic question, he said, was "Why would anyone, for any reason, make a concerted effort to place an oil refinery in a community committed to maintaining itself free of heavy industry?" The lines are drawn, he wrote.

> And even as the Governor repeats his assurances that he does not plan to force a refinery on any community—and the land agent of Olympic assures everyone they can have their land back for the asking—still the refinery moves ahead, under full power.
>
> If the opponents of the refinery want to catch up in this confrontation—and they are woefully behind—they had better watch carefully matters of tactics and strategy.

Speaking of strategy, Phyllis said, one of the pro-refinery strategies was to argue that the facility would bring significant tax advantages to the town. But the refinery opponents had been pushing back, arguing that any tax benefits to the town and its citizens of having the refinery would be minimal, because much of the facility would not be taxable under current state tax laws, and that services for the influx of workers and their families would overwhelm the town's resources. SOS had provided *Publick Occurrences* with a 1970 study of the economic implications of a refinery proposed for Tiverton, Rhode Island, a small town on Narragansett Bay that was somewhat larger than Durham, but facing similar environmental concerns. Phyllis had included the whole report in the December 14 issue.[101] The conclusion had been that in the short run, there could be a lowering of tax rates, but "in the longer run the refinery could turn out to be a net tax loss for the community." In addition, there was the possibility of reductions in land values, danger to marine-oriented activities, and environmental degradation. Publication of that study undermined the tax bonanza argument being made by Olympic and the governor.

On the day after Christmas, however, the town's counsel, Attorney Joseph Millimet, delivered to the Board of Selectmen a three-page letter offering his legal opinion on the tax issue, which contradicted the SOS argument.[102] Phyllis was writing the story (as usual, without putting her name to it), quoting Millimet that "the town of Durham would in all likelihood receive very substantial additional property taxes from the location of the refinery there, but the exact amount would have to be determined by an analysis of the nature of the refinery." The attorney admitted that his opinion was preliminary "in the sense that I have made no attempt to make an exhaustive study of the subject." He suggested that "before any final decision is made, it will be necessary to pursue it in considerable depth."

As Phyllis and her group drank their beers, they reflected on the impact of that opinion, however preliminary Millimet said it was. Obviously, it would shake up the anti-refinery activists. They knew that if the townspeople became convinced Durham would get a substantial tax relief from the refinery, many voters could be swayed to support its construction. Already, a pro-refinery movement had begun, initiated by Tommy Thompson, the man who had gathered signatures on some two hundred petitions and presented them to Onassis personally. That was the other front-page story for the current issue, this one written by Jay McManus.

WHY A FARMER WANTS A REFINERY

"Tommy" Thompson, leader of the group known as "Save Our

Refinery," has roots deep in the soil which Aristotle Onassis plans to take on Durham Point.

Generations of Thompsons have coaxed crops from the rocky earth and raised dairy herds since the 1700s. Thompson's own family farmed two hundred acres on Packers Falls Road in Newmarket, until the fire in the spring of 1969. Thompson and his family were awakened one night by the roar of flames which destroyed their house, the barn, and fifty-five head of cattle.

"I wanted to start again," Thompson recalled in an interview. But it was a $100,000 loss. And even if the insurance had covered it all, that $2,400 in taxes made it foolish to rebuild."

For Thompson, now maintenance supervisor for the Oyster River School District, the only way of life he knew had suddenly ended. Thompson, his wife Shirley, and their children, now live closer to town on two acres of land...

It's no secret Thompson wants to sell that two hundred acres on Packers Falls Road. "Probably to some developer," he said with a shrug. "Why not? I'm losing control of it year by year."

Although he can't document it, Thompson is convinced that an oil refinery on Durham Point would drive land value and wages up—and taxes down. Something would be lost, but a lot more would be saved.

When Governor Meldrim Thomson announced the $600 million project, Nancy Sandberg ran up the black flag of Save Our Shores—and "Tommy" Thompson fumed. "The reason I jumped in, well, I got really uptight about SOS trying to speak for the whole town of Durham and steamroller Olympic out of town.

"SOS certainly wasn't speaking for me, or for a lot of other people I knew. I felt it would be a boon for Durham…. The reaction of a lot of seacoast residents I've talked to is: 'Durham's crazy! Why don't they want it?'"

At forty-six, Thompson obviously relishes his new role as spokesman. The issue has split the town down the middle, he said.

"It's friend versus friend. Land values, taxes, and wages are things that directly affect all of us. And I hope the majority feel that way by the time the whole proposal is in."

—Jay P. McManus

Phyllis told the group that while she agreed with Dick's anti-refinery editorial when it was published in the last issue, she still felt sympathy for people like Tommy Thompson. You couldn't blame him, she said, especially since his farm and house burned down. He just wanted to recover, and was hoping the refinery would be the golden goose. But it's not going to happen, Jay McManus said. If the refinery were actually built, Thompson probably wouldn't realize any benefits. His farm on Packers Falls Road was not in

the area where Olympic needed land, nor was it near enough to either downtown Newmarket or Durham for satellite businesses to locate. While he said he expected land values to increase, that was simply wishful thinking. Who would want to buy land and live anywhere near a refinery?

Phyllis drank to that. From her own years of living in New Jersey, what Jay said made sense. Anyway, she told the group, at least there's one business profiting from the proposal. Even if short term. Phil Bernier, who ran a small press in Newmarket, was printing bumper stickers—for both pro- and anti-refinery drivers. *YES for Durham OIL REFINERY*, and *NO REFINERY NO*.

Phyllis had interviewed him. How did he personally come down on the issue? "I'm impartial," he said. A prudent answer indeed.

18

MORE ON THE PETITIONS

On the first Sunday of the New Year, January 6, 1974, the SOS executive board gathered together in Nancy Sandberg's kitchen, at about seven o'clock in the evening, for a continuation of their weekly meetings that had been going on for several weeks, and which they expected would continue indefinitely. A blast of cold air accompanied each of the people who came in the door—Celeste DiMambro, Sharon Meeker, Alex Cochrane, Maryanna Hatch, Jeannette Congdon, Karen Mower, and Roger Wilson. They shed their outer clothes and shuddered in the warmth, laughing and talking about the weather and the Christmas holidays and their hopes for the New Year. It was a good group, Nancy felt, a genuine camaraderie forged by a serious threat to their lives. Cass Curtis, the vice-chair of SOS, would not attend. He told Nancy he could not continue because of other commitments. The logical choice to replace him was Celeste DiMambro, who was actively involved in the Outreach Committee with Sharon Meeker. Celeste was willing, so this evening they would make it official.

The only problem with the group was Roger, who had a lot of energy, but also possessed a stubborn streak that made the meetings difficult. It seemed that no matter what the issue was, it had to be resolved the way he wanted. Even if all the other members of the group had come to a consensus, Roger would cavil each item of the agenda or each decision of the group, often causing their meetings to extend much later into the evening than what everyone else wanted. He just couldn't seem to accept the views of the women if they disagreed with his own. Nor, it seemed, could he accept that a woman was the leader. Nancy had expected he would eventually mellow out. But that did not seem to be happening.

Once they had sat down and exchanged pleasantries about the holidays, the group agreed that Celeste would become the new vice-chair. Sharon reported that they now had more than five thousand signatures, including more than one thousand Durham voters. The petitions they had given to Dudley to deliver to the governor were, of course, only copies of the originals. The committee had agreed to tape all the petitions together, end-to-end. The next day, they would stretch them out all along Main Street to see how far they would go.

The meeting lasted almost to midnight, the group discussing numerous topics—what reports they could expect from the professors working with Karen on the technology committee, the efforts Sharon and Celeste and Maryanna were making to encourage citizens in other seacoast towns to join forces with SOS, Jeanette's research on the current New Hampshire tax laws that would affect an oil refinery, Alex's efforts to raise money for bumper stickers and flyers, and the extent of the pro-refinery movement led by Tommy Thompson. At the end of the meeting, after all had gone home, Nancy was exhausted. Roger's interminable arguments long after a consensus had been reached were making the meetings unbearable. She would talk with him again. At some point, she might have to take more serious action.

• • • •

On Monday, January 7, some forty or fifty men and women assembled in front of the Town & Campus store on Main Street, talking and laughing with great enthusiasm. Using the phone tree they had established weeks earlier, Celeste and Sharon had recruited these volunteers to help stretch the pile of petitions from one end of town to the other. It was cloudy and cold, but above freezing,

DAVID W. MOORE

with just a hint of snow in the air. There was little chance the petitions would be ruined by precipitation.

"Okay," Nancy said. "Let's go." Sharon grabbed the top pages in her gloves and held onto them, while Nancy began walking down Main Street, the papers unfurling from the stack in her arms. Volunteers spaced themselves along the sidewalk to hold the petitions off the ground. She walked past the Red Carpet, past Jenkins Court, down to Young's Restaurant in the middle of town, and continued on down the street past Shane's Mens Store, the Dry Cleaners, the Outback, Wildcat Pizza, the Corner Exchange, and across Madbury Road to the Post Office. She raised her hand to indicate she had come to the end, and all the volunteers down the line raised their hands, until a big cheer erupted from the crowd. Later someone would measure the distance: 288 feet from one end to the other. People snapped photos, and as cars turned from Main Street onto Madbury Road, they went under a section of the petitions held in the air by the volunteers.[103]

• • •

That evening, Celeste DiMambro presented the petitions to the Board of Selectmen at their biweekly meeting:[104] "During the past thirty days, volunteers have circulated a petition declaring: 'We, the undersigned, oppose the construction of the oil refinery, pipeline, and tanker uploading facility proposed by Olympic Refineries, Inc. for the Seacoast area.' More than five thousand townspeople, students, area residents, and people from elsewhere in New Hampshire and New England have signed this petition."

She added that the SOS volunteers contacted 1,517 Durham voters, of which 1,017 signed their names to the petition. "This sixty-six percent response is an indication of the sentiment that exists in Durham against the proposed refinery…We are presenting these petitions to you, the elected leaders of this community, in the hope that they will guide you in your dealings with a proposal that would do untold damage to Durham and the seacoast region of New Hampshire."

One of the selectmen, Larry O'Connell, the only declared opponent of the refinery, said that "Whether one agrees or disagrees with the thrust of the petition—I happen to agree with it—I must congratulate the group [for their hard work]. I have never seen petitions signed by so many people."

Selectman Jim Chamberlin was more cautious, congratulating SOS for their work, noting that "We're here to support ordinances as they exist." Another selectman, Owen Durgin, acting as chair in Alden Winn's absence, echoed his previously stated reluctance to have the Board take a definite stand against the refinery, saying, "Most of us have a very strong interest in the matter of Home Rule. We are extremely concerned that nothing transpires that by a technicality reduces the impact of Home Rule." And, as he had warned before, he said the selectmen had to be "extremely careful" not to take any action that "would provide an excuse for action by the state."

Celeste came away from the meeting reaffirmed in her conviction that the Board of Selectmen would not be of much help in fighting the refinery. Without SOS, the town would be doomed.

19

THE ECONOMIC BONANZA MYTH

The following Sunday, January 13, at the weekly meeting of SOS, Karen Mower had some good news. One of the volunteer members of her technology committee, Sam Reid, an economics professor in the Whittemore School of Business and Economics (WSBE) at the University of New Hampshire, had just completed a report on the refinery, which he had submitted to the Board of Selectmen the previous Friday. In it, he took aim at the town counsel, Attorney Joe Millimet, for the legal opinion he had delivered to the Board of Selectmen. Reid was brutal!

Karen had a copy of the report, which she said *Publick Occurrences* would publish in the next issue.[105] In his report, Reid tore into the attorney's three-page opinion: "While the distinguished special counsel termed his report 'preliminary,' it should also be considered superficial, inaccurate, and misleading." He went on to debunk the notion that either the town or the state would reap much tax benefit from the refinery. Much of what constituted a modern refinery, he argued, would be tax-exempt under current New Hampshire law.

"If we consider that a petroleum refinery complex consists of a technical machine, most of which is not currently taxable under New Hampshire statutes; numerous storage tanks, which the State

Tax Commissioner says are not taxable to the local community; substantial water and air pollution systems which are tax-free (including the real estate on which they are located) for a period of 25 years; there is not much left to be taxed at the local level except part of the real estate, the office building, some pipes of negligible value, the cafeteria, and a few other buildings."

In his cover letter to the selectmen, Reid noted, "It is clear that my opinion is quite different from that give [sic] you by the distinguished special counsel, Mr. Joseph Millimet of Manchester. The special counsel is quoted as saying 'the prospect of paying 90 percent of the town's taxes will be hard to ignore.' My examination of existing statutes and the nature of a refinery indicate that Durham may receive about twenty-nine percent in increased property evaluation. When increased costs of providing town services are considered it would appear to be sheer 'folly' to locate a refinery complex in the town under existing state statutes."

Nancy wanted to know, what did the selectmen think of the report? Mostly they take a wait and see attitude, Karen told the group. Except for Jim Chamberlin, a crusty old fogey if ever there was one.[106] "Who is this guy anyway?" he said about Reid. "I'm going to wait for Millimet. I'm sick and tired of all these would-be professionals telling us what we ought to do. I've got a good deal of faith in Joe Millimet. He's one of the most outstanding lawyers in the state on matters like this. If I had to choose whose opinion to take, it would be Millimet's."

Karen noted the report presented evidence that the anticipated tax windfall at the state level was also a "myth."[107] In fact, "the State tax outlook from a proposed refinery is even bleaker than the dismal local situation." The problem was the state's business profits tax, which would apply only to the refinery part of the oil process, and thus would exclude the area where the oil companies take most of their profits—at the crude oil and transportation end of the business. The refinery by itself, he wrote, would provide little additional profit to be taxed. And, despite what some lawmakers were proposing, the state would not be allowed to tax Olympic

Refineries on a per-barrel basis, because federal law prohibits states from imposing import taxes.

That was really big news, they all agreed. For weeks the *Union Leader* and Governor Thomson had been flacking the promise of immense tax savings for the town and the state. This report showed that the promise was a lie. They needed to get the Reid report distributed as widely as possible, as soon as possible. Many Durham citizens were still operating under the illusion that a refinery would bring substantial tax relief, and they needed to know that if anything, taxes were more likely to go up than down.

On a different matter, Sharon said she had contacted people in several seacoast towns, including Rye, where oil that had been piped from supertankers would be redirected north to Durham. While most were sympathetic to Durham's plight, they did not want to join SOS. Instead, they decided to form their own local organizations. She had talked with Peter Horne of Rye, who was opposed to the refinery and the proposed pipeline, but who recognized that the residents of his town were divided. Many wanted what they hoped would be substantial financial benefits from the operation, while others were afraid of the environmental impact. They wouldn't necessarily trust Durham residents when it came to doing what was good for Rye. The local group, which called themselves the Concerned Citizens of Rye, would hold a meeting the following week, when Olympic representatives would present the case for the refinery. Sharon had given Peter some names of anti-refinery experts provided by Karen and her technology group. Sharon said she would definitely attend.

The discussion became more animated when it turned to the actions of the selectmen, who had been invited by Olympic to visit the Golden Eagle Refinery in Canada so they could see what an operating refinery would look like. And Olympic would be paying for it. They all agreed it would be so unprofessional, a real conflict of interest, for the selectmen to accept the invitation. If they felt it was necessary to visit a refinery, the town should pay for it.

Nancy said she had spoken with Larry O'Connell, the only

selectman who had directly refused the offer and the only one who had come out against the refinery. He said he didn't think it would be useful for the selectmen to examine an operation that produces 250,000 barrels of oil a day, when the Olympic refinery would be producing 400,000 barrels a day. "If I were going to buy a Mack truck," he said, "I would not go out and look at a Chevy Vega."[108]

20

RYE SURPRISE

On Wednesday evening, January 23, Sharon Meeker headed down Route 1 to Rye. At the town's junior high school gymnasium, the Onassis men would be making yet another presentation about their proposed oil refinery. More specifically for Rye, they would focus on the underwater pipelines that would come in from Lunging Island, part of the Isles of Shoals nine miles off the coast, and the overland pipelines that would take the oil from Rye to Durham.[109]

Olympic's consultants included the usual suspects, Robert Greene and Peter Booras, along with Eugene Harlow, the engineer from F.R. Harris charged with designing a deep-water oil terminal for Olympic. Sharon had worked with Peter Horne, who would moderate the meeting, to come up with the anti-refinery experts: Frederick G. Hochgraf, a metallurgist in the UNH engineering department; John Kingsbury, director of the Cornell Shoals Marine Laboratory on Appledore Island, another of the Isles of Shoals; and Richard R. Kepplar, a petroleum management specialist for the Environmental Protection Agency.

What Sharon did not know was that the presentation would astonish the crowd, immediately creating opinions that would become as solid as the state's granite bedrock. A resident of Rye, Kit Baker was a commercial pilot who frequently flew into New York City. With all of the controversy over the exact nature of Olympic Refineries—whether it was in fact a legitimate company with any refinery experience, or maybe just a fig leaf for Onassis to find some way to pump up his oil transport business—Baker decided he could visit the company at its New York City address during a layover. Maybe he could find out something that would be of benefit to the town. He broached the notion to Horne, who thought it a great idea.

When Baker arrived at the midtown Manhattan offices of Olympic Refineries, he explained who he was to the receptionist, and said that he wanted to talk with someone about the proposed oil refinery in New Hampshire. Eventually, he met with one of the executives, who told him that everyone was too busy to spend any time with him, but they did have a film that explained how their pipelines were built and laid in the Middle East. That sounded fine to Baker. It was a short film, and at the end of the viewing, he could hardly believe what he had just seen. Before leaving, he expressed enthusiasm for the documentary, and strongly recommended that when the Olympic representatives came to Rye, they should be sure to show it. If anything would persuade the citizens of Rye about the import of the proposed pipeline, that film would do it. He decided not to tell Peter. It would be a surprise.

Sharon arrived at the gym a few minutes before the start time of 7:30 p.m. to find it packed with some eight hundred or so residents. The press and TV cameras were there, along with representatives from Rye and surrounding towns. A blank screen was set in the middle of the temporary stage, a podium in the center, and three chairs on either side. She recognized the three anti-refinery experts talking to each other, while only Peter Booras was there for Olympic. Then she remembered that from 7:00–7:30, Greene and Harlow were scheduled to debate a couple of environmentalists on the PBS station WENH—Channel 11, its studio in Durham. What a strategic blunder for Olympic, she thought. The two consultants wouldn't get down to Rye until almost 8:30, by which time Kingsbury, Hochgraf, and Kepplar would have had plenty of opportunity to convince the audience that a refinery would be a disaster. Olympic was even more incompetent than her husband, Dave, had surmised. Yes, they were a bunch of boobs.

The first hour went pretty much as Sharon expected. She had

heard all of the arguments against the refinery from these guys before, but once again found the presentations terrifying. First on the agenda was Hochgraf, who informed the audience about the frequency of oil spills, based on extensive research of operations around the world.[110]

"When I completed my initial study," the engineer said, "I was appalled by the numbers, so appalled I just sat on the figures for a week until I could find confirmation from another study calculated by an entirely different method. They both came up with the same results from totally different approaches." His statistics showed that if the supertankers pumped 250,000 barrels of oil a day, far below the 400,000 planned, 3,660 barrels a year would be spilled in the waters off the coast. Piping just 200,000 barrels of refined oil back to the supertankers would cause another 3,980 barrels to be spilled, for a yearly total of 7,640 barrels.

Then John Kingsbury, the marine biologist, gave the coup de grace: only one part per million of oil in seawater would kill lobster larvae.

The presentations continued until the end of the hour, at which time Peter called for a ten-minute break. Greene and Harlow had arrived, and now took the stage. Sharon thought they looked stressed and haggard, perhaps suffering from the strain of the debate they had just come from, or the constant negative reactions from citizens and local leaders. They clearly did not exhibit the enthusiasm she had seen them exhibit in other venues. Perhaps this was a good sign.

When the meeting resumed, it was Booras who took the lead.

"We are here to explain the benefits of the refinery to you as fishermen," he said. "The people coming here eat fish like anyone else—and I expect they will want to enjoy your products."

"If there are any around," boomed a voice from the back of the room.

"There will be plenty around, I assure you," Booras said unfazed. He was more than used to public skepticism. "As a responsible applicant, Olympic intends to take steps to see that there are no ill effects to the environment." Met with another skeptical reaction from the audience, Booras replied, "I live in Hampton [a neighboring town] myself a part of the year, and I certainly wouldn't want to see this area destroyed. But we shouldn't allow our fears to dominate decision before all the facts are in."

"When will the facts be in?" an audience member asked.

"In the coming weeks," he said.

What about Olympic bonding to compensate fishermen for spills?

"I really can't answer that," he said. "It's in the hands of legal people."

Another audience member asked Harlow how the need for unloading equipment would affect the coastline. "I can't forecast what the successful bidding contractor will do," he said, "but I can imagine there will be no great beachfront work in Rye."

What about the promise of jobs? Are there any contractors in southeastern New Hampshire qualified to build an oil refinery?

"I can't say because I don't know," said Booras. "Olympic wouldn't consider laying pipe with inexperienced men. But I am sure, with a shipyard in the area, there are many good welders and pipefitters."

Peter Tucker, an engineer and chairman of the Rye zoning board of adjustment, was frustrated with the vague answers. "When are you gonna answer our questions? You've been sayin' for two months now that your plans aren't ready. Well, people have been complainin' to me that there's a lot of questions but no answers!" The audience erupted with applause. He proceeded to grill Harlow about the extent of construction on the beaches, how long it would take to finish laying the pipe, if the town would have any control over the use of its beaches by the construction crews, if it would be necessary to prefabricate structures on the beaches, and what impact the construction would have on the coastline. Obviously irritated by the insistent questioning, Harlow said that expecting him to have specific answers before the completion of his feasibility studies was like "asking a man in the middle of a race if he was going to win."

Douglas Gray, chairman of the Rye Board of Selectmen, said, "Why aren't these studies done now?"

"We're only human," Harlow said. "We're working as fast as we can."

Someone yelled out, "What's the possibility of oil spills?"

Harlow hadn't been there when Hochgraf had presented the results of his studies showing the likelihood of thousands of barrels of oil being spilled into the fishing waters each year. "There are no studies on that, no figures available to us," he responded.

Later, one reporter described what happened next: "Hochgraf, still seated onstage, slowly rose, clutching his thick notebook full of figures he had been reading from. His face struggled against a lupine, maniacal grin. Slowly, for full effect, he swung his arm down in an underhand loop and lobbed the notebook to the floor at Harlow's feet."[111]

The audience went wild.

It was time for the twenty-minute film that Booras had brought with him from the Olympic Refineries headquarter in New York City. It was a documentary about the installation of the deep-water unloading port at Mina al Ahmadi, Kuwait. This was something new for Sharon, who thought she had heard all of the arguments that Olympic had to make about the benefits of a refinery.

The film opened in dramatic fashion, touting the technological marvel that was being constructed. The narrator was English, his upper class accent adding a serious quality to the undertaking. A few minutes into the documentary, the narrator said, "Occasionally, we run into stubborn rock." And then, BOOM! A huge explosion, rock and sand and water spewing into the air. Finally, when the debris had settled, scenes of humongous pipes

being dragged across the beach by large construction vehicles appeared on the screen. After a moment of silent shock, the audience broke into noisy incredulity.

Sharon was stunned. Did Booras really know beforehand what impact the film would have? On lobstermen? On a town that depended on its beaches for tourism, not to mention for personal enjoyment? How could anyone who knew anything about Rye have thought this would be a good demonstration of pipe-laying to show the town's citizens—blowing up the beaches and the fishing waters on which so many people depended for their livelihood? SOS itself couldn't have come up with a more dramatic argument against the refinery and the pipeline. She wondered what genius had recommended that Olympic show that film.

21

SAVING THE DREAM

Phyllis wasn't so sure this tack of hers would actually work out. Ever since she took over as publisher and realized the paper was losing money each week, she knew she had to get some financial help, and that the business school at UNH would be the best place to get it. But so far, she had been getting palmed off from one guy to the next, and she wasn't sure there was anyone there who actually knew anything about small businesses. First, she had gone to see the Dean, Jan Clee, to whom she explained her problems and said that she wanted to talk with someone who could give her advice. Of course, she would pay for any consulting work, she just needed some help quickly. Dean Clee was patient and understanding, but said that the kind of problems she had weren't his specialty, and that she should see the associate dean, who could help her. She thanked him, they chit-chatted some more, and he asked if she would like to have dinner with him. Taken aback, she just sat there, not knowing what to say. Did he expect her to say yes because he was helping her, when in fact all he was doing was sending her off to someone else? Besides, when in god's name would she have time anyway? Thanks, she said, but no, she wasn't into dating. No problem, he said, and indeed, he didn't seem to care one whit. It's like he was just out there fishing, casting his line to see what might bite, but ready to cast somewhere else if there was no nibble. Well, *that* didn't make her feel very special.

She met with the associate dean, also a nice man, and mercifully not on the make. She was grateful for that. But he, too, said he was not a good person to advise her. His field of teaching and research were related to macroeconomics. The big picture. Small businesses were not included in that field. The person who would definitely be of help would be the Chair of the Marketing Division, the most logical choice for her kind of problems. That sounded good to Phyllis, yes, marketing was certainly what she needed to increase circulation and increase her revenue, and she wondered how such a logical idea had somehow escaped consideration by the dean.

The Marketing Director was friendly, enthusiastic even, telling her that he thought *Publick Occurrences* was a wonderful paper, and that he was glad she had come to his department. He knew just the person she should see—Ray Belles, a businessman who was spending a year at the university and who would be able to answer all of her questions.

As she climbed the stairs to the third floor of McConnell Hall to meet with this Ray Belles, students passing her on the way down, she couldn't help reflecting on her own days at Douglas College. God, that was years ago—the excitement she felt at learning about...everything. She had majored in history and political science, and upon graduation got an internship in the United Nations, and after that at the Voice of America, where she broadcast programs in Spanish. She got a full time job at the Baltimore Sun, where she met Steve, but the paper frowned on fraternization among employees, so she had to find another job (in such situations, it was always the woman who had to leave) and was able to get on the staff of Jim Wright, Speaker of the House. What an incredible time that was, his old Texas buddies—Ronnie Dugger, Willie Morris, Larry King—congregating in his office, always with wild stories to tell, King referring to his wife as the Jolly Green Giant. Each time King was introduced to someone new and they talked about their college days, he would mention a different school, one time Harvard, the next time Princeton, then Stanford, until finally Phyllis said to him, "Larry, if you don't want to say where you went to college, why don't you just say so? You know, people are going to realize you're just lying." But that didn't bother Larry—he would just laugh and name another school. Years later, he got a Niemen Fellowship at Harvard, and subsequently wrote an article about it, "Blowing my mind at Harvard,"[112] for his buddy, Willie Morris, Editor-in-Chief at *Harper's Magazine*. Phyllis remembers Larry sending her a Xeroxed copy of the article, which mentions in the very first paragraph that Larry's college experience consisted of one semester at West Texas Tech. Pinned to the article was a cover note that read, "Are you SATISFIED, Phyllis?!"

She found Ray Belles's office, and with a bit of trepidation, and half-expecting that he would have yet another person to whom she would be referred, knocked on his door. He welcomed her and, she was pleased to note, did not suggest his specialty was in some other area of business or economics. After explaining a bit about her debt-ridden newspaper operation, she asked how he might be able to help her. First, he said, he would need to see her business plan. You're looking at her, she said. That brought a smile to his face (a pained one, she thought), but he didn't berate her and suddenly treat her as though she were a nincompoop. He was easygoing and professional, asking her some basic questions about costs. She described how the paper operated, her overall expenses for salaries, and printing, and distribution, and rent, and of course office supplies and upkeep on office equipment. After some discussion, he noted that at a subscription price of five dollars per year, and a single copy price of fifteen cents, given the circulation of about five thousand copies a week, half of which were annual subscriptions, the revenue simply didn't cover the expenses. Why, he wanted to know, did they set the annual subscription price so low?

To encourage as many people to read it as possible, she said.

And why did they publish it on Friday, instead of a day or two earlier, when they could get grocery store ads?

That was a good question, and she was candid—that Steve didn't want it published earlier, and that he really didn't want any ads, though of course he acquiesced when she actually brought ads to the paper.

Had they sought funding from other sources, foundations and the like?

Steve was opposed to anyone else having a stake in their operation. It was theirs, and they would do it by themselves.

What impressed Phyllis most about Ray was that he did not judge her, or the decisions Steve had made, harshly. He listened and thought about the answers and in the end suggested she should now think about other funding sources. He would help her with that, as well as with devising some new marketing plans to expand readership. The one thing she could do now would be to increase the annual subscription price. They discussed how much, and finally settled on a thirty percent increase, from $5.00 to $6.50 yearly. She would leave the single copy price at 15¢. The annual rate was still a savings of about fifteen percent over a single copy price.

When she left the office, she found herself feeling rejuvenated and more hopeful than she had been. It was a useful meeting that gave her some ideas she could implement for the paper, and Ray was an unusually sensitive and attentive listener. She knew, of course, that nothing more than a formal consulting relationship would ever come of their interactions. Ray was a businessman, for god's sake, no doubt a conservative Republican opposed to government programs, and she was so far from that, a liberal Democrat who strongly supported Johnson's war on poverty, the civil rights act, and voting rights act. She had even participated in the March on Washington with Martin Luther King, Jr., in 1963, as well as the Selma to Montgomery marches in 1965. She couldn't imagine Ray doing something like that. Still, she looked forward to seeing him again, and to hearing what professional advice he could give her about saving *Publick Occurrences*. Maybe they'd have a glass of wine while they discussed it.

• • •

When Phyllis got back to the office, her mind was filled with a million thoughts. It was Wednesday already, and there were lots of stories that needed to be edited, as well as decisions that needed to be made about the operation of the paper itself. She would have to alert readers about the price increase, of course, which she and Ray had agreed would start with the February 15 issue, two weeks away. They'd alert them again the following week, offering readers a last chance to buy a subscription at the current rate before implementing the change the week after that.

There was another, more painful decision Phyllis had to make about whom to list on the masthead. On page four of every issue, in the lower left hand corner, was a box that listed all the major contributors to the paper—the publisher, editor, advertising manager, account representative, the reporters, the general manager, and the artist, Bob Nilson. This week, though, she was going to add to that list the name of Bill Graham, under "Design," for his continued work in helping to place the stories for maximum visual effect. When she and Dick agreed to that change, Dick had once again pressured her to add her own name as publisher. But she said absolutely not. She didn't want her personal life revealed to the public, which of course it would be if people saw a change in publishers. It was the next name that tore at her very being, her id screaming "No!" at the idea of adding Shaunna to the list, her superego demanding that she do it anyway, because it was the right thing to do. Despite concerted efforts, Dick had not been able to find someone else who could run the compugraphic machine. Shaunna did a good job—an excellent job, actually—and she was bright and eager to do even more to help the paper. Phyllis would not sacrifice the paper because of her own personal problems, so they kept Shaunna. In fact, this week she was also the author of a page two story about regional planning, and it was good. Dick had most of the interaction with Shaunna, but Phyllis could be professional about it, compartmentalizing her personal feelings and her professional duties, and would talk to the young woman when necessary. It was only right that she be listed as part of the masthead. Still, Phyllis could not escape the almost unbearable irony of it all, Steve working at a weekly paper in North Conway, actually earning money, as was Shaunna, and here she was, Phyllis Bennett, with Steve's surname, and with Steve listed as publisher, helping him survive by employing his soon-to-be wife, even as she was actually losing money. Life is certainly one strange beast.

When she ignored her personal problems, life was actually great. The vision she had for the paper—to serve the local communities with information they needed and did not get from any other source—was being played out in spades. This week they had three blockbuster stories—the gas shortage causing long lines of motorists and hurting the local gas stations; the evidence that the governor was reneging on his pledge to honor Home Rule, which wasn't exactly a surprise, but nevertheless confirmed the worst fears of the anti-refinery activists; and the successful effort by Olympic to pressure a family to sell Lunging Island, where the supertankers would off-load oil.

Not as crucial as these stories, but also important, was the issue about the role of the Board of Selectmen in the refinery controversy. Dick was preparing an editorial critical of the members who were not showing strict impartiality, but favoring Olympic. Apart from that, the governor had complicated the matter by giving one of the selectmen a plum appointment in what everyone, except the selectman himself, could see as an attempted bribe. Thomson had unseated the chairman of the State Board of Registration for Professional Engineers, and appointed Durham Selectman Malcolm Chase in his place, despite the recommendation from the state's Society of Professional Engineers for two other candidates. When asked if he thought political considerations had influenced the governor's action, Chase said, "I don't think the governor would stoop that low."

She wondered how difficult it was for him to keep a straight face while saying that.

There were other stories—the warrant articles to be voted on at the March town meeting in Newmarket, and separately in Durham; the fight between the university and the governor/*Union Leader* over the attempts of gay students to have an organization on campus; waste recycling programs being introduced in four local towns; the problems of funding regional planning; professional profiles of the men who constituted the Olympic "team"; a possible plan to revive the B&M Railroad to run through Durham. Not to mention the local calendar: *Mary Poppins* at the Franklin Movie Theater in Durham on Friday and Saturday, *Mash* on Monday and Tuesday. What would Durham and the surrounding towns do without the paper?

An idea came to her. Perhaps she should point out to the readers of *Publick Occurrences* just how fortunate they were to be getting local news. Maybe with tongue in cheek.

BLOWING OUR OWN HORN

We have been getting many encouraging letters and comments on our coverage and some topical issues. They have been very welcome and helpful.

However, we have performed several significant journalistic services which have captured little attention and elicited no acknowledgements whatsoever.

Perhaps you overlooked these things and, if you save your back issues of our paper, you may want to look these things up.

1. We never mentioned—even once—the international military alert called by President Nixon for some reason or other.

2. We used not one paragraph of valuable space—and not one moment of our readers' valuable time—on the White House program known as Operation Candor. Readers of newspapers and magazines elsewhere found themselves immersed in the problem of figuring out what Operation Candor was, then if it were operative, then if were still operative, then finally if it were ever operative. Our readers, happily, avoided the entire process.

3. Finally, a reader of *Publick Occurrences* never had to read or worry about Kahoutek. No features, no editorials, although we did, reluctantly, print some meeting notices announcing public talks by short-sighted speakers on the subject.

We figured Kahoutek had about it something of the fraud from its very beginning. Beware of ballyhoo is a rule you can follow whether you are looking up at the skies or down at Washington.

Anyway, with a year as bad as this one, and all its leftovers spilling into the present one, we figured that a major comet would be a wasteful omen.

Therefore, if you want to know what happened to the international alert, to Operation Candor, and to Kahoutek, you will have to read elsewhere, where the subjects were brought up in the first place.

As far as *Publick Occurrences* is concerned, they never were. Now that represents three good reasons in support of the price of a subscription.

22

THE OTHER GREEK

On Friday, February 1, Chris Spirou called Dudley and told her he wanted to come to Durham the next day to talk with her about an urgent matter.[113] He wouldn't say anything to her about the subject, wouldn't even give her a hint. She would find out everything when he got to her house. It was a strange thing for Chris to do. Dudley had been working closely with him for the past several weeks, as he was preparing for the special vote of the House in early March. He

was lining up speakers to oppose House Bill 34 and to support her own bills calling for Home Rule, while she was coordinating with the GOP leadership for the hearings on her bill, which would occur a few days before the full House vote. She couldn't imagine why he would be playing coy with her now. But Chris was a unique personality, an amazing man in many ways, especially his ability in one-on-one meetings to persuade people of his positions. It wasn't just his non-stop talking that, by itself, probably convinced some people to go along rather than have to undergo yet another intense interaction with the impassioned Greek from Manchester. It was also his detailed knowledge of New Hampshire history and the legislative process that made his encounters so successful. She would go along with his game, whatever it was.

It was snowing on Saturday morning when he completed the drive from Manchester to Durham. That he would venture out in the snow, and on a Saturday morning no less, rather than wait until the next day, or even a few days later, was itself testimony to how important he must have thought the meeting would be. A friend of Dudley's, Jane Kaufman, a member of SOS and a talented pottery artist, had arrived earlier, the two of them enjoying coffee as they waited for Chris. After an introduction and some polite chatter, Dudley asked what was so important that he wanted to discuss.

The day before, Chris said, he had been interviewed in the morning on the PBS station in Durham—yes, WENH, Channel 11—about the prison reform bill they had passed. "You remember that?" he said. She did. "You remember how that came about?" Not really. It all started, Chris recounted, after he was elected rep from Manchester. Before he was even sworn in, he got a call from the Speaker of the House, Marshall Cobleigh, who wanted to see him right away. He was in Governor Peterson's office, along with the state's Attorney General Warren Rudman. When Spirou arrived, Rudman told him that the prisoners at the state prison had rioted and taken fifteen hostages because they were upset about the conditions in the prison. The riot leaders, who had been residents of the district in Manchester now represented by Spirou, said they would not negotiate with anyone in government but him. They only trusted Chris Spirou to convey their views honestly and to tell them the truth about what the government would do. Spirou agreed to meet with them, though Rudman warned him that the men were murderers. After meeting with the prisoners, and going back and forth between them and the attorney general's office, he obtained an agreement. The rioters released the hostages.

The next year, Meldrim Thomson was governor, and Spirou was head of a committee to look into prison reform, as he had promised the prisoners. He intended to hold hearings in the prison itself, but Thomson didn't like the idea. There would be no hearings in the state prison, he said. Spirou told the governor that perhaps Thomson didn't understand the state constitution—the Legislative Branch of government was separate from the Executive Branch, and as a legislator, Spirou could hold hearings wherever he wanted. And he definitely intended to hold hearings in the state prison. "What are you going to do, Governor? Send the state police to arrest us?" Thomson said, okay, Spirou could hold hearings in the state prison, as though he—the governor—were granting permission rather than recognizing the legislator's constitutional right. After the hearings, the legislature eventually passed a prison reform bill, signed by the governor, and that's why Spirou had been interviewed on public television—to explain the background of the problem and the substance of the bill.

"But that isn't why you're here," Dudley said.

No, Chris acknowledged. Being filmed on TV was not what he wanted to talk about. That was simply why he happened to miss talking with William Loeb the previous morning, who had desperately wanted to see him.

Now Dudley's antenna was on full alert. "Why in the world would Loeb want to see you?" she asked.

"That was the very question that I asked myself," Chris said. After he drove back from the TV filming Friday morning, he went to the Merrimack Restaurant, and was eating lunch when one of the waiters came over to him and said, "Hey, Chris. You got a phone call." "Naturally, I was surprised," Chris said. He hadn't told anyone where he was going. So, how would anyone know he was there?

He went to the restaurant office to find out who was calling him. "Hi, Chris, this is Paul Tracy from the *Union Leader*."

Chris said nothing for a few seconds, not believing that anyone from the *Union Leader*, much less the managing editor, would want to talk with him. The editorial writer, Jim Finnegan, had been after him with scathing criticisms almost from the second he had declared his candidacy for the House, so what could possibly prompt an interest from them now? "How do I know you're really Paul Tracy?" Spirou asked.

The man said, "I can assure you I know who I am."

Chris said, "Give me your phone number." Tracy did. It looked like the *Union Leader* number Chris knew well, but he was skeptical that the man was really calling from there. "I'll call you back," Chris said. And when he called the paper's number, Paul Tracy answered. OK, thought Chris, so this probably was the managing editor of the newspaper that always treated him like shit. What did Tracy want?

"The boss has been looking for you," Tracy said, the boss obviously being William Loeb. "He wants to talk with you. He was here this morning trying to get in touch, but couldn't find you. So, I finally tried you at your favorite restaurant." Merrimack was a Greek restaurant, so it was a reasonable guess. "Can you come over?"

When he got to the offices of the *Union Leader*, Tracy was there, as was Jim Finnegan and another executive of the paper, Bob Anderson. Loeb was not there. Spirou couldn't help but wonder what the heck was going on that he warranted such a high-powered triumvirate. Tracy said, "The boss was here this morning with Aristotle Onassis, but they had to leave. They want you to head up the refinery." Spirou was speechless. It was such an unexpected response that he was having difficulty believing it was real. "You could make up to $1 million," Tracy said. There were a lot of questions that came to Spirou later, such as the details of how he would be paid, whether it was $1 million a year salary or a one-time payoff, or what? "You'd have to resign from the legislature, of course, and become full-time head of Olympic Refineries."

Spirou said, "Can I have until Monday to think about it?" Of course, Tracy said. Then all three told him what a great job he would do, and what an honor it was to be considered for such an important job by one of the most successful and powerful businessmen in the world. Despite his astonishment at the offer, he was not duped into thinking that it was his superior management skills, or extensive knowledge of the oil industry (of which he knew almost nothing), that led to this meeting. "It was not Onassis," he told Dudley. "It was Loeb. He is the one in charge."

Spirou left the *Union Leader* building in a daze, even walking down the street in the wrong direction. But he knew he had to tell Dudley. She had a right to know.

"What are you going to do?" she said.

"I'm giving it serious consideration," he said. "If they meet my demands. I want a yacht, so I can sail up and down the shore with my Greek sailor's cap and my blue blazer."

"Oh, god, no!" Dudley said. "Chris, you can't be serious."

"Why not?" he said. "You've got all these people on Durham Point, selling off the land where their parents and grandparents died, just to get some money. Why shouldn't I take advantage of the situation? It's not my family buried here."

"But they were lied to," she said. "They didn't know it was going to be a refinery."

"If not a refinery, then a development. Something. The fact is, they wanted the money. They were willing to sell. My finances could use the money, too."

He waited defiantly for a few minutes, then said, "Stop crying! Do you really think I would do that? If I was from Sudan, or someplace like that, I wouldn't care. But I'm from New Hampshire. I have roots here. My mother was born in Manchester, her parents came here in 1910. She went back to Greece for a while, but I came here with her when I was thirteen. And I know the refinery would be the worst disaster ever, not just to the seacoast, but to New Hampshire. My state."

"So what are you going to tell Tracy?" Dudley said, who in fact was not crying, though the incredulity registered on her face may have given Chris that impression.

"I'm going to tell him that even though my economic demands tell me I should do it, my constituents of the state that elected me won't let me do it."

Later, after he had gone, Dudley wondered what had

prompted Chris to come all the way over to Durham just to tease her with the possibility that he might go to work for Onassis. Yes, he was a tease, always in a kind way, but the more she reflected on this performance, the more she realized it was not just to pull her chain, but to have her recognize what a sacrifice he was making in opposing the refinery. A million dollars was a lot of money, far beyond what anyone in his position (or her position, for that matter) could imagine. The offer would have tempted anyone, and perhaps especially Chris, at age thirty, who had no visible means of support. If he was living off his family, the money would have been a godsend. How could he refuse? Yet, she knew he would. It wasn't his roots in New Hampshire that gave her such confidence, nor his deference to the constituents who elected him, as he claimed. It was rather his character. Who he was. Buying off Chris Spirou would never happen.

23

SOS PANIC TIME

With only a month until the annual town meeting, Nancy was overwhelmed. She had felt anxious about the first public meeting of SOS in early December, realizing the importance of the role that SOS, and she as head of the group, had in informing the public about the problems of an oil refinery. Until then, she had blithely accepted the chairmanship, just assuming everything would work out. But suddenly she realized how crucial her role was. She spent hours going over the format for the meeting, checked again and again with Robin Mower about the speakers, and made sure Sharon Meeker was getting the word out to the town. For the first time, she genuinely felt the burden of being the leader, and feared how awful the consequences would be if somehow she failed. She was so much in the public eye that if she made some serious mistake, it would reflect badly not just on her, but on the whole SOS effort. That's why she had gone to the Onassis reception in Bedford after getting an insultingly late invitation, even though she was convinced the whole thing was a farce.

The feeling she had now was different—she wasn't nervous about what to do, nor was she anxious that she wasn't capable of leading SOS. She felt comfortable in her role, and she was gratified by the wonderful support she was getting from so many people. She realized that delegating responsibility to the board members, and the volunteers working with them, was exactly the right approach. They were all responding in more positive ways than she ever could have imagined. What she worried about now was the confluence of events that seemed to be working against their efforts. After the Onassis visit, which she thought on balance had helped the anti-refinery effort, she was convinced the town would strongly reject the refinery. And Dudley insisted that the town really needed a powerful message of rejection in order to convince the legislature not to override Home Rule. A close vote, even if a majority against the refinery, could allow the legislature to weasel its way out of supporting Home Rule. But now, with so many bad things happening, Nancy was having doubts about how strong the vote might actually be. There was so much that needed to be done in such a short while.

If she had to list the myriad of worries that were running through her mind, at the very top would be the severe shortage of gasoline. The "Oregon plan" of allocating gas in accordance with the numbers and letters on a license plate was not placating a lot of motorists. She had heard numerous stories of irate drivers in Durham trying to get gas and getting angry at the gas station owners who themselves were being hurt by the shortage. Some owners limited gas to two dollars per purchase; others would sell all the gas customers wanted, and when the allocation ran out, would close for the day. When drivers complained, invariably the owners said *support the refinery*. It was maddening. The information was out there: Durham would *not* benefit from having an oil refinery, because gas is allocated on a federal level. There were long lines of cars trying to get gas even in New Jersey! But the myth remained. Get an oil refinery, and the gas shortage will disappear. Nancy worried that the myth would influence many town voters.

Also high on her worry list, though it was another problem she couldn't influence, was Olympic's success in getting Lunging Island. She had read the news in *Publick Occurrences*,[114] and it troubled her because the tactics that were used showed how absolutely determined Olympic was to get its way, regardless of what the citizens might prefer.

One of the Isles of Shoals, Lunging was to be used by Olympic for supertankers to off-load crude oil and upload refined oil. The island itself was only about two and a half acres. It had no running water or electricity, but it had been in the Randall family for close to half a century, family members coming there every year during the summer months. One of their sons, Richard, a Vietnam veteran, was buried there. Another son, Ray, continued to join them every summer. They had a home on the island called "Honeymoon Cottage," named when the famed nineteenth century writer and artist, Celia Thaxter, had spent her honeymoon there. When the Randalls had first been approached about selling the island, Peter Booras—that lying businessman from Keene—told them it was for a resort development. They told him they were not interested in selling for any reason, or at any price. They were visited again, this time by George Stamatelos, who said he was representing Booras. By then, the Randalls had heard about the sales on Durham Point, but Stamatelos denied that his interest in purchasing Lunging Island was related to an oil refinery. He claimed he didn't know why Booras wanted the property. Eventually, Stamatelos admitted the obvious. And later it came out that the man and his son-in-law had been working "undercover" for Onassis for months, purchasing options in the Portsmouth area.

Despite definite refusals, Stamatelos returned again, and again, each time with a slightly different offer, but with a basic purchase price of half a million dollars. The island was evaluated by the Town of Rye as worth $65,000. On Stamatelos's fifth and last visit, Robert Randall was prepared. He had been advised by his attorney that Olympic could probably get the island by eminent domain, and in that case, the price would be fair market value—not anywhere close to what Olympic was offering. Randall had his own list of demands in addition to the purchase price, including a requirement that Olympic pay for transporting Honeymoon Cottage off the island to another location. Stamatelos balked, Randall got angry and said he wouldn't sell under any circumstances, and Stamatelos came back with a hard-nosed threat. This was his last visit. Either they agreed to a contract that evening, or they would meet in court. Olympic *would* get the island. And Randall would not get half a million dollars for it. Not even half that amount. Stamatelos then informed them that Olympic was actually after all of the Isles of Shoals, and that he already had options on two of them, while a third was "listening." That convinced the Randalls. They had to sell. If the other island owners were caving, what chance would they have? So, they signed.

A few days later, they learned that Star Island Corporation, owner of most of the other islands, had adamantly refused to sell anything to Olympic and was actively engaged in opposing the oil refinery with all of the resources at its disposal. But the deed was signed. "It's like a death in the family," Prudence Randall said. "You have to face it, but still you can't accept it…I just can't conceive of not having it to go back to." When she said that to Stamatelos after signing the contract, he said, "Cheer up—maybe it won't go through."

This tactic of the Olympic men—to play nice until they don't get their way, and then turn hardball—was exactly what Sharon had predicted to Nancy all along. Not that Nancy needed much convincing. She had become much more skeptical over the past several weeks.

• • •

The most serious problem SOS faced in the near future was the long-anticipated Olympic presentation of its refinery plan details. For weeks, the Onassis men had been claiming that all of the questions people had about the environment and jobs and impact on the community would be answered, once they had time to finalize their plans. Now here it was, just a month before the town vote, and Olympic was postponing its presentation from the middle of February until the end of the month. SOS feared that Olympic would be able to makes its case with slick slides and superficial promises just days before the vote, giving anti-refinery activists no real chance to examine the details and rebut the claims where possible. To a reporter for *Publick Occurrences,* Nancy had made it clear that she believed the delay was not an accident. It was deliberate. The longer Olympic waited, the better off they would be. SOS had to do something to neutralize the Olympic advantage.

They had one strong advocate on the Board of Selectmen, Larry O'Connell, who was doing his best to make sure the anti-refinery advocates got as much time at the presentation as did Olympic. But the chairman, Alden Winn, was bending over backward to be "fair" to Olympic, each time citing some vague court case that went against a town's decision to exclude a business because the town had not treated the business fairly. But the town's attorney, Joseph Millimet, had already assured the selectmen that nothing they had done would cause a court to rule against them. Winn was an old Yankee, conservative to the point of inaction.

Olympic wanted a four-hour block of time to make their presentation: one hour each for an introduction, description of on-shore facilities, description of off-shore facilities, and a summary to include an analysis of the refinery's impact on the community. No time was suggested for people to ask questions. If people wanted time to ask questions or rebut some parts of the proposal, it would be in a separate meeting after the Olympic presentation.

At the meeting of the Board of Selectmen, which Nancy had attended to make sure SOS's position was represented, Larry O'Connell suggested that instead of four hours for Olympic alone, the company be given two hours and the public two hours. Maybe it could be just ten minutes for an introduction, then half an hour for each of the other three topics, with the public given half an hour to ask questions. As expected, Winn didn't want to shortchange Olympic, and suggested it be given two and a half hours of the four. The selectmen argued back and forth over how much time should be given to each side, then at the suggestion of Malcolm Chase, the man who had just been appointed to an engineering board by Governor Thomson, the selectmen decided to "sit down with Olympic" to come up with a format.

Nancy was furious. Why should Olympic have a say in how much time the public should be given? She wanted the selectmen to follow the reasonable suggestions outlined in *Publick Occurrences*[115]:

1. That Olympic be held to its promise to produce all available plans and other information by mid-February as originally promised.

2. That this information not be held up while details of a public meeting are worked out, but that it be presented in writing and to the press at a full press conference attended by the appropriate Olympic technical advisers and Olympic corporate representatives authorized to speak on policy matters on behalf of the company, town officials, representatives of the governor and representatives of SOS which is a de facto organization of a considerable body of the citizenry, and SOR representatives if there are such.

3. That the public meeting be held at least ten days after that press conference so that an adequate period of public study and debate can take place.

4. That the public meeting be held and turned over entirely (or almost entirely) to questions from anybody who has one, and that this meeting end when the questions end.

We question the value or the fairness of a question period at which the questioners will be quick studies forced to gulp down four hours of raw data then try to spit back the sharpest, most appropriate questions....

The original presentation in writing, the period of public scrutiny and debate, and the full and long question session ought to give the public a rather good idea of what is being proposed for this area by Olympic Refineries.

The SOS board had little confidence that all of the suggestions, however reasonable, would be followed. To hedge their bets, they had decided to hold another town meeting of their own, scheduled several days before the Olympic presentation. But they were all worried. How could they rebut specific problems without knowing exactly what Olympic was planning? Still, they couldn't afford not to try, and there were some new developments since the first meeting on December 4 that would make this meeting not just a rehashing of what was covered earlier.

Other worries that weighed on Nancy's mind included a presentation for the first time to concerned citizens of North Hampton, which bordered Rye on the south. The citizens were a bit late in taking up the issue, finally realizing that their fishermen use the same waters as the Rye fisherman, and that the currents from oil spills off Rye Beach would inevitably mingle with the waters off Hampton Beach. It had taken some time for Sharon to persuade people there to hold a meeting, but now they were, and SOS was providing the speakers from Karen's bevy of experts.

Finally, there was the continuing saga of Roger Wilson, the board member who just couldn't accept the group consensus if it contradicted his own views. And, unfortunately, that scenario occurred quite frequently. Nancy had talked with him after the first meeting in January, and he seemed to understand that he should be more cooperative. He had been elected secretary back in October, but that didn't seem to be what he wanted to do, and so after the New Year he was made the legal coordinator, but that didn't seem to help much, either. He was still unwilling to concede an argument until far beyond the time when all the other members of the board had come to an agreement. Nancy didn't know if it was a sex issue, that he just couldn't accept the authority of women, or whether he had some other problem with the group. But it really didn't matter anymore. Her main concern was the unproductive hours the board spent trying to accommodate his feelings. The time had come for her, as head of SOS, to do something about it, as distasteful as that might be.

That evening, she called his number. "I don't think it's working out with you on the board," she said to Roger.

"What does that mean?"

"We've talked about this before. I'm not going into it again."

"What are you saying?"

"You're not welcome to come to any more meetings."

"You can't do that!" Roger said, his voice rising. "I was elected by the SOS members. At the Congdon's house. You can't fire me."

"You're not being fired. You weren't ever hired. This is a volunteer organization. I'm simply telling you: don't come to any more meetings."

"Who gives you the right to do that? I was voted onto the board."

"I've already talked with the other board members. They all agree with me."

"I'll protest. Take it to the SOS membership."

"I don't think so. You know they'll support me and the board. You'll just embarrass yourself."

There was a long silence. Finally, he said, "This is emasculating."

So it was a sex issue after all. "I'm sorry you feel that way," she said.

She hung up and breathed a sigh of relief. Well, that's one less worry, she thought.

She had plenty left.

24

AS RICH AS CROESUS

When Phyllis came across the article in the *Boston Globe Sunday Magazine*[116] in late January about the oil refinery controversy in New Hampshire and the coverage it was getting from her own newspaper, she was stunned to read, "With a pick-up crew of local journalists, many of them part-time, *Publick Occurrences* would soon prove itself the most enterprising newspaper in New Hampshire." Her first thought: Yes! Someone in the profession finally recognized the unique contribution that the paper was making in the service of democracy. Her second thought: it's nice to get praise, but what she really needed was financial help. It was the second thought that prompted her to find out who at the *Globe* controlled the money. She discovered that the paper had been incorporated into Affiliated Publications, and that the president was John I Taylor, a man in his early sixties who had started working for the paper almost four decades earlier. This was the time, she thought, to do what she had always argued to Steve was essential, and what the UNH business professor Ray Belles had confirmed was necessary—ask for funds to support the paper. If *Publick Occurrences* was seen as so enterprising, perhaps she could somehow work with the *Globe*, justifying some infusion of money from the Boston paper. At best, it was a long shot, but given the positive article, it was certainly worth a try.

Phyllis wrote a letter to Taylor, mentioning the article in the magazine section and asking him if he would be willing to meet with her to discuss some possible areas of cooperation. She mailed the letter, and two days later got a call from him personally. Yes, he said, he was eager to meet her and talk about her paper. They agreed to meet at a downtown restaurant on Friday, the only weekday that Phyllis really had free, after she picked up the printed copies for the week in Plaistow and brought them up to Newmarket for distribution. That meeting was tomorrow. In the meantime, she had to finish editing articles for the current issue.

The most startling article she had read outside of her own paper was in the February 1 issue of *Forbes* magazine, which focused on Onassis. It provided a perspective on the reputed richest man in the world that she had not previously considered. She deliberated over whether to edit or describe it, or at least explain who Croesus was. In the end, she simply republished the article without comment. It would be up to the readers to figure out the literary reference. She would add only a headline at the top of the page.[117]

FORBES MAGAZINE ON BUSINESSMAN ONASSIS

FORBES

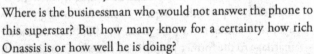

IS CROESUS LOSING HIS TOUCH?

Reversing the style of most people, Aristotle Socrates Onassis lives a private life that is very public and a public life that is very private. While the strobe lights flash around Onassis and his wife, his business dealings are wrapped in mystery.

This has been very useful to Onassis. Where is the businessman who would not answer the phone to this superstar? But how many know for a certainty how rich Onassis is or how well he is doing?

Onassis says he is sixty-eight; others say he is well into his seventies. But the big question is: can Onassis be slipping? Some suspect so. More than half of his sixty tankers are in the spot market; that is, they are rent for single voyages, rather than under long-term lease. Spot rates, $40 a ton for voyages from the Persian to the US only four months ago, have fallen to $7.50 a ton, barely a break-even level. Once-bullish stock market operators are now beginning to wonder if there will be any market for the tonnage they have been ordering at such a furious rate in recent years.

In the rest of his fleet, too, Onassis is having his difficulties. The big oil companies, which own forty percent of the world's tankers and charter most of the rest, have been raising the yellow caution flag on renewing long-term charters. Onassis has tiffed with the majors for years. And there have been scattered reports of some oil companies attempting to drop charters by claiming *force majeure* because of the Arab embargo.

On top of this, bunker fuel is short. "Those that have it, by and large the oil companies, aren't letting it move," says a prominent New York shipbroker. And Olympic Airways, Onassis's 23-plane international fleet, is feeling the same ills as all the international airlines—dwindling travel and soaring costs.

In this troubled context, Onassis's proposal to build a giant oil refinery in New Hampshire becomes highly significant. Why would Onassis, who made his money in shipping oil, now want to refine it? Can it be that he needs a captive market for his ships, that his old role as shipper is becoming obsolete?

The refinery would cost $600 million. Located at Durham near the Atlantic shore and served with a big offshore tanker terminal, it would be the single biggest new refinery project in the US. New Hampshire's ultra-conservative Governor Meldrim Thomson, Jr. is an all-out backer of Onassis and full of scorn for the environmentalists blocking the project.

Perhaps Governor Thomson will deliver for Onassis, but it is unwise to count an Onassis deal until it is hatched. His big deal to expand the Greek economy fell through two years ago, after a long run in the press. In 1968, two days after his marriage to the former Jacqueline Kennedy, Onassis flew from Skorpios to meet with George Papadopoulos, Greece's then dictator, and firm up a $400 million deal. Onassis was to provide his homeland with a refinery, power plant and aluminum complex in return for a contract guaranteeing business for his tanker fleet. But Onassis couldn't deliver the total financing package, even after First National City Bank had given the Greeks a $7-million guarantee; nor could he assure a source of low-priced Arabian crude.

People close to Onassis say that he now has good lines to the country's new dictator, Brigadier General Dimitrios Ioannidis, Chief of the Military Police, but there is no more talk of giant deals in Greece.

So, too, with a long-ago Onassis deal to gain a monopoly over Saudi Arabian oil shipping. In 1954 Onassis sealed a pact with the then Saudi king, Ibn Saud Bin Abdul Aziz Al-Saud, brother of the present king. The deal would have set up an Onassis fleet with the right eventually to transport all Saudi oil. But the powers of the world, the big oil companies and the British and American governments, killed the deal.

Will the New Hampshire refinery fare better? Or will it be a headline maker rather than a moneymaker?

Unlike the ill-fated refinery in Greece, the one in New Hampshire probably would command big bank and insurance company financing if Onassis turns up with a contract for Arabian crude. There is a rumor floating around the oil industry these days that Onassis is fronting for the Organization of Petroleum Exporting Countries. Onassis neither confirms nor denies the rumor, which, if anything, adds luster to his image.

Constantine Gratsos, Onassis's major domo, claims oil sources for Onassis in Saudi Arabia, Iran and possibly Abu Dhabi. However, tanker operators contacted by Forbes are skeptical. "The Arabs are loaded down with good offers," says Elias Kulukundis, president of Burma Oil Tankers, a subsidary of Burma Oil, Inc.

Nobody thinks Onassis is down to his last penny. In fact, the Onassises are not even down to their last island or town house. But even with his skill at avoiding income taxes, his style of living is a constant strain on his finances; one report said he personally spent $20 million during his first year of marriage to Jacqueline Kennedy Onassis.

If the New Hampshire deal, like the Greek deal and the Saudi deal before it, turns out to be just a golden red herring, certainly Onassis's credibility and his Croesus reputation will suffer. "It's a different ball game than when Ari started out," says a longtime acquaintance who insists on anonymity. "The deals are too big now for a lone wolf to handle. You have to have partners and an open corporate balance sheet to get the financing. And that just isn't Ari's style."

The glitter of the Greek shipowers may be giving way to the glow of the oil sheiks.

The next day, after completing her newspaper run from her home in Brentwood to Plaistow to Newmarket and back to her home, Phyllis looked over her limited wardrobe to find an outfit that would impress. Appearance probably wouldn't matter too much, she thought, but then again, she knew it did matter. People's judgments are often instantaneous, and while she might be able to change a poor evaluation to a positive one over time, she didn't have that kind of time. Taylor would see her and if she looked like a dodo bird, it was all over. Then she thought maybe she was obsessing too much. He had, after all, called her the very same day he had read her letter, or so he said on the phone. So, he must be impressed with the paper. Certainly, she didn't need to worry a whole lot about how she looked. On the other hand....

When she arrived at the designated restaurant, she was wearing a white dress and heels. The maître d' led her to a table with a gray-haired man in an elegant looking suit, who stood on her arrival and introduced himself as John Taylor. She addressed him as Mr. Taylor, but he insisted she call him John. A waiter asked if they wanted anything to drink. Taylor looked at her, waiting for her to make a decision. What should she order? Was he going to order something alcoholic, and if she did and he didn't, what would that look like? Do people usually drink wine or cocktails for *lunch*? She didn't want to ask, didn't want to look like a hick, but he was waiting, the waiter was waiting, she needed to say something. It occurred to her that people drank orange juice or tomato juice with vodka in it for breakfast, so certainly it would be okay for her to have something similar for lunch. Besides, she thought it would look cool, a woman in control. And so she made the fateful decision: "Bloody Mary, please." Taylor ordered a glass of wine.

They talked, looked at the menu, got their drinks, and talked some more. The waiter returned to take their orders just as Phyllis was raising her glass to drink. Smack! He hit her arm and the glass jerked forward, the tomato and vodka mix spilling all over Taylor's suit, Taylor jumping backward to no avail, Phyllis holding the guilty glass, its contents mostly gone. The waiter apologized profusely, offering Taylor a clean napkin, which he took to wipe off his face and hands. Patting his wet suit, he gave out reassuring sounds that it was okay, but Phyllis knew it wasn't okay, what a stupid thing to do, who drinks Bloody Marys for lunch anyway? She apologized, but Taylor said no, it wasn't her fault, and after all, it wasn't life or death, just a drink, so don't worry about it. But she did, and would never forget the incident, always wondering how uncool could anyone be to order a Bloody Mary for lunch?

They talked and Taylor was encouraging, telling her that *Publick Occurrences* could be affiliated with the *Globe*. It was an experiment he was trying—to work with other newspapers in the area to bolster local content. Within that framework, he could provide her some money and allow her to insert her newspaper into the New Hampshire edition of the *Globe*, thus giving her wider distribution. They would not sign anything formal. He would send her the check, and he trusted her to continue with the kind of work she was doing. He was delighted to have her as an unofficial partner. And if things worked out, there would be more money as well.

When she got home, she was still riding high, her spirits reinvigorated, her faith in the paper's future restored. She would have to tell Ray Belles. He would be impressed, she was sure. After all, *she* was impressed with what she had accomplished: an initial grant of $250,000, no strings attached. She felt as rich as Croesus.

25

FINAL PREPARATIONS

The rain was heavy, the air cold, a generally miserable night for SOS's second open meeting on Tuesday evening, February 19.[118] Nancy had been worried that the weather would discourage people from coming, and it appeared she was right. Less than half the number who had turned out in December attended this new presentation. While not unexpected, it was still a bit disappointing, though it was quite possible the weather wasn't a factor. It could be that many people had already made up their minds, or maybe they felt they had already heard enough and now wanted to hear what Olympic had to say. That was the opinion of Save Our Refinery activist Tommy Thompson, who sat through the first half of the meeting, but then left at the intermission. He thought the smaller audience was reassuring for the pro-refinery group. It showed, he said, that people were going to wait until they got more information from Olympic Refineries next week. He seemed to believe that if people were still waiting for more information, they hadn't been persuaded by all the arguments SOS had provided thus far, and were therefore likely to be convinced by Olympic that a refinery was a good thing for Durham.

Whatever the reason for the lower turnout, the material itself that SOS presented at this second open meeting was mostly new, and the people who attended—many of whom Nancy remembered from the last time—seemed engrossed in what the speakers had to say. She had started off the evening herself by welcoming everyone and thanking them for taking the time to come and listen. She

noted that the Olympic presentation had been delayed, and that it was now scheduled for the following Wednesday and Sunday, almost two weeks later than originally scheduled. That left just two days for everyone to absorb all the information Olympic would throw at them before being asked to vote on the matter at the Annual Town Meeting the following Tuesday. "It is no coincidence that the Olympic study is late," she said, pointing out that the delay meant there would be no time for SOS to have a post-Olympic presentation to challenge the company's detailed plans. "How different is New Hampshire's approach to the oil refinery compared with Maine?" she asked rhetorically. "There the government has committed $1.7 million for a study of just an oil terminal development, while our governor is rushing headlong into embracing a gigantic and complex refinery project, with no money at all for a feasibility study to determine if, when, and where a refinery should be constructed in the state." She called upon on all present to contact as many senators and representatives as they could in order to neutralize the effort that Olympic was making by hiring three lobbyists.

Other speakers that evening included Sam Reid, who elaborated on his economic report challenging claims that the refinery would be a tax bonanza. His report had already been published in *Publick Occurrences*, but it was possible some of the people hadn't read it. And it was worth reiterating the major conclusions anyway, since the *Union Leader* and governor and even the Onassis men continued to assert there would be a big reduction in property taxes with the refinery.

John Beckett talked about the bills being considered during the special legislative session. Usually Dudley would be called upon to talk about what was happening in Concord, but she deferred to Beckett, a Republican rep from Durham who was going against the governor in opposing the refinery. It would be good for people to know that opposition included reps from both parties. Beckett noted that Dudley's Home Rule bill "confirms the traditions of the state," but will possibly be exposed to a "strong effort to defeat or amend its meaning."

A hydrologist, Francis Hall, talked about the water needs of the refinery, but admitted it was difficult to do much analysis since Olympic had not yet settled on how much water they expected to need.

Jim Horrigan, an economics professor at the UNH business school, took issue with a state report from the Department of Resources and Economic Development (DRED) that the refinery would produce some 15,000 jobs. That number was vastly inflated, he said. In fact, the likely number of new jobs was less than one-tenth that number: 1,300. How did DRED come to its conclusions? The estimate, he said, had been lifted from a study done by Massport for Massachusetts, which assumed a "permanent construction work force." For that to apply in Durham, it would require the construction of a new refinery every three years!

One of the more chilling presentations came from Arthur Martin, who was the co-chairman of a committee in Maine promoting regional cooperation among the six New England states. Thomson, he noted, was the only governor in the region to refuse to participate in that effort. Then he reported that as a naval architect, he was convinced that the supertankers in the Onassis fleet were simply not safe. "A supertanker requires up to three miles to come to a halt from cruising speed. Sometimes they veer as

much as one half mile off course while stopping." Given the limited maneuvering space near the Isles of Shoals, and also the fact
that the Portsmouth Harbor shipping lane crosses the proposed
terminal area, he said, "a half-mile error could be disastrous."

The one piece of good news came from Leo Allen, an aide to
the Majority Leader of the Massachusetts State Senate, William
Bulger. The senator, Allen reported, believed that pollution from
the refinery in Durham could affect Massachusetts waters, and that
regional planning for oil refineries was essential to avoid environmental disaster. Thus, the Bay State was moving toward legal action
to halt the refinery. Nancy doubted such an effort would be effective in the long run, but the very fact of a long legal battle might
help to deter Olympic from trying to build its refinery in Durham.

• • •

The following Sunday evening, the SOS board members spent
little time fretting over the possible reasons for the low turnout
of their second informational meeting. There was nothing they
could do about that now anyway, and they had more pressing
issues to deal with. The next day, Olympic would be unveiling
its scale model of the refinery, presumably to demonstrate how
easily the gigantic facility could be integrated into the Durham
community. "Yes!" Sharon said. "Just like a Christmas tree!" The
board members laughed.

The unveiling would be in Concord rather than Durham.
SOS needed to have someone in the capital city to examine the
model. John Hatch, a local artist, had made an eight-foot-square,
three-dimensional topographic model of Durham in 1965. His
wife, Maryanna Hatch, who had replaced Roger Wilson as SOS
secretary, suggested that perhaps Durham would want to cart that
model to Concord to provide a realistic look at how much the oil
refinery would dominate the small town. The board members had
no confidence the Olympic model would be accurate.

• • •

Then, on Wednesday, Olympic would make its long-awaited pitch to the town, and everyone on the board knew how crucial that would be. They didn't like the format. It would be Olympic talking and people questioning, a horrible and unfair way for Olympic to control the flow of information. But the townspeople would ask hard questions. Karen and Celeste and Sharon had all been working on getting people to address the issues SOS had been harping on for weeks, questions that the Olympic men had been dodging, claiming they needed time to complete their plans. For each issue, SOS had someone who would demand an answer—on the requirements for water, what provisions Olympic had made for the inevitable oil spills, how Durham and the state could expect special treatment in getting heating oil and gasoline given the federal allocation policy, how many jobs Durham could realistically see, where Olympic would store the refined oil, how many petrochemical satellite industries there would be, and whether or not Olympic was going to abide by their promise to respect Home Rule. Celeste vowed that she would press Olympic on that last question. They had promised many times, and Onassis himself had

promised, not to force a refinery where it wasn't wanted. But they were pulling back from their promise, and she wanted to make it clear to everyone what Olympic and the governor were doing.

Karen had some good news. Olympic had sought some UNH consultants from the engineering college and from the business school, but all had refused. She had already enlisted the aid of all the faculty who might be able to help with the refinery issue, so Olympic's effort to buy off some UNH faculty was dead in the water.

Other good news had been reported by *Publick Occurrences* the previous Friday. The Baudet family was holding out on selling options to Olympic, which apparently felt that the property was critical to their plans.[119]

> The 210-acre farm owned by Carmelia Baudet stretches in an unbroken parcel from Route 108 westward to the B&M Railroad, where it fronts the track for over half a mile.
>
> The push to acquire the farm—which would give Olympic access to the railroad—began last July when George Pappademus, the Nashua realtor, offered $300,000 plus the value of the buildings and life tenancy in the house to Mrs. Baudet and her son Norman. Pappademus said that the land would be used for a housing development, according to Norman and another son, Wilfred. (Pappademus has since claimed that he didn't know what his clients were planning for Durham Point.)…
>
> Mrs. Baudet, with the support of her sons, has rejected all offers out of hand….Of all the landowners under pressure to sell to Olympic, Mrs. Baudet appears on the surface to be among the most vulnerable. And yet she has never wavered in her resolve to keep the farm, which has been in the family over fifty years.
>
> She will be eighty-four years old next week. She said in an interview with *Publick Occurrences* that her wish is to "stay on the farm until I die," and then "turn the farm over to Norman."
>
> Mrs. Baudet is a shut-in. Her son Norman, forty-two, spends much of the day looking after her. He took over man-

agement of the farm at the age of seventeen, when his older brother Wilfred, now fifty-seven, moved to Dover to work for General Electric. Mrs. Baudet's husband died when Norman was still a small child....

The house itself, the barn and the grounds reflect the tidy and frugal lives of Mrs. Baudet and her son.

No miscellaneous pieces of farm machinery to collect snow in the barnyard. No trash cans. No tool handles poking through the snow. No shed doors hanging from a single hinge. No tar paper flapping in the wind. Nothing which bespeaks negligence or waste.

The only luxuries are three fluffy cats which sit silently on the porch, basking in the sun and watching with little interest the approach of visitors.

In the front yard is a statue of the Virgin Mary in the traditional pose of welcome.

Inside, the themes repeat themselves: tidiness, frugality, faith.

Sitting at a bare, simple table in a long, sparsely furnished living room, Norman expressed optimism about continuing on the farm, despite his and his mother's current problems. "I'm not worried about making a living," he said....

Asked what he would do if Olympic purchased the farm, he seemed unable to visualize an alternative life for himself, despite the money he and his mother would receive. "I'd be out on the street, I guess," he said.

His mother was more definite. "I couldn't stand the bulldozers and the noise," she said. "I'm so nervous, I can't see straight."...

As the interview with the Baudets drew to a close, Wilfred looked around the table and said, "Money is no good if you're not happy."

On Monday, Olympic unveiled its scale topographic model of the oil refinery at the State House in Concord. Nancy didn't go, because of so many phone calls she was getting from the media, but John Hatch went and called to tell her that the town needed to take his scale model to Concord so people up there could see

the real impact of the refinery on the town. Olympic had a slick model, he admitted, and it made the whole facility look like it was enclosed in a natural habitat and would be invisible to the rest of the residents. But there were many incorrect details about the roads and housing divisions in the area, making it appear as though the refinery was less intrusive than it would actually be.

Apparently, several other Durham residents had gone to the unveiling as well, and had also come away with a negative impression of the model's details. When Nancy called Alden Winn, he said the Recreation and Parks Division was getting a truck to cart John Hatch's model up to Concord. Hatch had outlined on his scale model where all the optioned properties lay, showing a much greater impact on the town's geography than the Olympic model.

Nancy read about the ceremony the next day in the *Manchester Union Leader*,[120] which described the Olympic mockup as a "ten by eleven foot geodetic model, designed for eye-level viewing to picture the relationship of the refinery to any particular point of the surrounding terrain." It required more than five hundred man hours to construct at an estimated cost of $30,000 to $40,000. Standing next to the model was Governor Meldrim Thomson, along with Constantine Gratsos and Nicholas Papanicolaou, a young man who had just recently joined the Onassis team to replace Peter Booras as the face of Olympic. The governor was effusive: "This is an auspicious moment in New Hampshire's history. I hope that it augurs the building of an environmentally safe and economically successful Olympic refinery in our state...with this detailed model and the great depth of facts that will be presented to the people of New Hampshire, Olympic is demonstrating its faith in the future of our state and the wisdom of our people." He then portrayed the possible acquisition of an oil refinery as though it would be a momentous achievement both for the country and the state. "New Hampshire's history is filled with instances like this where our people have led the nation in great goals of national progress."

Refinery supporters echoed the governor's fulsome praise.[121] House Minority Leader Ernest Coutermarsh, a Democrat in favor of the refinery regardless of what Durham voters might want, said he was "very impressed with the visual display" and that "it had many pluses to be gained for our state." Executive Councilor James Hayes, a Republican from Concord, liked "the exclusivity of the location as shown by the model" and said the refinery "doesn't

194

appear objectionable." And Maurice Read, another proponent of the project, said that he couldn't see how the refinery "would interfere with anybody." The most unrestrained praise came from Roger Crowley, the Democratic nominee for governor who lost to Thomson a year earlier, but was appointed by the victorious Republican to be director of the Governor's Crime Commission. The model itself, he claimed, refuted any environmental objections opponents might have. The rendering "was excellent. It appears the refinery would not have an adverse impact on the environment."

This was exactly what Nancy and the SOS board had feared—that the model would, by itself, be treated as evidence that the refinery would not be harmful to the environment. And, of course, there was no indication in the model of where the petrochemical plants, projected by Olympic, would be located.

The only negative comments in the report came from Chris Spirou, who said he was not impressed. He thought the refinery project "looked massive." And he wanted to know why it was being displayed in Concord first, not in Durham. It wouldn't be transferred to the town until Wednesday, the very day that Olympic was giving its long-delayed presentation.

An Olympic spokesman replied, "This affair concerns the state government and since we're here at the invitation of the governor, out of respect to him, we decided on showing it in Concord first. He deserves all the merit of the project."

Well, Nancy thought, that shows where Olympic thinks the power is. It's more important to please the governor than the citizens of Durham. She intended to prove Olympic wrong.

26

DUDLEY'S HEARING

Dudley was feeling anxious and depressed.[122] These were not new feelings for her. They had occurred frequently over the past several months, but, on Tuesday evening, February 26, the day before the legislative hearing on her bill, HB 18, when she was preparing her testimony for the committee, they were occurring in spades. What still seemed unbelievable to her after all these months was that she, a freshman legislator of the minority party, should be the focal point of the opposition to the refinery, when there were so many other, more experienced legislators who could have filled that role. And she feared that she wasn't doing a good job in marshalling the opposition. Yes, Chris Spirou was working behind the scenes, and he was a really big help, but as he suggested to her, she was the point man in the campaign. And she couldn't help wondering if she wasn't letting him down, along with all the other opponents of the refinery who seemed to be counting on her. The confrontation with the governor over the petitions troubled her. She was haunted by the picture of her looking like a hysterical woman clutching wads of paper, the caption underneath reading, "I was badly treated." How professional did that look?

It wasn't the first time she had looked foolish—or at least had been portrayed that way by the press. Her very first foray into the legislative process, on her third day as a member of the House in early January 1973, was even worse. She was testifying before the Judiciary Committee on a bill that would specify penalties for possession of drugs. It occurred to her while listening to other testimony that something was wrong with a law that provided incentives for addicts to beat and rob people to get money for drugs. So, she suggested to the committee that if the legal penalties were removed, and addicts could go to the pharmacy to get a gram when they needed it, the problems of crime would be lessened. Decriminalization of drug use could be supplemented with treatment programs. As far as she could recall, no one had ever paid much attention to anything she had ever said in her life, so she was stunned when her comments elicited an uproar of condemnation. The tag was seemingly everywhere: *Dudley Dudley favors legalization of marijuana. What a foolish/stupid idea!* Her colleagues, and of course the press, especially the *Union Leader,* tore into her. Right from the beginning of her service as a rep, she was dismissed as a lightweight or, even worse, as a kook.

Doubting her ability to lead the fight against the refinery was only one of the things that made her anxious. She was also apprehensive, almost to the point of paranoia, about the seemingly thousands of lobbyists hired by Onassis. As she jokingly told a reporter for *Publick Occurrences,*[123] it seemed she was hallucinating them in every state house closet. In one case, there was a man she saw who was frequently in the office of the House Minority Leader, Ernest Coutermarsh, a supporter of the refinery. *That man's in there every day! Why? Why?* As it turns out, he was not a lobbyist for Olympic, but a man requesting help for his wife, who was appealing the loss of a government job.

Still, her anxiety over Olympic's power was reinforced when she read that Tex McGrary, the PR guy from Texas, was given $1 million to run an advertising campaign in the state. She also read that Olympic had just bought off Marshall Cobleigh, the highly respected Majority Leader of the House until he retired last year. The same with William Craig, a former chairman of the state Democratic Party and minority leader in the House. Both hired by Onassis with separate, impressive-sounding titles. Both trying their best to convince their former legislative colleagues that the state needed a refinery. And if that wasn't enough, Olympic had also tried to buy off Chris Spirou with $1 million. How many other politicians had Onassis tried—in his own words—"to seduce with money"?

In the meantime, she was generating bad news story after bad news story. Of course, all people who opposed the refinery were castigated by Loeb and the *Union Leader*, though she seemed to generate more criticism than most. She recalled one of the publisher's responses to a citizen who had written a letter opposing the refinery: "People such as yourself who oppose the refinery are kooks. You don't know a damn thing about refineries. You have fallen for scare talk by some university nuts who used you and played you for a sucker." And that was tame. Name calling was Loeb's way of dealing with people who disagreed with him—they were jackasses and fools, and she was Mrs. Fuddy Duddy and Deadly Dudley, and the "women of Durham" opposed to the refinery "were beating their small breasts." At one level, his remarks were so juvenile as to be humorous, and she and Nancy and the other women of SOS had all chortled over the outrageously sexist comments, but over time, the constant stream of invective began to wear on her.

She remembered one afternoon a couple of weeks earlier when she read one of the *Union Leader*'s editorials, referring to her as "Mrs. Thomas Dudley" and the "Durham housewife." After fuming about it for some time, she finally grabbed the phone and called the newspaper. "I have only one complaint," she told Jim Finnegan. "Please don't call me Mrs. Thomas Dudley."

"But we have to let our readers know you're a woman," he said. "After all, you do have an unusual name. Okay, what about Representative Mrs. Thomas Dudley?"

Dudley exploded.

"Well, we've hit on a sensitive point, haven't we?"

Finnegan knew as well as she did that the constant references to her as an appendage to her husband, and as a housewife, were intended to demean her qualifications, not to provide relevant information. How relevant was it, anyway, that she had ovaries rather than testicles? Besides, if the readers really needed to know she was a woman, the pronoun "she" should provide a clue for even the most obtuse *Union Leader* reader. Finnegan was just spewing garbage, as he typically did. Yet, she had blown up, and she knew that was what Finnegan and Loeb relished—to torment their opponents.

In an interview with a reporter, she had speculated that perhaps the reason Loeb and Finnegan were especially antagonistic toward her was that in 1969 she had been active in opposing the incarceration of two black Marines at the Portsmouth Naval Prison, simply for saying Vietnam was a "white man's war." Her actions, along with help from Chris Spirou and others, had pressured the Navy to set the men free. The *Union Leader* went bananas over that. In addition, she was a McGovern delegate in 1972, the presidential candidate who was charged with supporting "acid, abortion, and amnesty." And then, of course, she was from Durham. Loeb hated Durham and UNH. Dudley often wondered what in his past made Loeb feel so antagonistic to people with education.

Later, Dudley would learn from a writer for *Esquire*, who reported on the Onassis oil refinery controversy, that Loeb did indeed harbor special resentments toward her.[124] "There are a lot of people I don't like," Loeb told the reporter. "But Dudley Dudley, I hate."[125] It shocked her that he had admitted his deep aversion for her, and she wondered what in Loeb's past caused him such fury when a woman dared to challenge him.

Unfortunately, the tone set by Loeb and his paper reverberated throughout the state. Dudley was subjected to a steady stream of obscene letters and phone calls, both of which often included threats, which were a major factor in her occasional bouts of depression. She admitted to the reporter from *Publick Occurrences*, "I can't stand the heat...I don't think I'm much of a politician. And I don't think I've been very effective this session."

Yet here she was, preparing for a hearing on her bill designed to protect Durham, and all the other cities and towns in the state, from being forced to accept an oil refinery. How in the world did she become the Joan of Arc of New Hampshire?

• • •

Early the next morning, Dudley drove to Concord for the hearing.[126] It had been delayed until February 27 at her request, because she wanted to see what the other bills might contain. In the meantime, she had withdrawn a second bill that she had originally proposed, which would have prohibited a refinery and its pipelines from being classified as a public utility. Currently, it was up to the discretion of the energy siting committee to make such a determination, and her bill could easily be amended to say the opposite of what she wanted. It seemed better to focus on just her Home Rule bill, rather than get involved in arcane arguments about what constituted a public utility. The truth was, as she told a reporter, "Frankly, I was in over my head. I didn't have the technical knowledge to see it through, and I didn't want the wrath of the Public Utilities Commission."[127]

When she arrived at the Legislative Office Building (LOB), across the street from the back of the State House, hundreds of people were demonstrating in the cold, wearing anti-refinery buttons and holding anti-Olympic signs and placards. She was pleased to see the protestors and thankful for the hard work that Nancy Sandberg and her SOS volunteers had done to get out the crowd. To accommodate everyone, the venue had to be changed from the LOB to the city's American Legion building, where some three hundred spectators crowded into the auditorium. Dudley spoke first, appearing nervous at the beginning, but rising to the moment, her voice strong, her words clearly articulated.

"Aristotle Onassis, Peter Booras, Governor Thomson, and William Loeb want to build an oil refinery in New Hampshire," she said to the crowd. "It would swallow up one-fifth of the town for which it is presently proposed. It would cover four square miles. The proposed refinery's tank farm and truck dispatching terminal will be located on the final approach to the main northwest-southeast runway of Pease Air Force Base. If a plane ever crashed into that refinery, and there have been four crashes so far at Pease, the whole area for miles around would look as if it had been hit by an atomic bomb. I don't believe any community should be asked to take that risk against its own best judgment."

She took issue with the governor's latest stand on Home Rule. The governor, she charged, had reneged on his promise that Durham would not be forced to accept the Olympic refinery. She read the governor's letter to Alden Winn, and quoted from the Bedford press conference, where Thomson made it clear he would respect Home Rule. She reminded the audience of the controversy in Salem, New Hampshire, where the town citizenry had been opposed to allowing Sunday horse racing at Rockingham Park. And the state had agreed to abide by local sentiment. "The same principle should be applied to Durham," she said. "My bill is an affirmation of the New Hampshire I grew up in, where the most important event of the year was our annual town meeting, where local citizens got together to thresh out local problems. This bill shouldn't be necessary, but it is. New Hampshire people are in danger of jeopardizing one of their most cherished rights—that of local self-determination. If Durham is forced to accept the refinery, then democracy is dead."

After she finished speaking, the audience cheered. Other speakers followed, some thirty in all, most of whom echoed her emphasis on the importance of Home Rule, and her fear about the potential loss of democracy if the state forced Durham to accept what it didn't want.

Peter Horne of the Concerned Citizens of Rye said that his town, where the proposed pipeline would be laid, had stood for Home Rule since its founding in 1623, and that principle "is still in the hearts of those who have lived here all their lives." He also condemned the pressure being brought on two women in Rye who were refusing to sell land that Olympic said it needed for the pipeline. One Olympic representative had even approached a local minister, asking him to urge his parishioners to sell land to the refinery company. "The minister had a place for him to go," Horne said. The audience laughed.

Fishermen from Portsmouth, Hampton, Rye, Kingston, New Castle, and Seabrook all chimed in with their concerns about the effect of the refinery on the fishing industry.

A state representative from Rochester said his city would gladly accept a refinery, requiring Olympic Refineries to extend their pipeline only ten miles. He couldn't understand why Onassis hadn't taken up the offer.

Then came Attorney Charles Douglas, legal counsel to Governor Thomson. He noted that the governor supported the concept of Home Rule in principle, but the issue of a refinery had statewide implications, and it was much too crucial to be left to one small town to decide for the whole state. Scattered boos could be heard as he finished that statement. He went on to say that the governor wanted the question of locating a refinery to be presented before all the citizens in a statewide referendum.

Attorney William Craig, recently hired by Olympic to serve as its legal counsel, was the next speaker. "Look," he said, "I'm a native. My children were all born here, and I hope they stay here. But unless we encourage industry, we'll have nothing to induce them to stay here." He talked more about the benefits of the refinery, then said that people had to be realistic. With respect to the refinery, he said, "Home Rule is already by the boards. The Site Evaluation Committee, established in the last legislative session, already has the discretionary authority to decide where a refinery will be sited."

But moments later, Attorney Edward Haffer, representing the state's attorney general, took issue with Craig's interpretation of the recently passed Site Evaluation legislation. According to Attorney General Warren Rudman, Haffer said, current law already prohibits building a refinery in Durham, unless the town changes its zoning ordinances to favor one. So, HB 18, Dudley's Home Rule bill, would apply only to those cities and towns without zoning ordinances.

• • •

On her way back to Durham, Dudley reflected on what had happened. Haffer's testimony had convinced the committee that her bill would be limited in its effect. If the attorney general was correct, Durham was already protected. But she knew there was a catch. In fact, there were two of them.

First, Olympic could challenge the attorney general's interpretation in court, and there was no assurance that the courts would honor local zoning ordinances. The court might well interpret the legislation the same way as Attorney Douglas had—and since Douglas had crafted the wording of the law for the legislature the previous year, his opinion might well prevail.

Second, even if current law did protect Durham, a separate law could give the Site Evaluation Committee the authority to override local ordinances. And, unfortunately, that's exactly what HB 34, sponsored by House Majority Leader George Roberts, could become.

Roberts insisted that all he wanted to do with his bill was streamline the process of evaluating a refinery, so that instead of requiring a company to appear before several legislative committees, it would appear before only one consolidated committee. And Dudley trusted Roberts when he said his bill was not intended to favor a refinery. But she knew that the governor and his supporters wanted to amend HB 34 to achieve exactly that goal. In fact, Olympic representatives had just the day before requested that the House Environment and Agriculture Committee approve a provision in HB 34 specifying that state approval would override local rejection of a refinery. The committee had declined to do so, but a minority report, sponsored by Representative Maurice Read, called for an amendment giving the Site Evaluation Committee override authority. That amendment would be voted upon by the full House next week.

The fight over Home Rule had shifted. No longer was it her Home Rule bill, HB 18, that would determine the fate of the refinery, but HB 34 and the effort to amend it.

Sometime later she would have to think about the implications of this shift and what it might mean to her strategy. Right now, she needed to think about the Olympic Refineries presentation for this evening in Durham. Nancy Sandberg had attended the morning hearing for HB 18, but left early, whispering to Dudley that she needed time to prepare.

"You look worried," Dudley said.

"I am worried," Nancy said.

That made Dudley worried as well.

27

OLYMPIC REFINERIES PRESENTATION

Nancy *was* worried.

She explained why to a reporter from *Esquire* magazine as they drove from Concord back to Durham after the hearing on Dudley's Home Rule bill.[128]

First, Olympic now seemed to have gotten its act together, compared with the earlier meetings it had up and down the seacoast, especially the fiascoes in Durham and Rye. Though Dudley had specifically mentioned this morning that Peter Booras, along with Onassis, Thomson, and Loeb, wanted an oil refinery in the state, Booras was actually out of the picture. He was being investigated by the attorney general for possible violations of election laws in his run for the US Senate in 1972, and Olympic had dropped him. It was good Dudley had reminded people of Booras's participation, because he was a controversial figure, but he had recently been replaced by Nicholas Papanicolaou, also Greek, and a much smoother representative, just twenty-five years old, with a Harvard undergraduate degree and an MBA from Columbia Business School. He was the new shining face of Olympic. And he was more organized. As a consequence, Olympic's recent presentations had been going much better.

Second, the sheer frequency of Olympic presentations, and their ad campaign promising more jobs, lower tax rates, and a plentiful supply of gasoline and home heating oil was having an effect. People seemed more willing to accept what Olympic was saying about the improvement of refineries—that the modern facilities were not as environmentally damaging as the older ones, and that the new refinery wouldn't be dirty and smelly. Perhaps, people were coming to believe, the Durham refinery really would be "clean as a clinic." Nancy couldn't know for certain, of course, how much of an effect the new Olympic image might be having, but she was worried that any effect could be fatal. The town needed to make a strong statement to the state to avoid being steamrolled by Thomson, Loeb, and Onassis.

She talked strategy with the reporter, telling him how SOS planned to put the Olympic consultants on the defensive. The format agreed to by the Board of Selectmen was to allow Olympic to make its presentation in the first and third hours of the evening, with the second and fourth hours reserved for questions and answers. The same four-hour format would be repeated the following Sunday for the second half of the Olympic presentation. The company had distributed a summary document of its refinery proposal on Monday, claiming its more detailed technical reports—some fifty in all—were still at the printer, and wouldn't be available until the second scheduled meeting on Sunday. What an excuse! A multi-million-dollar operation didn't have enough *printers*? Nancy told the reporter, of course it was not an accident that Olympic had delayed again. She felt it was part of their ongoing manipulative efforts to prevent Durham citizens, and the SOS experts, from having time to fully understand what Olympic intended to do.

The SOS strategy was to upend the meeting format, which implied that each Q&A session was limited to asking questions only about the material presented by Olympic in the previous hour. But that gave too much control to the Onassis men. Who knows what part of the refinery project they would discuss in that first hour? It didn't matter. SOS had lined up people to ask the hard questions that Olympic had continually refused to answer. And they would ask those questions in the first Q&A session, regardless of what had been discussed the previous hour. If, at the start of the presentation, SOS could make Olympic look incompetent or even deceitful—and the SOS board had developed some questions that

might well accomplish that objective—the result could undermine the company's credibility overall.

The meeting would be held in the UNH Field House, local officials believing that as many as four thousand people from around the seacoast might attend.[129] Ultimately, about seven hundred attended in person, many people apparently changing their minds about coming once it was announced that New Hampshire Network, a local public television station, would cover the event from beginning to end. Nineteen Olympic consultants, each with his own expertise, ready to provide answers to any questions the citizens might ask, sat on stage facing the audience. Robert Greene of Purvin and Gertz, the main consulting company hired by Olympic to find an appropriate site for the refinery and oversee its construction, sat in front, behind a table. The other men, all in dark suits and ties, spread out behind him.

Officially, the meeting was hosted by the Board of Selectmen, with the Board Chairman, Alden Winn, moderating. At the beginning, he cautioned the audience to listen politely and that they would have an opportunity to ask questions.

Greene began the Olympic presentation by giving a brief overview of the project and by revealing for the first time that Pease Air Force Base had agreed to allow the necessary pipelines to cross under its property. He also cited some of the benefits of the refinery. It was just as Nancy had feared. He was making claims that had long since been rebutted. "The Environmental Protection Agency in Boston," he said, "has agreed that a refinery in Durham would mean a better assurance of oil products in the New Hampshire area." On the topic of taxes, "the refinery would mean taxes in Durham would be lowered by two-thirds." Apparently, Nancy thought, Greene believed if you repeat a lie enough times, people will come to believe it, especially if they wanted it to be true.

He was followed by Eugene Harlow, executive vice president of F.R. Harris engineering company, who outlined four steps that he said would eliminate or minimize oil spills at the Isles of Shoals, where the unloading terminal would be located. Part of the process included a navigation system that would be based on Star Island, which surprised Nancy. She had not heard that Olympic had obtained an option there.

Captain Otta Meyer, a retired superintendent of ship handling for Mobil, elaborated on the communication system. There would be two sea islands constructed by Olympic about a mile west of the Isles of Shoals, toward the coast line. The supertankers would navigate to those islands with the aid of a radio scanner and radio communications center located on Star Island. Again, Nancy was surprised at the apparent claim that Olympic had obtained rights to Star. How had it happened and she had not heard of it?

The first question in the Q&A session came from Celeste DiMambro, as SOS had planned. "Does Olympic's promise still stand, mainly to uphold the wishes of the people of Durham, and if not, how are we expected to believe any of your other promises?" The audience roared its approval.

Papanicolaou came to the front of the stage, looking a bit nervous, and said, "Olympic is bound to listen to the authority with the power in the state. It will be up to the state or local government

whether Olympic will build a refinery in Durham." Several people booed his non-response.

Jim Horrigan from the UNH business school asked if Olympic even existed as a company, and if so, who owned it, and where did it get its money? Papanicolaou announced that in fact, Olympic had been incorporated in the state that very day, and that "ownership of the company rests entirely with the Onassis family." He added that statements on the corporation's officers, directors, and credit rating could be obtained from the First National Bank of New York. Horrigan pointed out that this was exactly the same statement Olympic had made when Governor Thomson first revealed Olympic's proposal back in November. How could people trust that this new claim wasn't in error also? Papanicolaou admitted it was a mistake to make that claim back in November, but that it was valid now.

Trembling with emotion, Evelyn Browne came to the microphone. She was the woman who had refused to sell her 170-acre property she called "Salty," but had agreed to option Ambler Acres, about a fourth the size, believing the claim by George Pappademus, the real estate agent, that the property would be used for a private residence. When she discovered the truth, she was outraged, and said she would go to court to overturn the contract. And now she was outraged again, this time on behalf of the Baudet family, with whom she was close friends. She had examined the scale model of the refinery in the Memorial Union Building at UNH, and found that it included a railroad spur running through the Baudet property. "They have held out against Olympic, despite tremendous pressure," she said. "They have not signed an option to their land. And they never will!"

The audience burst into cheers.

Greene apologized and acknowledged that "we certainly have made some mistakes in the model."

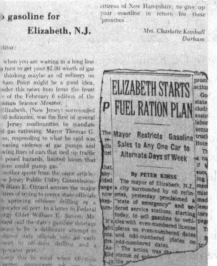

Another angry citizen had strong words for Olympic. Barbara Rutledge of Dover, a member of the Star Island Corporation, took issue with the claims by Joseph Bonasis and Eugene Harlow that Olympic would use Star Island for a communications center. "Olympic doesn't have an option on Star Island," she said. And as a member of the Board, she could tell them unequivocally that "Star won't sell you one inch of land at any price."[130]

Again, the audience cheered. Alden Winn cautioned people, "Please. This is not a political rally. Let's not turn this into a farce. The eyes of the state are upon you."

But that did not deter another cheer when Representative Dudley Dudley came to the microphone and confronted Greene on his claim that Durham would get special treatment when it came to obtaining gasoline and home heating oil. "It is one of the most dishonest and damaging myths," she said, "and it has been proven false numerous times. As everyone should know by now, gasoline and heating oil are distributed according to a federal allocation program, and the criteria for distribution do *not* include where the oil is coming from."

If states could benefit from having refineries, she said, the federal allocation program would have to include Texas and New Jersey, but "the price of gasoline is as high in those two states as it is here, and in many cases higher. Also, fuel is no more plentiful there than in New Hampshire either." She referred to an article in *Publick Occurrences*, which showed a news clipping that reported Elizabeth, New Jersey, had started a fuel ration plan, clear evidence that a refinery brought no special benefits to local towns. She went on to say that the EPA was not in charge of the federal fuel allocation program, so she had no clue why anyone from that organization would promise special consideration if Durham were to accept a refinery.

"So, let's be clear," she said. "The promise that Durham, or the seacoast, or the state of New Hampshire will get special treatment if a refinery is located here is simply false. Don't believe it."

Speaking in favor of the refinery was Tommy Thompson, head of Save Our Refinery, who said that it would cause lower property taxes. "Right now, Durham is a town where its own workers can't afford to live because of high property taxes." He talked about his

own experience, when his farm burned down and he didn't have the resources to start again. But he thought the refinery would increase property values and bring many other benefits to the town. It would be a modern facility that would not damage the environment. "SOS doesn't speak for the farmers and people who have lived in Durham for generations," he said. "We should welcome the refinery, which other towns would love to have."

A short, square-built woman in L.L. Bean boots and jacket took the microphone. "I'm Clif Horrigan," she said. "A grad student in hydrology." Nancy knew she was the wife of Jim Horrigan and the mother of two young children. She had gone back to school to pursue a field of study she had abandoned when she got married. "Mr. Greene, your plan calls for six thousand gallons of freshwater per minute, right?" After he agreed, she said, "Where are you going to get six thousand gallons of freshwater per minute?"

Greene hesitated, then walked back to his bevy of experts, whispered with them for a few seconds, and finally came back to the front of the stage. "We think we'll need just three thousand gallons per minute."

Nancy was taken aback. Just like that, he could reduce the water requirement in half? How much time had Olympic actually spent preparing their plans, anyway?

Undeterred, Horrigan asked, "Where are you going to get three thousand gallons of freshwater per minute?"

Again, Greene hesitated, then went back to his experts, and returned seconds later. "Actually, we believe we'll need just 1,500 gallons per minute."

The audience went wild, erupting in laughter and hoots and boos. Nancy couldn't believe it. In a matter of less than a minute, Olympic had cut its water requirement by seventy-five percent!

The noise continued for a while, Chairman Winn trying to calm the audience and warning them again that the eyes of the state were upon them.

When calm returned, Horrigan said, "Where will you get

1,500 gallons of freshwater per minute?" The sheer persistence of the grad student's question made everyone laugh again.

This time Greene did not return to his experts to come up with yet another figure. He said Olympic would expect to use about ten percent of the water from the Lamprey River. Anticipating Horrigan's next question—how they might obtain that much water from a river that perhaps was already being used to full capacity— he admitted that Olympic still needed to get permission to use the water. And if they couldn't get all they needed, the company would acquire effluent water from secondary sewage treatment facilities in the region.

By the end of the first Q&A session, Nancy was satisfied that SOS had accomplished its objective of questioning Olympic's credibility. The next two hours went more calmly, although in the second Q&A period, Greene was put on the spot again when a questioner wanted to know how he was going to resolve the inconsistency between EPA policy and Olympic's site selection. The EPA opposed refineries in unique environmental areas and along coastlines or in wetlands.

"We received notice of the EPA statement on February 11," Greene said. "No such policy existed when we selected the site." He would now have to take that statement into consideration. He also acknowledged that his company's choice of a refinery was not based on regional planning, but on an airplane flyover to find the nearest suitable site given the terminal location at the Isles of Shoals. Durham Point was close to Rye and mostly unsettled, requiring a minimal length of pipeline.

The following Sunday, at the beginning of the second four-hour presentation, Alden Winn read a statement of rebuke to Olympic Refineries unanimously endorsed by the Durham Town Board of Selectmen. It was critical of actions taken the previous week during the bill hearings in Concord:

> Since the refinery was first proposed, the Board of Selectmen
> has understood that the Olympic Company recognized its

obligation to satisfy voters of Durham before they would attempt to construct a refinery in our town.

To construct a refinery here, they would have to persuade the town to amend its zoning ordinance. For this reason, and because as public officials, we felt it was our responsibility to cooperate in making all the facts objectively available to our citizens; we have expressed no official Board opinion on the refinery issue.

We are now disturbed to discover that an Olympic representative has proposed to amend HB 34 in a way which would force acceptance of the refinery on a town—any town—even if the vast majority of citizens in that town were opposed to it. From this we can only conclude that however skillful they may be in business, the Olympic people have no understanding of the form of government we cherish in New England.

We think they will find that our system of government is more important to our way of life than any conceivable benefits to be derived from a refinery.

Like the rest of citizens, not only in Durham, but in all of New Hampshire, we deeply resent this change of heart on the part of Olympic.

We want to inform them that we will resist all efforts on their part, or on the part of any of their supporters, to deprive us of our right of local self-government.

The crowd loudly applauded the statement, this time Winn allowing the audience's boisterous expression without a warning about the eyes of New Hampshire upon them. The two hours of presentation on Sunday focused on the "minimal" impact the refinery would have on Durham, though skepticism was evident in most of the questions posed to the Olympic experts during the two Q&A sessions. As noted later in *Publick Occurrences,*[131] "question after question set off bursts of applause from the audience." Tommy Thompson was the only person to express a favorable opinion from the floor, arguing that the refinery was needed "because of the critical shortage of fuel," still believing that Durham would get preferential treatment if it agreed to accept the refinery. He decried the hostile questions of other audience members as a "political decathlon." Celeste DiMambro could not restrain herself from making one last comment to the Onassis men, who had promised to respect Home Rule and then had cavalierly abandoned their promise when they didn't get their way. "Leave your number at the front desk," she said to Greene. "And don't call us. We'll call you."

* * *

Nancy couldn't have been more pleased at the outcome of the two-day event. But there were signs that all was not well. Both presentations drew only about seven hundred people, many of whom came from the surrounding towns and cities. Yes, she knew that TV coverage by the New Hampshire Network may have depressed turnout, but maybe the opponents constituted a "silent majority." They stayed home for the event, but would come out to vote later. Did the presentation actually change anyone's mind? Was the audience so negative that it would cause a backlash?

That was the premise of the editorial in the *Union Leader*, which portrayed the audience and the questioners in a negative light. While Finnegan lauded the professionalism of the Olympic experts, and even of Alden Winn's performance as moderator, he came down hard—as expected—on the audience and the questioners:[132]

> And yet, for the opponents of the refinery, the entire performance may have proven a public relations debacle. No citizen of any perception who attended or viewed on television Wednesday night's meeting could have failed to grasp the essential point: Not only was every question—except two—hostile to the refinery concept, but also it was obvious that most of those posing questions had already made

up their minds and were more interested in harassment of the officials on stage than in soliciting answers.

In fact we wonder why the thought did not occur to some of those who were strutting like peacocks and playing to the gallery at the UNH Field House that their performances were being witnessed by a far larger gallery of TV viewers.

THE ONE-SIDED PERFORMANCE CONSTITUTES THE BEST ARGUMENT CONCEIVABLE OF WHY SUCH A MOMENTOUS DECISION, ONE AFECTING THE ENTIRE STATE, CANNOT BE LEFT EXCLUSIVELY IN THE HANDS OF A RELATIVELY SMALL GROUP OF PEOPLE, MANY OF THEM TRANSIENTS, WHO OBVIOUSLY DON'T GIVE A TINKER'S DAMN ABOUT THE BEST INTERESTS OF THE STATE OF NEW HAMPSHIRE.

In just three days, Nancy and SOS would know how effective their campaign over the past several months had been.

28

THE TOWN SPEAKS

On Monday, March 4, as the *New Hampshire Times* reported, "The bombardment began at dawn."[133] When thousands of people throughout New Hampshire opened their morning *Union Leader*, an eight-page supplement fell out. Screaming from the top of the front page, in red, was the headline, "HELP BRING A REFINERY TO NEW HAMPSHIRE!" On the bottom was another headline highlighted in red: "THE ANSWER IS UP TO YOU!! Call your legislator TODAY!"

The same supplement was included in the afternoon editions of the state's other nine daily newspapers. The insert was unsigned, which violated state law, but everybody knew who had paid for it. Just one day before town meetings were to be held across the state, and just three days before the legislative vote, Olympic Refineries was making a final push to convince the state legislature to locate a refinery in Durham.

On the front of the supplement was a photo of Olympic's geodetic model of the refinery in Durham, with two articles underneath—one that reported a *Boston Globe* poll showing majority public support in the state for the project, and the other explaining the reasons "Why N.H. needs the Refinery in Durham." On the inside were numerous additional articles with headlines that hyped the refinery's historical and economic importance: "Refinery Could Create 15,000 Jobs," "A Top Team of Engineers: 'To Be The Cleanest Ever Built,'" "Oil Refinery Hoped to Relieve $50 million Wage-Profit Loss," "Our Golden Opportunity" (authored by Governor Thomson), "Labor Leaders Favor Durham Site," "An Historic Moment," and "*Hampton Union*: Proponents Confident."

In the middle of the insert, under the headline "How You Can Support An Oil Refinery: Call Your Legislator Now!" was a two-page listing of all 424 state legislators—four hundred House members and twenty-four Senators—with their home phone numbers. On the last page was a facsimile of a telegram, dated February 28, 1974, from the head of the Federal Energy Office, William Simon, to Governor Thomson:

> Congratulations on the progress you are making in New Hampshire toward the construction of a refinery in your state. This forward step and the progress with the proposed nuclear generating station will substantially help our country achieve energy independence by 1980, in accord with the president's goals. You may be assured that when your refinery becomes operational, the additional availability of heating oil and gasoline will be of substantial benefit to the citizens of your state and region.

Olympic also had radio ads on all 90 plus New Hampshire stations, except for one that rejected them, because the station manager felt they were so one-sided, refinery opponents should be given equal time.

Reinforcing the Olympic effort, Governor Thomson suggested that the people of New Hampshire could use the town meetings on Tuesday to convey their support for the refinery. Emboldened by the *Boston Globe* poll published a few days earlier, which showed support for construction of a refinery in New Hampshire by a margin of sixty-five percent to nineteen percent, Thomson sent a letter to approximately 220 town moderators across the state asking them "to request an expression of opinion of voters in your community." Though most town meeting agendas had already been finalized, the people of the town could raise issues at the end of a meeting under "other business." At that time, Thomson wrote, he hoped that a town citizen would request that all voters be asked to express their opinion on this question: "Do you favor the construction of an oil refinery in New Hampshire so long as it meets all environmental requirements?" The governor acknowledged that "such a vote, if taken, will not be legally binding on anyone, but would offer an expedient means of obtaining a state-wide referendum to guide your elected representatives in Concord when considering legislation pertaining to the proposed refinery." He went on to say, "I can think of no better time for our citizens to utilize the forum offered by our town meetings to express their feelings about this crucial issue."[134]

• • •

Nancy Sandberg was angry when she saw the Olympic supplement. The whole production was filled with lies and misleading statements, the same prevarications and misrepresentations SOS had been battling since the refinery announcement was first made. The telegram by William Simon was a new one, but it erroneously reinforced the notion that Durham and New Hampshire would get preferred treatment in obtaining heating oil and gasoline. As energy czar, even Simon couldn't change the federal allocation law by fiat. Besides, it was simply inconceivable how a refinery that depended on oil from Arab countries would "substantially help our country achieve energy independence by 1980, in accord with the president's goals." If anything, the Onassis project would weaken efforts to achieve energy independence. And the claim that the refinery would create 15,000 jobs had been rebutted long ago by Jim Horrigan's analysis that the total was more like 1,300. Even the *Globe* poll was misleading. Yes, people may want an oil refinery, but at the expense of Home Rule? The poll didn't ask about that.

Nancy spent the day on the phone, discussing strategy with other SOS board members and with Dudley, and pointing out the distortions in the supplement to the press. Sharon Meeker assured her that for the legislative vote on Wednesday, there would be numerous anti-refinery lobbyists in Concord. Peter Horne from

Rye and several representatives of the fishing industry would be there, as would people representing environmental concerns.

Dudley was aghast at the extent of the advertising effort. It reinforced her worst fear—that Onassis might be able to use his vast wealth to buy approval for his refinery project. She was most concerned that the supplement's misinformation would mislead legislators around the state who hadn't seen all of the evidence published in *Publick Occurrences* that refuted the alleged benefits of the project—the increased jobs, the greater availability of heating oil and gasoline, the financial benefit to the state. And even if the refinery were the "cleanest ever built," it would still be dirty and harmful to the fragile ecosystem in Great Bay.

She also worried that the last-minute push by Onassis might influence some of the citizens of Durham. By now, she suspected, most people had made up their minds, especially after seeing the Olympic presentation the previous Wednesday and Sunday. But the deluge of radio ads and the repetition of lies in the supplement could persuade some town residents that the refinery might not be so bad after all. This was not good. Durham needed a strong statement of rejection.

• • •

Town Meeting Day was on Tuesday, but Durham officials postponed discussion of the oil refinery until the following evening at 7 p.m., so that this day could be devoted to normal business—election of town officials and voting on budget and zoning articles. Polls were open as usual from 8 a.m. until 7 p.m. But throughout the state, town moderators confronted the request by the governor to take their town's pulse about the refinery.

• • •

Wednesday was a legislative day, and Dudley spent most of it in

Concord, lobbying her colleagues, as well as voting on several bills brought before the House. The votes on Speaker Roberts's bill, HB 34, and Dudley's Home Rule bill, HB 18, were not scheduled until Thursday, but Nancy and several SOS board members also spent the day in Concord, arguing their case against the oil refinery to any of the four hundred reps willing to listen. The corridors outside Representatives Hall were teeming with lobbyists from both sides of the refinery issue, the environmental and fishing industry representatives having shown up in force to counter the seemingly ubiquitous Olympic supporters. Outside the State House, radio ads continued to bombard listeners with exhortations to contact their reps to support the refinery. With so many House members, and the ramped-up pressure from Olympic, it was impossible to discern a consensus either in favor or opposed to the project.

• • •

That evening, Durham residents came in droves to the Oyster River High School gymnasium for the second day of the annual town meeting, scheduled for 7 p.m.[135] Cars jammed the parking lot, an overflow extending from the high school back down and then up the road to the middle school. While anyone could attend, only registered voters were given a red voting ID card once their names had been verified on the voter checklist. A long line formed outside the gym, the largest turnout in Durham's history. Fortunately, the weather was unusually warm, temperatures into the fifties. So many people showed up that Town Moderator Joseph Michael requested all non-voters to move into the cafeteria, where loudspeakers had been installed. On stage, the selectmen sat facing the audience, while several media crews surrounded the moderator, who would not allow media coverage until the voters had granted permission. Two rows of tables off to the sides were filled by reporters chatting among themselves. It wasn't until 7:48 p.m. that everyone had been checked and settled, and Michael called the meeting to order.

The tension was palpable, the audience trembling with excitement and expectation.

The moderator announced that several media organizations wanted to cover the proceedings and that he wanted the voters to make the decision. Would they permit coverage by film cameras? If yes, he said, raise your voting ID cards. A sea of hands holding cards shot into the air. Now, if no, raise the voting ID cards. Only a scattered number of hands were raised. He repeated the process for coverage by radio equipment, and for still cameras. In each case, the show of hands indicated overwhelming approval. Microphones and cameras had already been placed on and around the stage, and now they could be activated.

Before getting to the main issue, Michael said, he wanted the voters to be aware of a news release from Pease Air Force Base issued that very day. He introduced Major Pierce and Captain Griswold, who announced that—contrary to the statement by Robert Greene last Wednesday at the Olympic Refineries presentation—Pease had not agreed to allow Olympic pipelines to cross the base. In fact, no one at Pease had even received a request for such authority. While the officials there had been informed that Olympic's plans called for an easement for the pipeline, Olympic representatives had been told they should explore other sites for the pipeline before asking for permission to construct it through the base. Cheers and applause reverberated in the gym as the two officers smiled and left the stage.

Michael announced that the vote on the refinery would be by secret ballot after a motion had been made about the refinery and enough time had been allocated for people to express their views. As moderator, he was exercising his authority to limit the debate to one hour, and he requested that each voter who spoke limit their comments to two minutes. He called for a motion.

Selectman James Chamberlin moved that the Town vote to amend the Durham Zoning Ordinance to permit an oil refinery. Selectman Lawrence O'Connell seconded the motion. The first speaker was Nancy Sandberg.

She read a scathing attack on Olympic Refineries. "Olympic is a company we can't trust. Just last week, we witnessed a presentation that didn't begin to answer our crucial questions. Important issues have been evaded and dodged. They say they will create thousands of jobs. That's not true. They say they will lower our tax rates. That's not true. They say they will build a refinery that's clean as a clinic. We all know that's not true. They admit there will be oil spills and pollutants released into the air. That's not the kind of 'clean' clinic I want to go to! And I am outraged—we should all be outraged— at their attempt to override Home Rule.  Tonight we should make our voices heard loud and clear—No Refinery in Durham!" The audience stood and gave her loud and sustained applause.

Tommy Thompson spoke next, saying that Olympic Refineries had presented plans to the cities and towns of the State for a clean,

safe refinery on Durham Point. "Olympic consultants have demonstrated that they do have the know-how to construct and operate a new type of clean modern refinery located and built in such a manner as to safeguard both our land and sea environments. I urge you to vote on the basis of the known facts, rather than on the basis of emotion or hysteria." Polite applause followed his statement, punctuated by a single loud boo. Michael immediately condemned the rudeness, and the audience reacted to the rebuke with loud applause. No such impropriety occurred again throughout the evening.

In all, twenty-two citizens offered their views about the refinery. Only two besides Tommy Thompson praised the project—one, because he thought it would bring tax relief; the other, because she felt it would bring new jobs. Selectman O'Connell spoke against the motion, which he had seconded only to help get it on the floor for debate. As she approached the microphones, Evelyn Browne received an ovation for her earlier feisty repudiation of the Olympic contract she had signed under false pretenses.

The last speaker was Representative Dudley Dudley, who was greeted with a long round of applause. She compared Durham to the Titanic, which could see only the tip of the Olympic iceberg and faced a more dangerous situation than was visible. She accused the company of concealing the truth about its proposal, just as it had concealed the truth about its intentions when purchasing options on Durham Point. "It keeps changing its mind on how much water it needs, on how many jobs will be created, on whether it has a guaranteed source of oil, on whether Arab countries may actually own part of the company. It either doesn't know what it's doing, or doesn't want us to know. Or maybe both!" She castigated Olympic for "promises that the refinery would not be forced on the community against its will, now retracted and replaced by

a massive advertising and lobbying campaign to override local option. And the Governor supports this effort. We need to send him the strongest message we can that we intend to hold onto our precious tradition of local option—to the limit of our energies."

The audience jumped to its feet with cheers and applause. Abandoning his strict impartiality in the matter, the moderator said to her, "This ovation indicates the town's warm affection for you."

In the next hour, voters obtained paper ballots and deposited them in the ballot box. Once everyone had voted, the ballots were counted while most people remained in the gym. Finally, some two hours after voting had begun, Michael stood before the microphones to announce the results.

"In favor of the motion, 144 votes. Opposed, 1,254 votes."

A thunderous cheer could be heard, some people said, as far away as Concord.

29

CONCORD SPEAKS

The next morning, as Dudley drove to Concord, she heard on the radio that very few towns in the state followed Governor Thomson's request to vote on his specific refinery resolution. She was confused at first, because the day before she saw the headline in the *Union Leader*, "Town Meetings Favor Refinery."[136] As it turned out, the headline was technically correct, but it failed to indicate that almost all the towns who favored the refinery also amended Thomson's resolution to say that no town should be forced to accept a refinery against the will of the citizens. This was definitely good news! Thomson's ploy to rally the troops against Home Rule appeared to have failed.

Also good news was the vote from Rye. Among the several warrants on the town's ballot was Article 4, which asked voters whether to rezone Lunging Island—where Olympic would build its supertanker port—as a single resident district. By an overwhelming margin, the town voted in favor of the warrant, with 1,073 citizens for, and just 194 opposed. North Hampton and Hampton also voted decisively against the oil refinery. With those three neighboring towns opposed, it would be difficult for Onassis to find a location for his pipeline.

Still, Dudley realized that all of those votes could be overturned in Concord. Olympic was not letting up. Radio ads continued to air throughout the state, and pro-refinery lobbyists would be out in force at the State House again today. On a less important, but still infuriating, note was the apparent decision by the *Union Leader* to adopt the Finnegan solution on how to refer to her, so that readers could discern that she was female. The paper's State House reporter, Donn Tibbetts, referred to her in the morning's paper as "Representative Mrs. Thomas Dudley."[137] What Neanderthals! She knew they were trying to get under her skin. And, unfortunately, it was working!

The morning's House agenda was unusually full, leaving little time for lobbyists to buttonhole various representatives in the corridors outside Representatives Hall. And the mood was ebullient, a frisson of excitement not typical of legislative sessions. The House quickly passed bills to establish a Food Grant program, improve a Flat Grant welfare system, approve a bond issue to study reinstituting service from the Boston and Maine Railroad, increase retirement benefits for police and firemen, approve a pay raise for state employees, and authorize hitchhiking. It was as though the reps wanted to rush through all of these bills to get to the main event.

It was time for a long lunch break, the session to resume at 3 p.m. Predictions of the outcome on the refinery issue varied, several legislators suggesting a close vote, others convinced the legislature would bend to the will of the Onassis-Loeb-Thomson triumvirate. Dudley heard that Gratsos viewed the Durham town vote against the refinery as a "little local difficulty," and was confident that the legislature would be immune to local pressure groups. His words: "They've got to vote down this Home Rule nonsense. You can't run a state with every two-horse town able to tell its government to get lost."[138] Marshal Cobleigh, the former Speaker turned Olympic lobbyist, said the vote outcome "looks pretty good." The scale model was back in the State House, where Onassis's men were cornering reps to show them how clean and unobtrusive the refinery would be. Anti-refinery lobbyists were equally plentiful, Nancy Sandberg among them, making their last-minute pitches.

It was just after 3 p.m. when House Speaker James O'Neil banged his gavel for the afternoon session to begin.[139] This was the time of reckoning, when all of the efforts by Dudley and Chris Spirou in the Legislature, by Nancy Sandberg and SOS, by the voters in Durham and Rye and other seacoast towns, would either succeed or fail. Dudley's heart was pounding. The stakes were immense. She wondered whether the House would actually permit Onassis to build the nation's largest oil refinery on Durham Point, four hundred thousand barrels a day, along with a port for supertankers off the Isles of Shoals and pipelines bringing crude oil through Rye—creating an industrial wasteland in southeastern New Hampshire. Would the House really bend to the influence of Onassis's immense wealth, to the bullying tactics of William Loeb and the *Manchester Union Leader,* to the false promises of Governor Meldrim Thomson, or would it listen to thousands of voters across the state?

She sat in her assigned chair, barely able to contain her anxiety, and observed, along with all the other House members and the throngs of spectators in the gallery, Speaker O'Neil turning his gavel over to Deputy House Speaker Kimon Zachos. O'Neil said he intended to take sides on the issue, and thus, by custom, was relinquishing his authority to a representative who would serve as a neutral presiding officer.

At that point, everyone was aware that there were two bills to be considered: HB 34 sponsored by Majority Leader George Roberts, and HB 18 sponsored by Rep. Dudley Dudley. The Roberts bill, to be considered first, would bring any oil refinery proposal under the jurisdiction of the Site Evaluation Committee, but—as currently written—would not affect Home Rule.

HB 34 was officially reported to the House by Representative Elizabeth Greene of Rye, who chaired the Committee on Environment and Agriculture. At that point, as everyone had been expecting, Representative Maurice Read moved to amend the bill to give the Site Evaluation Committee authority to override local ordinances when it considered where to locate "energy production and distribution facilities"—i.e., an oil refinery. If passed, the votes in Durham and Rye would be rendered meaningless.

This was exactly the situation that Dudley had feared right in the beginning, when Thomson first revealed the Onassis proposal—and promised it would not be forced on any town against its wishes.

"Because of the extreme emotionalism being generated on this issue, some key facts are being overlooked," Read said in defense of his amendment. "At no time in the history of this state capitol building have our predecessors in the House been confronted with such a momentous decision. The strength of our country is an abundant supply of energy and now our country's energy foundation is being eroded."

He pointed out that the price of heating oil was soaring and supply dwindling. "Motorists have to wait in long lines for a few gallons of gasoline. Most people want more heating oil and gasoline. They think an oil refinery built locally will help the situation, and they want to take up Aristotle Onassis on his offer." He went on to say that it would be unfair to allow the voters of Durham to keep a refinery out of the state.  "The man or woman waiting in gas lines in Claremont is as much concerned as the one waiting in gas lines in Rye. One of the key points in our democratic system is being challenged." People who believe that Durham and Rye should be allowed to reject the Onassis refinery, he argued, "would substitute the will of the minority for the will of the majority."

Representative Chris Spirou rose to say that the Read Amendment would not only override Home Rule, but would give the Site Evaluation Committee power over local zoning ordinances. "I'm a Greek bearing a message," he said. "If the Read Amendment passes, Olympic could build an oil storage facility in Manchester, and the citizens of Manchester would have nothing to say about it."

As the *New Hampshire Times* later reported, "Ever since the beginning of the Special Session, Chris Spirou has turned all his considerable political talents toward defeat of the Onassis oil importation scheme. Like a wily fox, Spirou has been, it seems, a dozen places at once, bolstering doubtful representatives, filling them full of arguments to justify an anti-refinery vote to the boys in the fire station back home. It is Spirou who has put together the team of speakers who take the microphone today to urge defeat of the Read Amendment. And if the amendment wins, he is prepared to lead a series of parliamentary assaults aimed at amending the amendment to death, even if the maneuvering takes all night. Spirou is the field marshall who carries out the anti-refinery strategy on the House floor today, and his performance is masterful. Hardly a sentence is muttered all afternoon about killing the refinery to save the environment. Instead, it's kill the refinery to save Home Rule."[140]

Other speakers took turns at the microphone. By arrangement with House leadership, there were fifteen speakers in favor of the refinery, fifteen speakers opposed. Supporters cited increased jobs and more availability of heating oil and gasoline. Some reiterated Read's argument that it would be unfair for one or two towns to prevent a project that would benefit the whole state. One speaker even suggested that Durham's opposition was really a class policy intended to prevent blue collars workers from living in the town.

Refinery opponents stressed Home Rule, with Roberts himself saying, "We have never before overridden local zoning for the benefit of a private corporation and we shouldn't do it now."

Speaker O'Neil argued that there was no need for the Read Amendment. "The conditions exist to site an oil refinery in New Hampshire without this amendment."

Then, as the *New Hampshire Times* later reported, "A hush falls over the throng when Dudley Dudley of Durham steps forward to speak. Everyone wants to hear the woman who, almost singlehandedly, may cost one of the richest men in the world more than $2 million he has already sunk into promoting the Durham Point refinery project. Ever since the refinery bombshell burst in New Hampshire last fall, Dudley Dudley has been one jump ahead of Onassis and his New Hampshire operatives. Last December, when she went to Meldrim Thomson's office to present him with a petition containing four thousand names opposed to a refinery on Durham Point, the Supreme Executive Magistrate threw her out of his office. Today Dudley has her revenge. She is the architect of the strategy being played out today."

Dudley felt jittery, but under control. She had prepared and she was now ready. She recited the Read Amendment to the House, paused, and then made her argument. She talked about the long history of the legislature going back some three hundred years. She recounted stories of how the legislators had struggled in the face of Royal opposition to maintain their right to speak for the people, and how that principle of representation had seeped to the local level, to the cities and towns all across the state, and how Home Rule had emerged as a fundamental part of the state's political culture. She denounced the Read Amendment for undermining that culture:[141] "Make no mistake that the effect of this wording is to override the century-old tradition of Home Rule in the State of New Hampshire; that tradition which is the very bedrock of democracy in New Hampshire; that tradition which our Municipal and County Government committee has upheld in its recent deliberation; that tradition which town meetings from Colebrook to Seabrook are carrying forward this week; that tradition which, when challenged, calls the people of New Hampshire to its defense in 1974 as it did in 1776." She then called on the representatives to throw out the foreign invader attempting to build this refinery, just as two hundred years ago the people of New Hampshire threw out King George III. "I want to urge you to vote no on this amendment and ask you to consider your vote on this matter as a positive one—a vote *for* your neighbors and friends, a vote *for* your town, a vote *for* your city—and most of all a vote *for* the maintenance of Home Rule in our whole state from Coos to the sea."

She had barely finished speaking when Representative Tony Smith, a Republican from Hampton, a seacoast town that voted against the refinery on Tuesday, rushed into the Hall and asked the presiding officer to make a special announcement from the governor's office. Deputy Speaker Zachos agreed, and Smith announced that Governor Thomson had just moments ago received a telegram that was important for all to hear. It read as follows: "I can assure you that if New Hampshire had a refinery now, the price of fuel to your consumers could be less and the availability of supply to your people greater than at present. Signed, William E. Simon, Federal Energy Office."

There was a ripple of surprise among the House members. The new telegram was similar in substance to the telegram that had been included in the eight-page supplement Olympic paid all the daily newspapers to include the previous Monday. But the promise of cheaper and more abundant fuel, if New Hampshire had its own refinery, was much more explicit. Dudley was stunned that Simon would make such a statement. She knew it was a lie, plain and simple.

The announcement was timed perfectly. There was no opportunity to rebut the Simon telegram. It had been three hours since Zachos had assumed the duties of presiding officer, and he now called for a voice vote. This implied Zachos expected an overwhelming consensus, which could easily be discerned by how loudly people shouted their preference. Dudley's heart sank. She knew that most people believed the Read Amendment would pass. The call for a voice vote, especially after the last-minute announcement from the governor's office, seemed to confirm the worst.

The hall was quiet again. Zachos's voice boomed, "All those in favor, say aye." The response was deafening. Dudley felt like she had been kicked in the stomach. She saw Chris Spirou's glum face and realized that he, too, saw imminent defeat. They had both heard voice votes in the House before, and whenever one side would produce such a loud response, it meant the overwhelming majority was in favor. There was only so much voice power. The other side could include only a relatively few people.

"All those opposed, say no." A thunderous roar filled the chamber. Dudley was stunned. The look on Spirou's face was instantly transformed to exhilaration.

Zachos called for a standing vote. This allowed a precise count without recording the preference of each member. Standing for the Read Amendment: 121 representatives. Standing against the Read Amendment: 209 representatives.

Pandemonium broke out in the Hall of Representatives. Spectators and reps alike loudly cheered the results. Dudley waved wildly to Nancy and the SOS members in the gallery. Five conservative Republicans called for a roll call, to force each representative to go on the record. Several reps scrambled to leave the Hall, but Zachos ordered all exits locked. Four escaped, and the rest were locked in and forced to vote and be counted.

The new vote produced an even more lopsided result: only 109 supported the Read Amendment; 233 opposed it. The margin in favor of Home Rule increased from 88 votes to 114.

With the defeat of the amendment, it took only a few more minutes to pass the original Roberts bill by voice vote. Minutes after that, HB 18, Dudley's Home Rule bill, was also passed by voice vote.

Home Rule was upheld. Durham was safe.

• • •

Later, Dudley and a small group of her fellow legislators went out to celebrate at an Italian restaurant in Concord. Just as they were seated, Dudley looked across the room and saw a table with many familiar figures. At that moment, they noticed her, rose, and walked over to her table. They were the men from Purvin and Gertz, F.R. Harris, Texas Instruments, Kling Associates—all Onassis consultants. They surrounded the table, looking sternly at Dudley.

Eugene Harlow of F.R. Harris said to Dudley, "We just want to tell you one thing."

She swallowed, knowing what they were going to tell her: The fight wasn't over. There was Newmarket or some other location where Olympic would go. "What?" she said.

"We just want you to know," he said, suddenly smiling, the other men all smiling as well, "that the right side won."

30

IMMEDIATE AFTERMATH

Dudley was convinced that the timing of the House vote, coming after the vote in Durham on Wednesday and the Annual Town Meetings on Tuesday, transformed what probably would have been a close vote on the Read Amendment to a landslide rejection. The last-minute exhortation by Governor Thomson for the towns to express their views on the refinery backfired. Instead of limiting their consideration to whether citizens wanted a refinery, towns throughout the state amended their views about the project with a caveat: no town should be forced to accept a refinery against its will. The expression of support for Home Rule was so widespread, including in Thomson's hometown of Orford, that most representatives simply couldn't avoid paying attention.

The Olympic insert in all the daily newspapers that provided readers with the telephone numbers of all the legislators might have backfired as well. Most of the calls that came in were against forcing a refinery on a town. One rep from Portsmouth claimed to have received 147 calls, all to protect Home Rule.

• • •

William Loeb was furious. At the Legislature. At Durham. At everyone with even a peripheral association with the University of New Hampshire. After having finally gotten his own man as governor, enticed the richest man in the world to propose a refinery in the state, and waged a vigorous fight with all the resources he could muster, the defeat in the House vote was unbearable. His editorial reflected his bitter anger:[142]

> The New Hampshire Legislature has just cast the stupidest vote of its career. It is a vote against progress in the State of New Hampshire.
>
> It is a vote of utter and complete selfishness, disregarding the best interests of the United States, which so desperately needs this new refinery...
>
> The vote at Durham illustrates the intellectual and moral bankruptcy of that campus community.
>
> The vote in the Legislature illustrates how stupid and narrow and selfish legislators can be...
>
> After that vote in the Legislature, this newspaper suggests that perhaps the New Hampshire state motto should be changed from 'Live Free or Die' to 'WHAT'S IN IT FOR ME?'

Governor Thomson apparently was constitutionally unable to understand how people might feel that the refinery would be an environmental blight. Speaking of himself in the third person, he insisted instead that one reason for the rejection "was that the governor was very active in this and his enemies saw an opportunity to discredit him. I think the Democrats saw an opportunity to gang up and tried to throw this down and they succeeded, but it's only a temporary victory. I'm sure the majority of people in our state are looking forward to the progress that we would have here if we had more energy."[143]

• • •

For the first ten days after the vote, the Onassis men were on hold.[144] All talks with other cities and towns were cancelled until Onassis would let the consultants know what he intended. Sometime later, Robert Greene of Purvin and Gertz, and Nicholas Papanicolaou, insisted the refinery project was not dead. The most frequently mentioned town for the refinery's location was Newmarket, which had voted in favor of the refinery and was adjacent to Durham.[145] There was also discussion about Olympic looking to construct a refinery in Rhode Island, or perhaps farther south. However, Nicholas Papanicolaou, now a vice president of Olympic Refineries, reassured refinery supporters that "Olympic hasn't abandoned New Hampshire." He added, "But we have no intention of going through another hassle or taking any more of the abuse we did in Durham."[146] Eventually, however, Olympic made no new efforts to locate a refinery in the state, or in any other state.

• • •

A week after the House vote, Dudley's Home Rule bill was taken up by the Senate's Resources and Environmental Control Committee. In hearings conducted in the seacoast area, the committee agreed to accept Dudley's amendment, which would restore the provisions of her original HB 18—requiring all cities and towns to conduct a vote of the citizens, or of the City Councils, to approve a refinery, regardless of whether zoning regulations already existed. The bill was sent back to the House for approval, and later signed by the governor.[147]

• • •

On April 12, a front-page story in the *Concord Monitor* reported that the last-minute telegram rushed from Governor Thomson's office, to be read by Representative Tony Smith to the House moments before its vote on the refinery, was a fabrication. Representative Kathryn Cushman, a Democrat from Canterbury, had been skeptical of the ploy, and sent a letter to the Federal Energy Office inquiring about the telegram. John W. Weber, assistant administrator, responded in a letter on April 2, 1974: "This is in reference to your letter dated March 10, 1974, pertaining to a telegram allegedly sent on March 7, 1974, to Governor Thomson.

A search of our files fails to disclose any information that the telegram you referred to was sent from this office."[148]

• • •

In the April 19 issue of *Publick Occurrences*, Phyllis Bennett finally allowed her name to be listed on the masthead as the newspaper's publisher.

The April 19 issue was also the last time that Shaunna McDuffee was listed on the masthead under "Production." The next week, she moved on to help Steve establish his own local weekly in Conway.

That spring, *Publick Occurrences* was nominated for a Pulitzer Prize, as was the paper's cartoonist, Bob Nilson.

Phyllis continued to consult with Ray Belles about the financial condition of the paper, and discovered that they shared much in common. They had subsequent meetings with John Taylor of the Boston Globe, who provided additional funds for the "most enterprising paper in New Hampshire."

• • •

In Durham, at the last session of its annual town meeting on the Saturday after the refinery vote, Article 40 was passed by an enthusiastic voice vote:

> Be it resolved that the 1974 Town Meeting of Durham expresses gratitude to those who turned back the mortal threat of Olympic Oil to the town: SOS (Save Our Shores) for mobilizing thousands of citizens in Durham and surrounding towns; the newspaper *Publick Occurrences,* for investigative journalism; the Durham Selectmen for manning the zoning and home rule defenses; Channel 11 ETV for televising to the entire state the Selectmen's two four-hour hearings for the refinery proponents; and, during the battle, those who provided inspired leadership—Evelyn Browne, Dudley Dudley,

and Nancy Sandberg; and that a copy of this resolution signed by the Town Clerk be sent to the named institutions and individuals.[149]

EPILOGUE

NANCY SANDBERG

Following the victory in the battle for Home Rule, under Nancy's leadership, SOS received a federal grant to run a year-long seacoast communities education program that focused on regional solutions for shared problems such as solid waste, water quality, energy alternatives, and public transportation.

Nancy's personal interests and education had always concentrated on American History and Material Culture. In 1979, she started her own business specializing in eighteenth and nineteenth century interior design. Over the next thirty years, she provided historically appropriate furnishings, fabrics, wall-coverings, hardware, and lighting fixtures to museums, historic homes, and businesses. For thirteen years she served on the Wentworth-Coolidge Commission to furnish and interpret the home of Provincial Governor Benning Wentworth.

As for the apple orchard she and Mal had started, they harvested ten varieties of apples and sold them out of their barn for a dozen years. Eventually, they found competing with the deer for the apples was a losing proposition, and turned their attention to other work.

Over the years Nancy's concerns for the Durham community

led her to participate on three different Master Planning committees, spend nine years on the Historic District Commission, and three years on the Zoning Board of Adjustment.

Since retiring she's worked with the Durham Historic Association (DHA) as President and, separately, as Curator of the DHA museum, where she is currently reorganizing the collection into eight periods that reflect four hundred years of Durham's history.

DUDLEY DUDLEY

Dudley was re-elected to the New Hampshire House of Representatives in 1974 and 1976. In 1978, she was elected to the five-member Governor's Executive Council, making her the highest-ranking woman who had ever held elective office in New Hampshire's history.

In 1984, she ran for the US House of Representatives from the First Congressional District, but was defeated and did not run for public office again. Nevertheless, she remained active in the State Democratic Committee and was made a lifetime member in 1997.

For eleven years she was executive director of the Women Legislators Lobby, dedicated to reducing US expenditures for weaponry and ending the nuclear arms race. She continued to be a political activist, opposing the nuclear power plant in Seabrook; working to reunite the parents of a Congolese family, whose children were refugees in Uganda; directing the First Congressional District office for Carol Shea-Porter in her first term; and endorsing Bernie Sanders in his quest for the presidency.

She served on numerous non-profit boards and received several awards for her service, including the University of New Hampshire's highest recognition for a citizen, the Granite State

Award for "outstanding contributions to the state," and the New Hampshire Democratic Party's Eleanor Roosevelt Award for her lifetime in politics and community service.

In 2016, on the fortieth anniversary of her election to the Governor's Executive Council, her portrait was unveiled in the Governor's Executive Council Chambers—where she had been photographed holding four thousand anti-refinery petitions underneath the painting of Thomas Dudley, shortly before being thrown out of the governor's office.

When first informed about the possibility of her portrait being hung in the Council Chambers, she thought it was too "pretentious." But Ray Buckley, the State Democratic Party Chair, persuaded her when he told her that as a young boy he had been inspired by the images of the male leaders, and he believed that "Every fourth-grade girl should walk in these halls and see the amazing women who have served their state."

PHYLLIS BENNETT

In the year after the battle for Home Rule, Phyllis moved into Durham and continued to consult with Ray Belles, their relationship blossoming into a forty-year partnership and marriage. Together they sought funding and creative ways to keep *Publick Occurrences* financially solvent.

Phyllis continued publishing *Publick Occurrences* until April 1975. It was a difficult time for small newspapers, and she could no longer afford to continue. Support from *The Boston Globe* dried up, because that paper, too, was facing financial difficulties and had to streamline its operation.

For the next four years, she worked at the newly formed

New Hampshire Humanities Council. In 1979, she joined the University of New Hampshire as the Associate Vice President in charge of University Relations, guiding that office for eight presidents over a twenty-three-year period.

She was a quiet power in state politics, working as a trusted advisor in both formal and informal capacities, and on countless political campaigns. She and Dudley became especially good friends, both of them highly involved in progressive causes. And, with their husbands, they loved sailing together on the very Great Bay that they had both helped to preserve.

In my interviews with Phyllis, she admitted she still harbored feelings of betrayal for Steve's leaving her in 1973, but she also recognized that he had stayed with Shaunna until he died, and that he had found love with her. The heart, she acknowledged, had a will of its own. She, too, had found love with Ray.

On July 21, 2015, after a bout of pneumonia, she was driving back to Durham from Manchester when she slowly drove off to the side of the road and died. A big hole was left in the hearts of everyone who knew her.

FORTIETH ANNIVERSARY MEMORIAL BENCH

In the fall of 2014, the fortieth anniversary of the defeat of the Onassis oil refinery, a granite bench was constructed to memorialize the town's battle for Home Rule, to be located on Durham's Wagon Hill Farm overlooking the Oyster River. On the bench are carved the words, "March 1974 Durham Says NO To Olympic Oil Refinery." J. Dennis Robinson,[150] an occasional contributor to *Publick Occurrences* and one of Phyllis's long-time friends, took a photo of the three heroes of the battle: Nancy Sandberg, Phyllis Bennett, and Dudley Dudley. The bench was the brainchild of Ed Valena, husband of the former Dale Rollinsford, one of the young women who had placed signs in the snow saying Ari Go Home.

ARISTOTLE ONASSIS

The December visit by the Greek shipping magnate was, according to John Meyer, one of the Onassis men, "a screw-up from beginning to end. Ari wasn't properly briefed, except for one ass-brained joke about the Governor's homemade syrup, which was meant to defuse the question of why we'd been buying up land secretly. Nobody bothered to talk strategy for the question-and-answer session with him, and even if they had, his consultant team was so unprepared it was unbelievable."[151]

Despite the disastrous visit, Onassis was not about to give up. As his biographer reported, in January and February, as the Olympic consultants prepared for their presentation to Durham and then for the House vote, Onassis was constantly on the phone to Gratsos, to Loeb, and to Governor Thomson, "kickin' ass."[152] Loeb told reporters that Onassis "wanted to hire the biggest law firm in New Hampshire. 'They have fourteen partners,' he'd say. 'They must be the best.'"[153] It was no doubt in response to Onassis's continual pressure that Gratsos hired Marshall Cobleigh and William Craig, and Loeb tried to get Chris Spirou to give up his political career to join Olympic. And it was that aggressive push that led to the final media blitz in the days before the House vote, which backfired.

After the House vote, which upheld Home Rule, almost everyone expected Olympic to continue with its efforts to locate a refinery in New Hampshire, and if not there, then in some other state. But Onassis was tired and had lost his enthusiasm for building his own refinery. Still contemplating divorce, and shifting his attention to his daughter Christina and problems he was having with Olympic Airways, he ordered his associates to abandon the refinery project. By the fall of 1974, he and Jackie were both consulting divorce lawyers. In December 1974, he caught the flu and later suffered from gallstones.[154]

On March 15, 1975 after a five-week hospital stay, he died—one year and one week after his hopes to build a refinery in Durham were dashed.

PHOTO CREDITS

Front cover	Bernie Casey
Back cover	Bob LaPree
Back cover	Meredith Bennett
Back cover	*Publick Occurrences* (*PO*)—Ray Belles
1	*PO*
10	Meredith Bennett
18	*PO*
33	Bob Nilson for *PO*
38	Bob Nilson for *PO*
44	Bob LaPree
55	Bob LaPree
87	*PO*
98	Ken Williams, *Concord Monitor*
101	*PO*
112	*PO*
122	*PO*
125	Bob LaPree
136	George Burke for *PO*
141	*PO*
142	*PO*
148	*PO*
156	*PO*
157	George Burke for *PO*
163	Bob Nilson for *PO*
166	Bob LaPree
175	*PO*
187	*PO*
181–184	Image and article reproduced with permission of Forbes Media, LLC 2018
190	*PO*

NOTES

1. Quoted and elaborated from "The Battle for Durham Point," *YouTube*. https://www.youtube.com/watch?v=vuruQX0VsvE. The elaboration is the sentence I added about the underappreciated leadership role of women.

2. Richard Nixon, *Radio Message About the State of the Union Message on Natural Resources and the Environment* (February 14, 1973), American Presidency Project, http://www.presidency.ucsb.edu/ws/index.php?pid=4101.

3. Unless otherwise noted, information about Onassis's life comes from Peter Evans, *Ari: The Life and Times of Aristotle Onassis* (New York: Charter Books, 1988).

4. Premise of the 1988 movie, *The Richest Man in the World* (http://www.imdb.com/title/tt0095780/), based on the writing of Peter Evans, Jacqueline Feather, and David Seidler.

5. Nicholas Fraser, Philip Jacobson, Mark Ottaway, and Lewis Chester, *Aristotle Onassis* (New York and Philadelphia: J.B. Lippincott Company, 1977), 338-39.

6. Ibid., 263-278, 297; and Peter Evans, *Nemesis: Aristotle Onassis, Jackie O, and the Love Triangle That Brought Down the Kennedys* (New York: ReganBooks, 2005), 150-170.

7. Fraser et al, *Aristotle Onassis*, 340.

8. Evans, *Ari,* 288.

9. Fraser et al, *Aristotle Onassis*, 340.

10. Ibid., 340-341.

11. Ibid., 341.

12. Leon W. Anderson, *To This Day: the 300 years of the New Hampshire legislature* (Canaan, NH: Phoenix Publishing, 1981), 25.

13. Anderson, *To This Day*, 75.

14. See the website of the State of New Hampshire (http://www.gen-court.state.nh.us/house/abouthouse/housefacts.htm).

15. Evans, *Nemesis*, 233.

16. Ibid., 268.

17. Ron Lewis, "Real Estate Blitz on Durham Point," *Publick Occurrences* (Newmarket, NH), Oct. 5, 1973.

18. This account was later published in "How Durham Point was taken," *Publick Occurrences* (Newmarket, NH), Dec. 14, 1973.

19. *Publick Occurrences* (Newmarket, NH), Oct. 5, 1973.

20. Tom Dudley, *My Life on Boats, Vol. I*, (self-pub, 2014), 24.

21. D. Allan Kerr, "1969 incarceration of black Marines drew Seacoast protests," *Seacoastonline.com*, Feb. 8, 2015, http://www.seacoaston-line.com/article/20150208/NEWS/150209335.

22. Tom Dudley, *My Life on Boats*, 58-59.

23. "A Bit of Naval Shipyard history…," *Fosters Daily Democrat* (Dover, NH), Dec. 17, 2014, http://www.fosters.com/article/20141217/GJOPINION_0102/141219515. See also, D. Allan Kerr, "1969 incarceration of black Marines drew Seacoast protests," *Seacoastonline.com*, Feb. 8, 2015, http://www.seacoastonline.com/article/20150208/NEWS/150209335. Photo comes from Tom Dudley, *My Life on Boats*, 58.

24. Tom Dudley, *My Life on Boats*, 59.

25. "The Circumstances of Public Affairs," *Publick Occurrences* (Newmarket, NH), Nov. 30, 1973.

26. *Publick Occurrences* (Newmarket, NH), Nov. 23, 1973.

27. "I couldn't think of a worse place to put it," *Publick Occurrences* (Newmarket, NH), Nov. 30, 1973.

28. *Publick Occurrences* (Newmarket, NH), Nov. 30, 1973.

29. Ibid.

30. Unless otherwise indicated, all of the information in this chapter comes from Kevin Cash, *Who the Hell is William Loeb?*.

31. "William Loeb, 75, Controversial Newspaper Publisher, Dies," *Washington Post* (Washington, DC), Sept. 14, 1981.

32. Cash, *Who the Hell is William Loeb?*, 52.

33. Ibid., 110.

34. Ibid., 307-308.

35. Information about Meldrim Thomson comes from the following: Cash, *Who the Hell is William Loeb?*, 264; obituaries in the *New*

York Times and the *Washington Post,* April 20, 2001; "Meldrim Thomson, Jr.," *Wikipedia,* https://en.wikipedia.org/wiki/Meldrim_Thomson_Jr. and "Gale Thomson," *Wikipedia,* https://en.wikipedia.org/wiki/Gale_Thomson.

36. All information about the elections comes from Cash, *Who the Hell is William Loeb?*.

37. Ibid., 214-15

38. Donald R. Dwight, "Meldrim Thomson, 89, Dies; Governed New Hampshire," *New York Times* (New York, NY), April 20, 2001.

39. See Cash, *Who the Hell is William Loeb?*, 374, and the obituaries in the *New York Times* and *Washington Post*, April 20, 2001. See also Gerry Nadel, "The Score from New Hampshire: Democracy 1, Aristotle 0," *Esquire* (New York, NY), July 1974.

40. "Former N.H. Gov. Meldrim Thomson hospitalized," United Press International, Aug. 24, 1991.

41. Nadel, "The Score from New Hampshire: Democracy 1, Aristotle 0," 185.

42. See Cash, *Who the Hell is William Loeb?*, 374.

43. Information about the meeting can be found in: "Refinery Details Asked," *Concord Monitor* (Concord, NH), Nov. 30, 1973; "Refinery Foes in Uproar: Local Officials Show Disgust, Leave Meeting," *Manchester Union Leader* (Manchester, NH), Nov. 30, 1973; "Oil Refinery Proponents Face A Tough Selling Job," *The Nashua Telegraph* (Nashua, NH), Nov. 30, 1973.

44. Most of the information about the activity on this day comes from "Trying to Do Good in New Hampshire," *Publick Occurrences* (Newmarket, NH), Dec. 7, 1973, 11-12. Information about the hike around the Adams Point Wildlife Management Area is found on the website: http://www.hikenewengland.com/AdamsPointGen1.html.

45. Author's note: I spoke with the Jackson Estuarine Laboratory Director, Arthur Mathieson, in the fall of 2016 about the visit. He has no record of what he said to the group, but said that in general he would have given them a history of the research that had been done there and he would have addressed the problems that an oil spill would have had on the ecosystem. I have reconstructed that presentation based on information that is relevant to the subjects he covered. The sources of information I used are: W. Jeffrey Bolster, ed., *Cross-Grained & Wily Waters: A Guide to the Piscataqua*

Maritime Region (Portsmouth, NH: Peter E. Randall, Publisher, 2002); UNH websites devoted to the Jackson Lab (http://marine. unh.edu/historical-timeline and http://marine.unh.edu/facility/ jackson-estuarine-laboratory); and a state website about Adams Point (http://www.wildlife.state.nh.us/maps/wma/adams-point.html).

46. "Great Bay," *Wikipedia,* https://en.wikipedia.org/wiki/ Great_Bay_New_Hampshire.

47. "Peter Booras: Trying to do good in New Hampshire," *Publick Occurrences* (Newmarket, NH), Dec. 7, 1973, 11-12.

48. Jay M. Smith, "700 meet in Durham; explore the problem," *Publick Occurrences* (Newmarket, NH), Dec. 7, 1973, 13.

49. This chapter is based on information from interviews with Dudley Dudley; "Refinery Spawns New Controversy," Associated Press, in *Concord Monitor* (Concord, NH), Dec. 18, 1973; Gerry Nadel, "The Score from New Hampshire: Democracy 1, Aristotle 0," *Esquire,* July 1974. Photo of Dudley Dudley is from *Concord Monitor* article, unattributed.

50. Associated Press photo.

51. "Refinery Spawns New Controversy," Associated Press, in *Concord Monitor* (Concord, NH), Dec. 18, 1973.

52. "An appeal to Gratsos—and his answer," *Publick Occurrences* (Newmarket, NH), Dec. 14, 1973.

53. Katherine Wheeler meant to write 2,500 to 10,000. Perhaps she did and the paper got the number wrong. Or perhaps she made the mistake.

54. Photo of Phyllis Bennett provided by Meredith Bennett.

55. "Olympic not yet a company," *Publick Occurrences* (Newmarket, NH), Dec. 14, 1973.

56. "Thomson, Winn swap letters," *Publick Occurrences* (Newmarket, NH), Dec. 14, 1973.

57. "Death Penalty, Refinery Bills Undergo Hearing," *Manchester Union Leader* (Manchester, NH), Dec. 14, 1973.

58. "Onassis Here Today," *Manchester Union Leader* (Manchester, NH), Dec. 19, 1973.

59. Evans, *Ari,* 285-86.

60. Ibid., 38-39.

61. Ibid., 43.

62. Ibid., 45.

63. Ibid., 139.

64. Elizabeth Grice, "Aristotle Onassis's yacht was a floating Xanadu that seduced them all," *The Telegraph* (London, UK), July 5, 2013, http://www.telegraph.co.uk/news/celebritynews/10162341/Aristotle-Onassiss-yacht-was-a-floating-Xanadu-that-seduced-them-all.html.

65. Evans, *Nemesis*, 1-9, 21.

66. Evans, *Nemesis*, 1-9, 21; Evans, *Ari*, 147-48.

67. Evans, *Nemesis*, 22-23.

68. Evans, *Ari*, 157.

69. Ibid., 160.

70. Evans, *Nemesis*, 38-39.

71. Ibid., 55-63.

72. Ibid., 62.

73. Ibid., 66-67.

74. Ibid., 76.

75. Ibid., 94-105.

76. Ibid., 114-132.

77. Ibid., 233.

78. Ibid., 208.

79. Ibid., 233.

80. Evans, *Ari*, 230-31.

81. Ibid., 266-67.

82. Ibid., 232, 252-53.

83. Ibid., 279.

84. Stuart M. Speiser, *The Deadly Sins of Aristotle Onassis* (Ozark, AL: ACW Press, 2005), 252-253.

85. Evans, *Ari*, 291.

86. Davis, 197.

87. Fraser et al, *Aristotle Onassis*, 351.

88. Ibid.

89. Evans, *Ari*, 289.

90. See Chapter 13 of this book.

91. Fraser et al, *Aristotle Onassis*, 345.

92. Information about this event comes from interviews with Dudley Dudley and Nancy Sandberg. It also comes from "Nancy Fails, Dudley Fumes, Tommy Beams and the Band Plays On," *Fosters Daily Democrat* (Dover, NH), Dec. 20, 1973; and "Onassis Visits N.H. Sites: Offers Clean Refinery," *Manchester Union Leader* (Manchester, NH), Dec. 20, 1973.

93. For a detailed record of the press conference, see "Text of Olympic Refineries-Onassis press conference in Bedford," *Publick Occurrences* (Newmarket, NH), Dec. 21, 1973, 12-13. See also, Gerry Nadel, "The Score from New Hampshire: Democracy 1, Aristotle 0," *Esquire* (New York, NY), July 1974.

94. Fraser et al, *Aristotle Onassis,* 345.

95. This anecdote comes from personal interviews with Dudley Dudley.

96. Fraser et al, *Aristotle Onassis,* 345.

97. Published later in an article, "SOS says no to Ari," *Publick Occurrences* (Newmarket, NH), Jan. 4, 1974.

98. "Selectmen-in-Waiting," *Publick Occurrences* (Newmarket, NH), Dec. 21, 1973.

99. Photo of Onassis in center, and to his left Governor Thomson and William Loeb, by George Naum, *Manchester Union Leader* (Manchester, NH), Dec. 20, 1973.

100. *Publick Occurrences* (Newmarket, NH), Jan. 4, 1974.

101. "A study of the economic implications of an oil refinery on a town," *Publick Occurrences* (Newmarket, NH), Dec. 14, 1973.

102. "The tax value of an oil refinery," *Publick Occurrences* (Newmarket, NH), Jan. 4, 1974.

103. Photo comes from *The Portsmouth Herald* (Portsmouth, NH), Jan. 14, 1974.

104. "Selectmen given petition by SOS committee," *Publick Occurrences* (Newmarket, NH), Jan. 11, 1974.

105. "Refinery tax boon—'myth'," *Publick Occurrences* (Newmarket, NH), Jan. 18, 1974.

106. "A case against the refinery as a tax benefit," *Publick Occurrences* (Newmarket, NH), Jan. 18, 1974.

107. Ibid.

108. Quoted in "O'Connell's dissent," *Publick Occurrences* (Newmarket, NH), Jan. 18, 1974.

109. This account of the Rye town meeting is a compilation of information from "Olympic spokesman to face Rye citizens," *Publick Occurrences* (Newmarket, NH), Jan. 18, 1974; "Few Olympic facts for Rye," *Publick Occurrences* (Newmarket, NH), Jan. 25, 1974; "Fisherman oppose oil on coast," *Publick Occurrences* (Newmarket, NH), Jan. 25, 1974; Lisa Moll, *Rye's Battle of the Century: Saving the New Hampshire Seacoast from Olympic Oil* (Rye Historical Society,

2016); and Gerry Nadel, "The Score from New Hampshire: Democracy 1, Aristotle 0," *Esquire* (New York, NY), July 1974.

110. Gerry Nadel, "The Score from New Hampshire: Democracy 1, Aristotle 0," *Esquire* (New York, NY), July 1974.

111. Ibid.

112. *Harper's,* Oct. 1970.

113. The information in this chapter comes primarily from an interview with Chris Spirou on Sept. 12, 2016. Photo by Robert LaPree, published in "Special session diary: Onassis refinery defeated, Home Rule stands," *New Hampshire Times,* Mar. 13, 1974.

114. "The Taking of Lunging Island," *Publick Occurrences* (Newmarket, NH), Feb. 1, 1974.

115. "Getting it together," *Publick Occurrences* (Newmarket, NH), Feb. 8, 1974.

116. Daniel Ford, "Durham, Onassis, and Oil," *Boston Globe Sunday Magazine* (Boston, MA), Jan. 20, 1974.

117. *Publick Occurrences* (Newmarket, NH), Feb. 8, 1974.

118. See "300 at Durham SOS meeting," *Publick Occurrences* (Newmarket, NH), Feb. 22, 1974. Photo by Judy Jarvis. Nancy Sandberg is in the front row, middle right, by herself.

119. "One family still holding out," *Publick Occurrences* (Newmarket, NH), Feb. 15, 1974.

120. "Refinery Model Unveiled at Capitol—To Be Shown Late in Week at Durham," *Manchester Union Leader* (Manchester, NH), Feb. 26, 1974.

121. "Viewers Praise Refiner Model," *Manchester Union Leader* (Manchester, NH), Feb. 26, 1974. See also "Rock Endorses Refinery Effort," ibid.

122. Information about Dudley's thoughts comes from "Dudley Dudley: a sense of community," *Publick Occurrences* (Newmarket, NH), Mar. 1, 1974, and from her personal notes that she used to give presentations about the events that happened during the Onassis oil refinery controversy.

123. "Dudley Dudley: a sense of community," *Publick Occurrences* (Newmarket, NH), Mar. 1, 1974.

124. Gerry Nadel, "The Score from New Hampshire: Democracy 1, Aristotle 0," *Esquire* (New York, NY), July 1974.

125. The quotation comes from personal conversations with Dudley Dudley, October 2016.

126. The information about the hearing comes from several sources: Gerry Nadel, "The Score from New Hampshire: Democracy 1, Aristotle 0," *Esquire* (New York, NY), July 1974; from "Dudley Dudley: a sense of community," *Publick Occurrences* (Newmarket, NH), Mar. 1, 1974; "Issue of Home Rule Dominates Hearing," *Manchester Union Leader* (Manchester, NH), Feb. 28, 1974; Kevin Cash, *Who the Hell is William Loeb?*, 399-400; "House Fight Set On Refinery Vote," *Concord Monitor* (Concord, NH), Mar. 1, 1974.

127. "Dudley Dudley: a sense of community," *Publick Occurrences* (Newmarket, NH), Mar. 1, 1974.

128. Gerry Nadel, "The Score from New Hampshire: Democracy 1, Aristotle 0," *Esquire* (New York, NY), July 1974.

129. Information about the Olympic Refineries Presentation is based on: Nadel, "The Score from New Hampshire: Democracy 1, Aristotle 0," *Esquire* (New York, NY), July 1974; "Olympic Answers Durham's Questions," *Publick Occurrences* (Newmarket, NH), Mar. 1, 1974; Cash, *Who the Hell is William Loeb?*, 400; "700 Attend Olympic Hearing," *The Portsmouth Herald* (Portsmouth, NH), Feb. 28, 1974; "Refinery Plans Presented," *Manchester Union Leader* (Manchester, NH), Feb. 28, 1974.

130. Photo is by *Portsmouth Herald* staff, Feb. 28, 1974.

131. "Plans unsatisfactory to Durham," *Publick Occurrences* (Newmarket, NH), Mar. 8, 1974.

132. "Good Show!" editorial in the *Manchester Union Leader* (Manchester, NH), Mar. 1, 1974.

133. Information about the Olympic Refineries advertising efforts on March 4, 1974, comes from "Special Session Diary: New Hampshire Refinery Defeated, Home Rule Stands," *New Hampshire Times*, Mar. 13, 1974; and from the supplement itself, which was archived with the *Manchester Union Leader* (Manchester, NH), Mar. 4, 1974.

134. See "Thomson Urges Refinery Query in Town Meetings," *Manchester Union Leader* (Manchester, NH), Mar. 4, 1974, and "Special Session Diary: New Hampshire Refinery Defeated, Home Rule Stands," *New Hampshire Times*, Mar. 13, 1974.

135. Information about the 1974 Durham Town Meeting comes from the minutes of the meeting (https://www.ci.durham.nh.us/sites/default/files/fileattachments/community/page/21531/1974_

durham_town_meeting_minutes.pdf) and from "Twelve Hundred Times 'No'," *Publick Occurrences* (Newmarket, NH), Mar. 8, 1974.

136. *Manchester Union Leader* (Manchester, NH), Mar. 6, 1974.

137. "Oil Refinery, Home Rule On Line Today," *Manchester Union Leader* (Manchester, NH), Mar. 7, 1974.

138. Evans, *Ari*, 295.

139. The description of the House session dealing with HB 34 and with HB 18 comes primarily from "Special session diary: Onassis refinery defeated, Home Rule stands," *New Hampshire Times,* Mar. 13, 1974. Other sources include "House Deals Blow to Refinery, Supports N. H. Town Rule," *Concord Monitor* (Concord, NH), Mar. 8, 1974.

140. Photo of Chris Spirou by Robert LaPre in *New Hampshire Times,* Mar. 13, 1974.

141. Dudley's words come from Cash, *Who the Hell is William Loeb?,* 401.

142. Cash, *Who the Hell is William Loeb?,* 402.

143. "Thomson Still For Refinery," *Manchester Union Leader* (Manchester, NH), Mar. 13, 1974.

144. "Talks Cancelled," *Concord Monitor* (Concord, NH), Mar. 9, 1974.

145. "Newmarket Site Eyed By Olympic," *Concord Monitor* (Concord, NH), Mar. 9, 1974.

146. "State Remains First Choice, Olympic Insists," *New Hampshire Sunday News* [Sunday edition of the *Manchester Union Leader*.] (Manchester, NH), Mar. 10, 1974.

147. "Rep. Dudley Proposes New 'Home Rule' Bill," *Manchester Union Leader* (Manchester, NH), Mar. 14, 1974.

148. Cash, *Who the Hell is William Loeb?,* 403-404.

149. "Anti-refinery efforts get praise," *Publick Occurrences* (Newmarket, NH), Mar. 15, 1974.

150 Books by J. Dennis Robinson can be found at https://www.amazon.com/J.-Dennis-Robinson/e/B001HCWTYA/ref=dp_byline_cont_book_1.

151. Evans, *Ari*, 290.

152. Ibid., 291.

153. Fraser et al, *Aristotle Onassis,* 346.

154. Gage, 342-344.

INDEX

A

Adams Point, 72, 76, 77
Ambler Acres, Pappademus's interest in buying, 7
Appledore Island, Marine Zoological Laboratory on, 78
Article 40, passage of, 237–238

B

Baker, Kit, 152–153
Baudet, Norman, 191
Baudet, Wilfred, 191
Baudet family, 191, 209–210
Beckett, John, at SOS meeting, 188
Beckwith, Marion, 6–7, 79, 85
Belhumer, Mr., efforts to purchase land and, 7
Belles, Ray
  Bennett, Phyllis, and, 159, 160–161, 237, 241, 242
  Publick Occurrences and, 180, 185
Bennett, Meredith, 10, 36, 90, 92, 138
Bennett, Patrick, 10, 36, 90, 92, 138
Bennett, Phyllis, 241–242
  Belles, Ray and, 159, 160–161, 237, 241, 242
  on Bennett, Steve as publisher, 163
  breakup of marriage and, 12, 13–14, 43, 90–92, 94, 95, 100
  on building of oil refinery, 41–42, 138
  death of, 242
  Fortieth Anniversary Memorial Bench and, 242
  founding of Publick Occurrences and, 15, 47. 10–11
  friendship with Dudley, Dudley Webster, 242
  hiring of Levine, Dick, and, 12, 13
  Home Rule and, 241
  on land purchase, 15–17
  marriage to Bennett, Steve, 137–138
  New Hampshire Humanities Council and, 241–242
  on Nilson, Bob's cartoons, 38
  Publick Occurrences and, 12, 13–14, 36, 92–95, 135, 185, 237
  as publisher of Publick Occurrences, 93, 95, 158, 161–165, 237, 241, 242
  Taylor, John I and, 180, 184, 237
  at University of New Hampshire, 242
  work at Baltimore Sun, 12
Bennett, Stephen, 180
  assassination of King, Martin Luther, Jr., and, 104, 105–106
  breakup of marriage and, 12, 13–14, 43, 90–91, 94, 95, 100
  death of, 242
  establishment of weekly paper in Conway., 237
  marriage to Bennett, Phyllis, 137–138
  Publick Occurrences and, 10–11, 12, 15, 36, 43, 47, 93, 94–95, 160–161

standards of integrity and, 136–137
work at *Baltimore Sun,* 12
work at weekly paper in North
 Conway, 163
Bernier, Phil, 143
Black Panthers, 21
Bonasis, Joseph J., 68, 210
Bonner, Tom, 53–54
Booras, Chris, 7, 85
Booras, Peter, xii, xiii
 on deep-water port and, 156–157
 Durham Point and, 70
 land purchases and, 4, 6, 38, 174
 oil refinery and, 69, 80–83, 200,
  205, 206
 Olympic Refineries and, 68, 69, 73,
  152, 153, 154, 194
 at open forum, 68–69, 73
 at Rye meeting, 154–155
 violations of election laws and, 205
Boston and Maine Railroad, 227
The Boston Globe, New Hampshire
 edition of, 185
The Boston Globe Publick Occurrences,
 185, 218–219, 241
The Boston Globe Sunday Magazine, oil
 refinery controversy in, 180
Bridges, Styles, 56, 57–58
Browne, Evelyn
 construction of anti-refinery
  messages on property of, 122–123
 at Olympic Refineries presentation,
  209–210
 passage of Article 40 and, 237
 refusal to sell "Salty" and, 6–7, 16,
  79, 209–210
Buckley, Ray, 241
Burke, George, 136
Burlington Daily News, 50

C

Callas, Maria, 116–117, 119, 120
Cash, Kevin, 47, 50, 54, 56
Chamberlin, James, 68, 69
 economic impact report and, 149

Onassis, Aristotle, and, 129–130
 on SOS, 147
 zoning ordinances and, 40, 223
Chase, Malcolm, 68
 land sales and, 16, 40–41
 as member of Board of Selectmen, 164
 Olympic Refineries presentation and,
  176–177
Christina (Onassis ship), 114–115,
 116, 117–118
Churchill, Winston, 116
Cleveland, James, censure Loeb,
 William, III, and, 53
Cobleigh, Marshall, 167, 197, 227, 243
Cocheco River, 23, 76
Cochrane, Alex
 as chair of Financial Committee of
  SOS, 29, 144
 land purchase and, 16
 as member of SOS, 144
Concerned Citizens of Rye, 150,
 201–202
Concord, New Hampshire, Olympic
 Refineries and, 226–233
Concord Monitor, 15, 61, 63, 65
Congdon, Jeannette
 Legal and Regulatory Committee
  and, 29
 research on New Hampshire tax
  laws, 145
 SOS meetings and, 28, 144
Congdon, Robert
 attempted land purchase and, 16
 SOS organization meeting and, 28
Coutermarsh, Ernest, support for
 refinery, 194, 197
Craig, William, 197, 202, 243
Crime Commission, Crowley, Roger, as
 director of, 195
Croesus, 181, 183
Curtis, Cass, as vice chairman of SOS,
 28, 144
Cushman, Kathryn, Olympic Refineries
 and, 236

D

Daniels, George, 20–21
Davenport, Walter, xiv–xv
Declaration of Independence (1776),
    signing of, xiv
Department of Resources and
    Economic Development (DRED),
    state report on new jobs created by
    oil refinery, 188
de Seversky, Alexander P., 131
DiMambro, Arna, 29
DiMambro, Arthur, 29
DiMambro, Celeste
    fight against oil refinery and,
        122–123, 145–147
    as member of SOS, 144, 145, 190
    Olympic Refineries presentation and,
        208, 215
    Outreach Committee and, 29, 144
    as vice chairman of SOS, 144, 145
DiMambro, Thea, 29
Douglas, Charles, 63
    on Home Rule, 202
    opposition to refinery and, 139
    power plant siting law and, 63,
        66–67
    testimony of, 203
Dudley, Becky, 20
Dudley, Dudley Webster, 240–241
    anti-refinery petitions and, 96–99, 128
    anxiousness of, 196
    campaign for state legislature, 22
    committee testimony of, 109, 196–197
    at Concord hearing, 200
    Concord's response to Olympic
        Refineries and, 226–227
    directing of First Congressional
        District office of Shea-Porter,
        Carol, 240
    at Durham Town Meeting, 224–225
    education of, 19
    election to Governor's Executive
        Council, 240
    establishing anti-pollution laboratory at
        University of New Hampshire, 126
    as executive director of Women
        Legislators Lobby, 240
    formation of SOS and, 29–30
    Fortieth Anniversary Memorial
        Bench and, 242
    friendship with Bennett, Phyllis, 242
    holding of elective office in New
        Hampshire, 240
    Home Rule and, 25–26, 83, 188,
        202–203, 205, 221
    legislative hearing on HB18 bill, 196
    marriage to Dudley, Tom, 19–20
    oil refinery and, 23, 41–42, 62,
        63–64, 65–67, 89
    Olympic Refineries and, 210–211,
        220–221, 226–233
    Onassis, Aristotle, and, 123–124,
        127, 129
    open forum meetings and, 67–68,
        69, 72, 73–74
    passage of Article 40 and, 237
    political experience of, 20–21, 240
    Portsmouth Naval Prison and, 199
    power plant siting law and, 66–67
    presidential politics and, 22, 199, 240
    prison reform and, 199
    qualifications for office, 198–199
    Read Amendment and, 230–231, 234
    as recipient for award for
        "outstanding contributions to the
        state," 240–241
    Sandberg, Nancy, and, 27–28
    Senate's Resources and
        Environmental Control
        Committee on Home Rule bill
        of, 236
    at Sheraton Wayfarer press
        conference, 124–127
    SOS meetings and, 27–35, 74, 188
    Spirou, Chris's decision not to work
        with Onassis, Aristotle, 170–171
    sponsorship of HB 18 by, 228
    as state legislator, 18, 19, 22–23, 240
    tour of Durham Point and, 75–83, 81
    work for McGovern's presidential

campaign, 21–22
Dudley, Joseph, 97
Dudley, Morgan, 20
Dudley, Thomas
  as acting attorney for SOS, 79–80
  building of oil refinery and, 23–24,
    65, 241
  formation of SOS and, 24
  Governor Dudley, Joseph as son of, 97
  Home Rule and, 83
  marriage to Dudley, Dudley Webster,
    19–20
  move to New Hampshire, 20
  Onassis, Aristotle, and, 133
  Portsmouth Naval Prison and, 20–21
  reading of editorial to, 134
  SOS petitions and, 97
Dugger, Ronnie, 159
Durgin, Owen, 68
  Home Rule and, 147
  on oil refinery, 41
  Onassis, Aristotle, and, 129–130
Durham, New Hampshire
  fight over oil refinery in, 35, 41–42
  gas rationing and, 30–31
  Olympic Refineries and, 211–212,
    217–225
  passage of Article 40 and, 237–238
  piping of oil over land to, 62
  recession in, 30
  zoning in, 63
Durham Historic Association (DHA),
  Sandberg, Nancy's work with, 240
Durham Point, 25
  character of, 8
  location of refinery on, 17, 18, 31,
    32–33
  Onassis, Aristotle's personal tour of,
    122–123
  Pappademus, George's purchase of
    land on, 32
  touring, 75–83
Durham Zoning Ordinance, 223

E

Energy siting committee, on oil
  refinery, 109
Environmental impact studies on oil
  refinery, 81–82
Environmental Protection Agency,
  Olympic Refineries and, 208
Equity Publishing Co., 55

F

Fagley, Peter at Publick Occurrences, 14
Faiman, Robert, on in-depth impact
  study, 39
Findel, George, on attempted land
  purchase, 14
Finnegan, James
  editorials of, 131–133
  on Spirou, Chris's candidacy and,
    168–169
First National Bank of New York, 209
Flat Grant welfare system, 227
Food Grant program, 227
Forbes (magazine), on businessman
  Onassis, 181–185
Ford, Dan, 85
Ford, Sally, 85
Fortieth anniversary of defeat of
  Onassis oil refinery, 242
Fosters coverage of land purchase and, 14

G

Gallowhur, George, 51
Gallowhur, Nancy Scripps, 51
Georgakis, Yannis, 118
Golden Eagle Refinery, visit to, 150
Gouvalaris, Anne, 126–127
Graham, Bill, Publick Occurrences and,
  162
Granite State Award for "outstanding
  contributions to the state," Dudley,
  Dudley Webster as recipient of,
  240–241
Gratsos, Constantine "Costa", xii–xiii,
  114, 115, 116

claiming of oil sources for Onassis, Aristotle, in Saudi Arabia, 183

Hatch model and, 193–194

Olympic Refineries, and, 73, 103, 243

Onassis, Aristotle, and, 81, 110–111, 119–120

search for oil refinery site and, xii–xiii

Wheeler, Katie and, 101–102, 120–121

Gray, Douglas, as chairman of Rye Board of Selectmen, 156

Great Bay, 23, 26, 37
as estuary, 64, 76
oil off-loading and, 72
shallowness of, 78

Greene, Elizabeth, Olympic Refineries vote and, 228

Greene, Robert, xii–xiii
debate with environmentalists and, 153
at Durham Town Meeting, 222
on oil refinery, 72, 73
Olympic Refineries and, 152, 207–208, 210, 212–213, 215, 235
at Rye meeting, 154
soil tests on Durham Point and, 71
as vice president of Purvin and Gertz, Inc., 68

Gregg, Hugh, 57, 58

Griswold, Captain, 222

Gross, Marty, 24, 66

H

Haffer, Edward, 202, 203

Hall, Francis, 188

Hampton, New Hampshire, 77
oil refinery and, 202

Hampton Beach, 177

Hansen, Bill, at *Publick Occurrences*, 14

Harlow, Eugene
effect of equipment on coastline, 155–156
environmentalists and, 153
Home Rule and, 233
oil spills and, 156
Olympic Refineries, and, 152, 208, 210

at Rye meeting, 154

Harmon, Lois, 138

Harris, Frederic R., Inc. (engineer firm)
Bonasis, Joseph J. as engineer for, 68
design of deep-water oil terminal and, 152
Home Rule and, 233
Olympic Refineries, and, 208

Harvey, William, 20–21

Hatch, John
anti-refinery messages and, 122–123
taking of scale model to Concord, 192–193
topographic model of Durham and, 189–190

Hatch, Maryanna
anti-refinery message and, 122–123
as member of SOS, 144, 145
as secretary of SOS, 189

Hayes, James, support for refinery, 194–195

Heath, Lester, ticket writing by, 42, 135–136

Hochgraf, Frederick G.
as anti-refinery expert, 153
as metallurgist, 152
testimony on oil spills, 154, 156

Home Rule, 24–26, 236
Dudley, Dudley Webster's bill on, 205
Fortieth Anniversary Memorial Bench and, 242
impact of, 147
legislative override and, 173
limits of approach, 83
NIMBY and, 83
principle of, 108–109
Read Amendment and, 229
Sandberg, Nancy, and, 239
Spirou, Chris and, 66
Thomson, Meldrim, and, 63–64, 201

Honeymoon Cottage, 174

Horne, Peter
of Concerned Citizens of Rye, 201–202
on Home Rule, 201–202

moderator during presentation with
Olympic Refineries, 152
on Olympic supplement, 219–220
opposition to oil refinery and, 150
Horrigan, Clif, 212–213
Horrigan, James
introductory comments, ix
issue with state report on refinery, 188
on Olympic Refineries and, 209, 219
SOS Town meeting and, 87
Hotchkiss School (Lakeview, CT), 48, 49
House Bill 18 (HB 18)
HB 34 determining fate of refinery,
not Home Rule bill, 204
legislative hearing on, 196
restoration of original, 236
sponsoring of bill by Dudley, Dudley
Webster, 228
votes on, 221, 233
House Bill 34 (HB 34)
attempt to amend, 203
in determining fate of refinery, 204
Olympic Refineries proposal to
amend, 214
Roberts, George's sponsorship of,
203–204, 228
Spirou, Chris and, 166
votes on, 221

I

Ibn Saud Bin Abdul Aziz Al-Saud, 183
Ioannidis, Dimitrios, 183
Isles of Shoals, 37
Appledore Island and, 78
docking of supertankers at, 77
limited maneuvering space near, 189
Lunging Island and, 152
off-loading crude oil and uploading
refined oil, 173–174
off-shore unloading facility because
of, 69
oil tankers on, 62
Olympic Refineries interest in
buying, 175
as possible site for oil refinery, xiii, 208

J

Jackson, C. Floyd, 78–79
Jackson Estuarine Laboratory, 76, 77–79
Jiddah agreement, 116
Johnson, Lyndon B., 20
Joint Rules Committee, Dudley's
testimony before, 109
Jones, Galen, SOS Town meeting and, 87
Judiciary Committee, Dudley's
testimony before, 196–197

K

Kaufman, Jane, 167
Kelly, Anne Gale, 55
Kennedy, Bobby, 16, 115, 117, 118
Kennedy, Caroline, 117
Kennedy, John F., 115, 116, 117–118
Kennedy, Joseph, 116
Kennedy, Jr., John, 117
Kennedy, Patrick Bouvier, 117
Kepplar, Richard R., 152, 153
King, John, 58, 59
King, Jr., Martin Luther
assassination of, 104, 105–106
March on Washington (1963) with,
161
King, Larry, 159–160
Kingsbury, John
as anti-refinery expert, 153
as director of Cornell Shoals Marine
Department, 152
on oil spills, 154
Kingston, New Hampshire, effect of oil
refinery and, 202
Kitfield, Connie, 6, 16
Kling Associates, Home Rule and, 233
Knox, Annie Reid, 50–51
Knox, Frank, 50
Konialidis, Costa, 112
Koulkas, Michael, 39–40

L

Lamprey River, 37, 76, 213
Langley, Mrs. Harold, 16

Langley Family, 6
LaRoche, Roland, attempted land
    purchase and, 16
League of Women Voters, 29
Levine, Dick, 162
    editorials of, 142
    Governor Thomson and, 139
    on local events, 138
    nomination for Pulitzer, 12
    at *Publick Occurrences*, 12, 14,
        36–37, 92–95, 100, 135
    work habits of, 12
Lewis, Ron
    on oil refinery proposal, 39–40
    as reporter for *Publick Occurrences*,
        14, 15–17, 101
Little Bay, 6, 8, 23, 77, 78, 79
Livanos, Athina (Tina), 114, 116
Livanos, Stavros, 114
Loeb, Jr., William, 48
Loeb, Penelope, child support for, 51, 52
Loeb, William, II, 48
Loeb, William, III, xii
    annulment of marriage to Nagy,
        Elizabeth, 49
    attacks on Bonner, Tom, 54
    backing of Powell, Wesley, 56–57
    biography of, 47
    childhood of, 48
    editorials of, 44, 45–46, 52–53, 58, 131
    education of, 48–49
    endorsement of King, John, 59
    finances and, 49, 51–52
    front-page denunciations, 52–53
    marriage to McAllister, Eleanore,
        50, 51
    marriage to Nagy, Elizabeth, 49
    newspaper ownership and, 47, 50,
        51, 56
    on oil refinery, 107–108, 198, 200,
        205, 206
    "old guard" Republicans and, 56
    Olympic Refineries and, 234–235, 243
    Onassis, Aristotle, and, 121, 130
    press coverage and, 111

regional planning and, 61
resolution to censure, 53
social scene in New Hampshire and, 51
Spirou, Chris and, 168, 169, 170
support for Pillsbury, John, 58
Thomson, Meldrim, and, 55, 59, 60
    on University of New Hampshire, 52
Loeb-Thomson-Onassis juggernaut, 65
Lunging Island, 72, 152, 173–174

M

Manchester Union Leader (*Union
    Leader*), xii, 11, 15, 35, 44, 46, 47
    on building of oil refinery, 62, 217–218
    Loeb, William, III, as owner of, 56
March on Washington (1963), 161
Marine Zoological Laboratory, 78
Marshall, Tom, 86–87
Martin, Arthur, at SOS open meeting,
    188–189
Mathes, Jacob, 3
Mathieson, Art, 76, 77–79
McAllister, Eleanor, 50, 51
McCarthy, Eugene, 20, 124
McCarthy, Joseph, 115
McDuffee, Jay, 11, 39, 124
McDuffee, Shaunna
    Bennett, Steve, and, 14, 42–43, 137,
        242
    as compugraphic machine operator,
        11, 36, 93
    Levine, Dick's interaction with, 162
    at *Publick Occurrences*, 36–37,
        94–95, 237
    work at weekly paper in North
        Conway, 163
McGovern, George, 21–22, 54, 199
McManus. Jay, 14, 140–142
Meeker, Dave, 5–6, 74, 84, 153–154
Meeker, Sharon, 5–6
    building of oil refinery and, 27, 28,
        31–34, 122–123
    deep-water unloading port and, 157
    getting word out to town about
        public meeting of SOS, 172

on joining forces with SOS, 145
location of refinery on Durham
    Point, 31–32
on outreach Committee of SOS,
    28–29, 74, 86, 89, 144
petition drive of, 145–146
Rye meeting and, 152–154
SOS and, 8–9, 144, 189, 190
strategy of, on Olympic supplement,
    219
Meyer, John, 243
Meyer, Otta, 208
Michael, Joseph, at Town Meeting,
    221–223, 225
Mighell, John, historic house, 28
Millimet, Joseph, 176
    on building of oil refinery, 69–70, 140
    economic impact report and, 148, 149
Mill Pond Dam, 76–77
Mina al Almadi, Kuwait, deep-water
    port at, 156–157
Moore, Ken, 16
Morris, Willie, 159, 160
Mt. Cube Farm (Orford, New
    Hampshire), 55
Mower, Amy, 29
Mower, Karen, 29, 34
    bevy of experts and, 177
    economic impact report and, 148, 149
    SOS and, 85–86, 144, 190, 191
    of technology Committee, 85–86
Mower, Robin, 29, 172
Mower, Todd, 29
Murphy, Maurice, 58
Murray, Minnie Mae, 100–101
Muskie, Edmund, 21
Muzio, Claudia, 113–114

N

Nagy, Elizabeth, 49
New Hampshire
    citizen participation in government
        in, xiii–xiv
    concerns over building of oil refinery
        in, 18, 19

elections in, 108
Executive Branch of, 168
General Court in, 108
Governor's Executive Council in,
    96–97, 108
Home Rule in, 24–26, 108–109
Legislative Branch of, xiv, 18, 22–23,
    168
Onassis, Aristotle's visit to, 110–111
prison reform and, 167–168
seacoast of, 32
Senate in, xiv
state constitution in, xiv, 22, 108, 168
state culture and, 108–109
state motto in, 25
town meetings in, xv
zoning in, xv
New Hampshire Humanities Council,
    241–242
New Hampshire Network, 207, 215
New Hampshire Times, on Read
    Amendment, 229
Newmarket, New Hampshire, 13, 181
    Olympic Refineries, and, 235–236
    zoning regulations in, 25
Nilson, Bob
    cartoons of, 14, 37, 38
    nomination for Pulitzer Prize, 237
    at *Publick Occurrences,* 14, 162
NIMBY, 8, 83
Nixon, Richard M.
    energy policy of, xi, 30, 31, 33–34
    impeachment and, 100–101
    international military alert called
        by, 165
    Omega project and, 119
North Atlanta flyway, 78

O

O'Connell, Lawrence, 68
    opposition to oil refinery, 41, 147,
        150–151, 176
    at Town Meeting, 223, 224
Oil refinery
    building of, on Durham Point, 17

citizens opposition to, 41, 122–123, 125–126

Dudley, Dudley Webster's editorial on, 63–64

environmental impact studies on, 81–82

need for in-depth impact study on, 39

negotiations between Onassis, Aristotle and Thomson, Meldrim, 46

Olympic Refineries presentation on, 205–216

SOS focus in opposition to, 107

Thomson, Meldrim's establishment of, 44–45

Oil spills, citizens concerns over, 63, 72, 79

Olympic Airways, 116, 182, 244

Olympic Refineries, 32, 33

Booras, Peter as spokesman for, 68, 69

environmental impact studies from, 81–82

facilities needed by, 62–63

as ghost company, 109

Gratsos, Constantine as face of, 73

incorporation of, into New Hampshire, 209

Manhattan offices of, 153

objective of questioning credibility of, 213

Onassis, Aristotle's ownership of, 64

open forum meeting on, 67–68

press conference on, 37

as private company, 103

public relations and, 74

radio ads of, 218

release of cartoon accompanying news release, 37

SOS meeting and, 176

unveiling of scale topographic model of oil refinery, 192–193

Omega project, xii, 119

Onassis, Alexander, 114, 118, 119–120

Onassis, Aristotle, 243–244

Booras, Peter, and, 81

building of oil refinery and, xi–xiii, xv, 35, 44, 46, 120, 182–183, 200, 205, 206, 244

Callas, Maria, and, 116–117, 119

children of, 114–115

cigarette manufacturing and, 113

decline of meeting with Sandberg, Nancy and Dudley, Thomas, 133

Dudley, Dudley Webster. and, 129

early life of, 112–113, 115–116

editorial on, 132–133

fleet of ships of, xi, xii

goals of, 112

Gratsos, Constantine, and, 110

Hoover, J. Edgar on, 115

investments of, 114, 116

Kennedy, Bobby, and, 115, 116

Kennedy, John F., and, 115

lifestyle of, ix, 112–113, 183

Livanos, Athina and, 114

lobbyists hired by, 197–198

marriage to Jackie, xi–xii, xv, 118–119, 182, 244

oil tankers of, 112, 114

Olympic Airways and, 116, 244

Olympic Refineries, Inc. and, 32, 64

Omega Project and, xii

personal tour of, 122–123

poor health and death of, 120, 244

press and, 111, 121, 124–125, 130–131, 181–185

Sandberg, Nancy, and, 128–129

Saudi Arabian oil shipping and, 183

son's death and, 119–120

Spirou, Chris, and, 169–170

Thomson, Meldrim, and, 110–111

treatment of women, 114

visit to New Hampshire, 110–111, 112, 121–122, 173

Onassis, Artemis, 118

Onassis, Christina, 114–115, 244

Onassis, Jackie Kennedy, 117–119

lifestyle of, 116, 183

marriage to Aristotle, xi–xii, xv, 32, 182, 244

press coverage and, 32

Onassis, Socrates (father), 113
O'Neil, James
  Olympic Refineries and, 227, 228
  Read Amendment and, 230
Oregon plan, 173
Organization of Petroleum Exporting
  Countries (OPEC), 183

P

Papadopoulos, George, 182
Papanicolaou, Nicholas
  Booras, Peter, and, 206
  Hatch model and, 193–194
  Olympic Refineries and, 193–194,
    208–209, 235, 236
Pappademus, George, 79
  Durham Point and, 32, 38, 70, 191
  interest in buying land, 5, 6, 7, 16,
    17, 32, 33, 38, 191–192
Paul, Rod, investigative reporting of, 61
Pease Air Force Base
  oil pipe lines and, 72
  Olympic Refineries and, 208,
    222–223
  tank farm and truck terminal
    location at, 200–201
Peterson, Walter
  denunciation of daughter of, by
    Loeb, William, III, 52
  election as governor in 1968, 59
  in 1972 state primary, 24
  support for sales tax, 59
Pierce, Major, 222
Pillsbury, John, 58
Piscataqua River, 23, 27, 76, 79
Plaistow, New Hampshire, 10, 42, 181
Portsmouth, New Hampshire, 77, 189,
  202
Portsmouth Naval Prison, 20–21, 199
Powell, Wesley
  Bridges, Styles and, 56
  campaign for governor, 57
  Murphy, Maurice, and, 58
  Senate campaign and, 56, 57
Power plant siting law, 63, 65, 66–67

Powers, John, 31
Prison reform bill, 167
Project Independence, 31
Pro-refinery lobbyists, 226
Publick Occurrences, 10–11
  affiliation with *Globe* and, 185
  articles on oil refinery and, 15–17,
    18, 19
  atmosphere in office of, 93–94
  Belles, Ray, and, 159, 237
  Bennett, Phyllis as publisher of, 12,
    13–14, 100, 158, 185, 237
  Bennett, Steve, and, 13–14, 43, 47,
    93, 94, 160–161
  compugraphic machine and, 10
  coverage of Nixon, Richard M.'s
    impeachment proceedings, 100
  as enterprising newspaper, 180
  Fagley, Peter, as General Manager at, 14
  financial problems at, 43, 180
  founding of, 10–11, 15, 47
  Hansen, Bill, as Advertising Manager
    at, 14
  Levine, Dick, as editor at, 12, 14, 100
  McDuffee, Shaunna at, 94–95
  mood in offices of, 36
  Nilson, Bob, as cartoonist and
    illustrator at, 14
  nomination for Pulitzer Prize, 237
  on oil refinery in, 65
  on Olympic's misleading supplement
    misinformation, 220
  publication of economic report on
    refinery, 148, 187–188
  reporters at, 14
  report on tour of Durham Point in, 80
  reprinting of *Forbes* magazine on
    Onassis, Aristotle, 181–185
  running of, 12, 92–95
  stories in, 140, 164–165, 191–192
  subscription price of, 161
Purvin and Gertz, Inc. (independent
  consulting engineers), xii–xiii
  Greene, Robert L. as vice president
    of, 68

Home Rule and, 233
Olympic Refineries, Inc. project and, 207–208, 235

R

Radio ads, 226
Radziwill, Lee, 117, 118
Radziwill, Stanislaw, 117
Randall, Prudence, 175
Randall, Ray, 174
Randall, Richard, 174
Randall, Robert, 174–175
Read, Maurice
  Olympic Refineries, and, 195, 228
Read Amendment, 203–204, 229–233, 234
Reid, Sam, 148, 187–188
Revised Statues Annotated (RSA), 66–67, 109
Roberts, George, HB 34 and, 203, 228
Robinson, Francis, 5
Robinson, J. Dennis, 242
Rockingham Park, 201
Rollins, Dale, 122
Rollins, Dan Ford, 122
Rollins, Sherwood "Woody," 6, 16, 122–123
Rollinsford, Dale, 242
Rollinsford, New Hampshire, 77
Roosevelt, Franklin Delano, 20
Roosevelt, Theodore, 48, 50
Rough Riders, 50
Ruckelshaus, William, 101
Rudman, Warren, 167, 202
Rutledge, Barbara, 210
Rye, New Hampshire, xiii, 77
  building of oil refinery and, 62, 152–154, 202, 226
  Concerned Citizens of Rye and, 150
Rye Beach, 177

S

St. Alban's Daily, 50
St. Thomas More Church, 86

Salmon Falls River, 23, 76
"Salty" (170-acre estate), 6, 7, 79, 209–210
Sandberg, Betsy, 4, 127–128
Sandberg, Malcolm
  apple orchard of, 239
  babysitting duties of, 84
  Nancy, as president of SOS, 8, 9
  offer to purchase land and, 2, 3, 4
  press conference at Sheraton Wayfarer and, 127, 128
  skepticism during Onassis, Aristotle's press conference, 127–128
Sandberg, Nancy
  anger on seeing Olympic supplement, 219
  as anti-refinery lobbyist, and Olympic Refineries, 227
  apple orchard of, 239
  attendance at hearing on HB 18, 204
  building of oil refinery and, 27, 33–34, 85
  as chairman of SOS, 8–9, 28, 84–85, 86–87, 96, 141–142, 144, 145, 172–173, 200
  concerns for the Durham community, 239–240
  Dudley, Dudley Webster, and, 27–28
  Durham Historic Association and, 240
  Durham Zoning Ordinance and, 223
  Fortieth Anniversary Memorial Bench and, 242
  Home Rule and, 239
  Meeker, Dave, and, 74
  offer to purchase land from, 1–9
  Olympic Refineries and, 177–179, 205–206, 208, 212, 215–216, 227–228
  Olympic supplement and, 219
  Onassis, Aristotle, and, 123–124, 128–129, 133, 172
  Onassis, Aristotle's reception and, 127–128
  passage of Article 40 and, 238
  public relations and, 85

second open meeting of SOS, 186–189
town meeting and, 86–87
Sanders, Bernie, 240
"Saturday Night Massacre," 100
Save Our Refinery, Thompson, Tommy,
and, 186, 211–212
Scripps-Howard newspaper chain, 51
Seabrook, New Hampshire, 77, 202
Senate's Resources and Environmental
Control Committee, on Dudley's
Home Rule bill, 236
Shea-Porter, Carol, 240
Sheraton Wayfarer, press conference at,
124–127
Simon, William E.
Olympic Refineries and, 218, 219
Read Amendment and, 232
Site Evaluation Committee, 202, 203,
229
Smith, Jay
oil refinery and, 138–139
stories of, 14, 39
Smith, Sam, 6
Smith, Tony
Olympic Refineries and, 236
Read Amendment and, 231–232
Smith College (Northampton, MA), 49
SOS (Save Our Shores), 8–9
Curtis, Cass as vice chairman of, 28
delivery of petitions and, 96–99
DiMambro, Celeste's work with, 29
Dudley, Tom as acting attorney for,
79–80
Financial Committee and, 29
formation of, 8–9, 24, 29–30
Hatch, Maryanna as secretary of, 189
informational meetings of, 189
Legal and Regulatory Committee
and, 29
Meeker, Sharon's work with Outreach
Committee, 28–29, 74, 86
meetings of, 74, 107, 186–189
Olympic Refineries presentation and,
206–207
opposition to oil refinery, 107

outreach committee of, 89
phone bank operation of, 34
presentation of refinery plan and,
175–176
public meeting of, 172
Sandberg, Nancy as chairman of,
8–9, 28, 34–35, 84–85, 141–142,
144, 172–173
secretary of, 189
study of economic implications of
refinery proposal for Tiverton,
Rhode Island, 139–140
Technology Committee and, 29
Wilson, Roger as recording secretary,
29
Spirou, Chris, 24
as behind-the-scenes worker, 196
as charismatic, 75
Cobleigh, Marshall's meeting with, 167
Dudley, Dudley Webster, and, 65–67
Hatch's model and, 195
Home Rule and, 66
Loeb, William, III, and, 168, 169
Olympic Refineries and, 198, 227,
243–244
Onassis, Aristotle, and, 169–170,
229–230
prison reform bill and, 167–168
Read Amendment and, 229, 232
tour of Durham Point and, 75, 80
Tracy, Paul and, 168–170
Squamscott River, 25–26, 76
Stamatelos, George, 174–175
Star Island, Olympic Refineries, 208
Star Island Corporation, 175, 210
Stiles, Norman, 16
Stone Church, discussion of local
events at, 138
Stratham, New Hampshire, 25–26, 77

T

Taylor, John I, 180, 184, 237
Texas Instruments, 233
Thaxter, Celia, 174
Thompson, Edward, Law Book

Company, 55
Thompson, Murell "Tommy"
  at Durham Town Meeting, 223–224
  as head of Save Our Refinery, 128,
    140–141, 145, 186, 211–212
  Olympic Refineries and, 211–212, 215
  Onassis, Aristotle's plans to take over
    Durham Point and, 141
Thompson, Shirley, 141
Thomson, Meldrim
  arch-conservative agenda of, 60
  building of oil refinery and, xii, 17,
    23, 27, 31, 32–33, 37–38, 44–45,
    46, 60, 62, 68–69, 98, 104–105,
    107, 125–126, 138–139, 150,
    200, 205, 206, 235
  call for gas rationing and, 30–31
  candidacy for governor, 59
  as carpetbagger, 55
  as chairman of Orford School Board,
    55–56
  delivery of SOS petitions and, 96–99
  Dudley, Dudley Webster, and, 99
  education of, 55
  election as governor, 54, 59
  environmentalists and, 61
  formation of Taxfighters, 56
  as governor, 60
  Hatch model and, 193–194
  Home Rule and, 25–26, 201
  legal practice of, 55
  Loeb, William, III, and, 55
  in 1972 state primary, 24
  Olympic Refineries and, 38, 84,
    176–177, 218–219, 226, 228,
    234, 236–237, 243
  Onassis, Aristotle and, 46, 110–111,
    121, 123, 124, 130, 131, 182
  prison reform and, 167–168
  Read Amendment and, 230–231
  Simon, William's telegram to, on
    opening Olympic Refineries, 218,
    219
  as ultra-conservative, 11, 23, 182
Thomson, Mrs. Meldrim, 131

"Thomson's Raiders," 55
Tibbetts, Donn, coverage of Olympic
  Refineries and, 227
Tiverton, Rhode Island, 139–140
Tobey, Charles, 56
Town Meeting Day, 84, 220
Tracy, Paul, 168–170
Tucker, Peter, 155–156

U

Ulrich, Gail, 87, 88
Underwood, Barbara, 18–19
University of New Hampshire,
  anti-pollution laboratory at, 126,
  131–132, 134

V

Valena, Ed, 242
Voice of America, 159

W

Weaver, Charles Graham, 50
Weber, John W., 236
Webster, Bob, 19
Webster, Daniel, 53
Webster, Polly, 19
Wentworth, Benning, 239
Wentworth-Coolidge Commission, 239
Wheeler, Katie, Gratsos, Constantine,
  and, 101–102, 120–121
Who the hell is William Loeb? (Cash), 47
Wilcox, Edith, 16
Williams College (Williamstown, MA),
  49
Wilson, Roger, SOS and, 29, 144–145,
  178–179, 189
Winn, Alden, 201
  as board chairman of Durham, 40,
    67–68
  on building of oil refinery, 98,
    104–105
  Durgin, Owen acting as chairman in
    absence of, 147

Olympic Refineries, and, 176, 207,
  210, 212, 213–214, 215
at open forum meeting, 70–71, 72, 73
taking of Hatch's model to Concord,
  193
Thomson, Meldrim's letter to,
  regarding not wanting an oil
  refinery and, 98
Town meeting and, 88–89
warning to residents about the
  precariousness of situation, 88
Winnicut River, 76
WMUR-TV, oil refinery
  announcement on, 62
Women Legislators Lobby, 240
Woodward, William, 16
Wright, Jim, 159

Z
Zachos, Kimon
  Olympic Refineries vote and, 228
  Read Amendment and, 231–233

DAVID W. MOORE is an award-winning author, and currently a Senior Fellow at the Carsey Center for Public Policy at the University of New Hampshire. He is also the polling director and frequent columnist for iMediaEthics.org, for which he won the 2015 and 2016 EPPY Awards for his news/political commentary. For twenty-one years (1972-1993), he taught political science at the University of New Hampshire, and for the next thirteen years he worked at the Gallup Organization as a senior editor of the Gallup Poll. He became affiliated with UNH again in 2008. He is the author of three non-fiction trade books, and the co-author of one cross-over trade/academic book: *The First Primary: New Hampshire's Outsize Role in Presidential Nominations*, with Andrew E. Smith (University Press of New England, 2015); *The Opinion Makers: An Insider Exposes the Truth Behind the Polls* (Beacon Press, hardback, 2008; revised edition in paperback 2009); *How To Steal An Election: The Inside Story of How George Bush's Brother and Fox Network Miscalled the 2000 Election and Changed the Course of History* (Nation Books, 2006); and *The Super Pollsters: How They Measure and Manipulate Public Opinion in America* (Four Walls Eight Windows, 1992; trade paperback 1995). He has published essays and articles in *The New York Times, The Nation, The Boston Globe, Public Opinion Quarterly, New York Newsday, Public Perspectives,* and numerous other books and journals.

www.davidwmoore.us

9 781635 761887